THE AESTHETIC
DIMENSION OF
THE MIND

THE AESTHETIC
DIMENSION OF
THE MIND

Variations on a Theme of Bion

Lia Pistiner de Cortiñas

KARNAC

First published in English in 2009 by
Karnac Books Ltd
118 Finchley Road, London NW3 5HT

British Library Cataloguing in Publication Data

A C.I.P. for this book is available from the British Library

ISBN: 978 1 85575 612 0

Translated by Philip Slotkin and others

Cover design by Eugenia Cortiñas

Edited, designed and produced by The Studio Publishing Services Ltd
www.publishingservicesuk.co.uk
e-mail: studio@publishingservicesuk.co.uk

Printed in Great Britain

www.karnacbooks.com

Heard melodies are sweet, but those unheard
   Are sweeter; therefore, ye soft pipes, play on;
Not to the sensual ear, but more endear'd,
   Pipe to the spirit ditties of no tone:

O Attic shape! Fair attitude! With brede
   Of marble men and maidens overwrought,
With forest branches and the trodden weed;
   Thou, silent form, dost tease us out of thought
As doth eternity: Cold Pastoral!
   When old age shall this generation waste,
      Thou shalt remain, in midst of other woe
Than ours, a friend to man, to whom thou say'st,
   'Beauty is truth, truth beauty', __ that is all you need
      Ye know on earth, and all ye need to know.

ODE ON A GRECIAN URN
John Keats

CONTENTS

To my husband Jorge
and to my children Julian, Luciano and Eugenia

ACKNOWLEDGEMENTS

I am deeply indebted to Dario Sor, from whom I have received and learned so much. I am also especially grateful to Elizabeth Tabak de Bianchedi, who first connected me with Bion's ideas and with whom I had many fruitful discussions. I am especially indebted for the priceless stimulus I have received from Didier Houzel, José Luis Goyena, James Grotstein, and Antonio Sapienza, through a valuable exchange of ideas, and because their acknowledgements of my developments of Bion's ideas encouraged me to write this book. I want also to express my gratitude to Marta Lilliencreutz, who generously revised the English translation. Finally, I would like to give my special thanks to my husband, Jorge Cortiñas, for his wonderful support and patience through many years, accompanying me, listening to my ideas, and reviewing my writings, and to my daughter, Eugenia Cortiñas, for the beautiful cover design.

ABOUT THE AUTHOR

Lia Pistiner de Cortiñas is a psychoanalyst, full member and training analyst of the Buenos Aires Psychoanalytical Association (APDEBA) and fellow of the International Psychoanalytical Association (IPA). She has a specialization in child and adolescent psychoanalysis. She is also a psychologist (PhD) and a lawyer (degrees obtained at the Buenos Aires University).

She gives seminars, and is invited to lecture and supervise in different public and private institutions in Argentine and in Paris, Rome, Sicily, etc. She teaches Theory of Technique and Psychopathology at APDEBA's Psychoanalytical Training Institute. She is professor of the seminar "W. R. Bion" for the career of Specialization in Psychoanalysis of the Institute of Mental Health (IUSAM-APDEBA) and gives post-graduate seminars on "Psychosomatic and over-adaptation" and "Introduction to W. R. Bion's ideas" at the Faculty of Psychology of the Buenos Aires University. She has written papers for Argentine and international publications, is co-author, with David Liberman, of the book *Del Cuerpo al Símbolo, Sobreadaptación y Enfermedad Psicomática* and has written, with Elizabeth T. de Bianchedi, the book *Bion Conocido/Desconocido*.

In this magisterial work, the author almost encyclopaedically reviews all of Bion's works and does so from the perspective (vertex) of the aesthetic dimension. She scans virtually all the essential elements of Bion's contributions and then details them at length, giving unusual clarification as she does so. Bion is hard for most people to read because of the density and complexity of his style. The author seems to do so effortlessly. Her choice to employ the lens of aesthetics to study Bion is helpful. The concept of aesthetics has hitherto belonged in the area of applied psychoanalysis, but since Bion and, later, Meltzer, the role of aesthetics has become the essence of the psychoanalytic process itself. Bion emphasized the value of creativity and imagination, which were the products of what he originally called "alpha-function" and later, dreaming. Alpha-function and/or dreaming intercept the sense impressions of our emotional experiences and transform them into creative, as well as more tolerable renditions of the original impending, emotional truth. Our emotions, when thus transformed and realized, become analogous to imaginative aesthetic creations. Aesthetics, for Bion, constitutes a "vertex" (perspective) of consideration of the analytic moment, much like the key which governs and constrains a musical composition. Lia Pistiner de Cortiñas's work is the conception of Bion's works written in the "key" of the aesthetic vertex.

The author introduces us first to Bion's innovative conception of the importance of emotions and of the faculties of the mental apparatus that apprehend them, among which are consciousness, attention, and reverie, each devised to render us more aware of our emotional life in regard to our relationship with objects as well as with ourselves. The first two constitute techniques for observation, the third, for detecting emotions in preparation for feeling them, i.e., allowing oneself to experience them. Emotions, unlike sensuous stimuli, are not visible or tangible and, consequently, must be apprehended by reverie, a waking dream state.

The author delineates Bion's conception of the "dimensions of the psychoanalytic object" (the unknown emotional truth of the psychoanalytic session): "sense, myth, and passion", each being techniques for apprehending the analytic object, which Bion also associated with "O," the "Absolute Truth" about an infinite "Ultimate Reality" that operates beyond the range of the senses. Thus, "sense" can be equated with observation, "myth" with the personal or collective phantasy that serves as a container and definer for the analytic object, and "passion", the analyst's emotional receptor function for detecting the psychoanalytic object. Together, the author states, they comprise the "aesthetic dimension" for apprehending the emotional truth of the analytic session.

The sweep of the author's investigation is commendable. She deals with the psychological birth of emotional experience, dreaming, truth, lies, the significance of prenatal experiences, catastrophic change, the caesura, autism, and then courageously ventures into a comprehensive understanding of Bion's three-volume *A Memoir of the Future*. Her references to novelists and poets and her credible clinical examples are noteworthy. This work constitutes an outstanding piece of Bion scholarship and interpretation. One comes away from it with a deep appreciation for the author's "dreaming" of Bion's work and for the light she has shone on many of Bion's more recondite themes.

James Grotstein

PREFACE TO THE SPANISH EDITION

In her book, Lia Pistiner de Cortiñas stresses the significance of the analyst's achievement to develop and use, within the session, his or her capability to "dream" the patient's "dream", even though this "dream" may be fragmented and mixed with symptoms. In her view, this quality in an analyst is the basic mental equipment in the clinical practice of psychoanalysis. Evidences of this subtle activity, which the author more specifically relates with dream-work-alpha, is presented via illustrations of her clinical practice, which we will find in the last two chapters.

The first chapter highlights the factors that favour "the psychological birth of emotional experience", and it is from there that the text grows in depth, allowing for an experiential comprehension of the strategies proposed by the author in her approaches to autistic barriers, encapsulations, and enclaves.

This depth is highlighted in the incursions she makes into the meanders of "dreams and lies" throughout the second chapter where, while presenting the functioning of "dreams and myths" (containers of variables and unknowns), she establishes an interesting comprehension of *the dream as a potential interpreter for the dreamer himself*. The dreamer's ambiguity reveals, at times, "hypocritical" dreams. The writings of Umberto Eco and Luigi Pirandello appear at the end of this chapter, and are used as supports to deepen possible reflections.

In "Prenatal aspects of the mind: science and fiction in the psychoanalytic game", the third chapter, the use of models from theatre and literature as "personifications" gains prominence. These appear as *aesthetic tools* that allow the analyst to obtain flexibility and binocular vision, and thus be able to escape from the usurpation and tyrannical control of the superego assassin of the ego. The analyst can thereby collaborate with re-establishing the conditions for the patient's viability, autonomy, and mental growth.

The fourth and fifth chapters allow one to accompany the analytical pair's approximations to *truth* in the emotional turbulences of *catastrophic change** and traverse *caesuras**, requiring the refinements of *negative capability** and an increased tolerance in the face of *uncertainties* in the moments of "helplessness, ignorance, and mobilization when having to face the pair finite–infinite". The reader will be aware that I marked terms with an asterisk (*) because they can be consulted in the author's "Glossary of some Bionian terms", an appendix at the end of the book.

I do not want to leave out the progressive maps of observational theories that Lia offers us and which will serve as an approximation to the new developments proposed by Bion in his trilogy, *A Memoir of the Future*. Thus, in the sixth chapter, the author selects an excerpt from Volume I of the trilogy, *The Dream*, and comments with great clarity on Bion's extraordinary fiction in which a "nebulous invasion" imposes itself like a galaxy on the mind and ends up "fragmenting and dispersing the pages of a traditional Bible".

In *2001: A Space Odyssey*, the seventh chapter, we find a delicate and distinctive tribute from a psychoanalyst to a film-maker: Stanley Kubrick. I say from a psychoanalyst to a film-maker because there, significant correlations are outlined in differentiating the meaning of maps, distinguishing them from territories, and this contextualization will provide the signalling of the supports needed for the construction of psychic reality through models endowed with vitality, models capable of promoting new meanings as well as of detoxifying a mind loaded with nuclei poisoned by "arrogance, stupidity, and fanaticism". Because of this, a careful reading of this chapter, then, is recommended, and also because we will find a work with the descriptors (science and fiction, dream, models, neothenia, evolution, and mental growth), linked to the importance that Lia attributes to them, inspired in her theoretical and practical experience.

I am grateful for the honour of having been invited by my friend, the distinguished psychoanalyst Lia Pistiner de Cortiñas, to offer my brief view on this valuable book, one which will certainly be enriching for the reader interested in clinical questions of contemporary psychoanalysis.

Antonio Sapienza
Sao Paulo, Brazil

Introduction: the aesthetic dimension of the mind and becoming oneself

This book was born through a combination of my encounters: with psychoanalysis, with imagination, and with some psychoanalytical authors, all of which inspired deep changes in my thoughts and my way of thinking. The chapters have been written over several years, and are personal elaborations of my clinical experience and of some psychoanalytical theories, which I chose because of their qualities for enlightening and providing instruments for my clinical practice.

Freudian inquiries revealed to us different configurations of the human personality and led to innovative steps towards understanding mental pathological functioning and also certain manifestations that are inherent to the human being, such as jokes, slips of tongue, and the mysterious world of dreams.

In 1911–1915, Freud elaborates his metapsychological papers. He decides not to publish the chapter on consciousness, which is now lost. My book contains inquiries about the development of a consciousness capable of *becoming aware*.

Freud opened up a new spectrum of investigation when he revealed the child within the man. Psychosexual development and psychic reality are different levels which interweave with a

network of object relations: with the parental objects and those of
the child with himself, issues that were already understood through
the intuitions of the Greeks in their mythical narratives, such as
those of Oedipus and Narcissus, that inspired Freud in his discovery of psychoanalysis.

The relation between cognitive and emotional development and
their roots in early psychic functioning were revealed by Klein's
investigations: not only the child is a profound and complex being,
but, also, the infant contains an unsuspected emotional world,
which is often terrifying. He lacks sophisticated forms of expression, such as words, for his anxieties, for his emotions.

Bion discovered maternal reverie, the function that "dreams",
transforms, and gives meaning to primitive terrors and emotions; a
function which is the indispensable mediator for the development
of a psychic reality and that also is able to discern another reality
that exists outside ourselves, with facts that we do not choose.

The mysterious α function is necessary for generating instruments that can deal with mental pain in such a way that it can be
faced and modified. Some mental pains are inescapable, others are
unnecessary; contact with internal and external reality allows discernment instead of evasion of pain, the latter having catastrophic
consequences for the development of the personality.

Psychoanalytic treatment can no longer be conceived only in
the framework of a cure, but also as the development of mental
functions and the means of becoming one with oneself. As the
infant needs maternal reverie for his mental growth, so the patient
needs—sometimes more, sometimes less—the analyst's α function.
This means an even deeper engagement with our work as analysts.

Compared to other animals we are born prematurely—what has
been called neothenia—and we have pre-conceptions and pre-emotions, that is, cognitive–emotional structures which are given to us
as a species. The direction that they acquire during their development depends on a dialectic interaction of factors; this book is about
those factors, which I will mention as the development of a consciousness capable of being aware in a relationship with a human
environment which nourishes mental growth.

My "encounters" with Tustin allowed me to discover the autistic world and opened up new perspectives in my clinical practice.
Treating autistic children and adult patients with autistic enclaves

stimulated my thoughts about the very serious capacity for play, which I include in the aesthetic dimension of the mind. This dimension enlightens the crossroads between psychoanalysis, art, and myth.

Keats' "Ode on a Grecian urn" tells us that truth is beauty and beauty is truth. Only twenty-nine years old when he died, Keats wrote poetry that is still alive and speaks to those who can hear it. Freud made his first steps with the interpretation of dreams, and Klein with children's play. Often, in our clinical practice, we meet people, adults and children, who neither play nor dream. Some of them live compressed in prostheses (exo-skeletons) and lack a place within them where they can feel that they exist and are real. Part of our current culture, with its stress on the importance of technological developments, turns its back on mental pain and on the forms of expression that can transform it. This book means to be an inquiry into the challenges of the developmental problems of a mutually beneficial, symbiotic container–contained relationship; that is, between the emotional experiences and the expressive capacities that might help to metabolize them.

What is essential is invisible to the eyes, said the fox to the Little Prince; the psychoanalytical object is non-sensorial, it is an animated object which is always changing. The emotions, which are part of our prenatal endowment, do not have colour, sound, taste, etc.; they do not have sense qualities inherent in them. One could say that, as the Platonic essences, they acquire sense qualities through their association with the unique experiences of life of each human being. Thus, Proust could suddenly "discover" his childhood memories in the taste of a madeleine soaked in tea, or Shakespeare could describe Othello's jealousy as "that green eyed monster".

If our eyes see colours and our ears hear sounds, consciousness is the sensorial organ for the apprehension of psychic qualities. Things have extensions: they have a measure, a weight, a form, a colour, etc. Sensuous impressions—images, ideas, words—are those which provide the dimensions, that is, the extensions for the psychoanalytical object.

I now want to consider this object in the two definitions that Bion gave, as a way of introducing the idea of the *aesthetic dimension of the mind*.

In *Learning from Experience,* he defines it with a formula in Greek letters: M (mu), represents the innate aspects, cognitive and emotional, ψ (psi), as the already acquired and already saturated aspect which must go along with ξ (xi) as a non-saturated aspect which has to remain open to future experiences, ± Y (gamma) which represents mental growth and its direction, which also can be towards deterioration.

This formula of a high level of abstraction—Bion is looking for a language that can show the distinction between the "thing" and the "no-thing" (Kant, 1781)—includes what is innate, which is still a mystery about which we can only make hypotheses, such as drives and tropisms, and what is acquired, which needs a healthy development and becoming able to evolve an aspect of the personality that is open to changes and new developments. We are not ants, and, in our condition of neothenic beings, we have a great spectrum of potentialities that can be developed. A living object which is in constant change can grow or it can deteriorate. In analysis, an element that shows the evolution of a personality is whether its direction leads towards growth or deterioration.

This formula finds its complement in a particularization that Bion describes in *Elements of Psychoanalysis,* where he characterizes the dimensions of the psychoanalytic object. The psychoanalytic object needs to have shadows, it has to acquire dimensions, that is, extensions in different domains, in order to offer the possibility of being intuited, registered, and investigated.

1. An extension in the domain of sense, which can be shared by patient and analyst, without being confused with the sensorial. This extension is related to the crucial differentiation between "dreams", hallucinations, and lies.
2. An extension in the domain of myth, which is not a psychoanalytic theory, but provides an "embodiment" to psychoanalytic pre-conceptions and intuitions. An interpretation needs to contain a myth or a model, as when one says to a patient that in her relationship with men she seems like "Little Red Riding Hood", who never discovers the wolf disguised as her grandmother. The mythic dimension allows discovering and formulating the configuration of the emotional experience of each patient, in its singularity, and also allows the finding out of its meaning.

3. An extension in the domain of passion, which Bion describes as a non-violent emotion, shared at least by two minds. It is a kind of communication that keeps the psychoanalytic object alive within the session, with detoxified emotions and without violence. As a model, I propose the mother–infant relationship, when the infant's emotions resonate in the mother and she returns them within an L (love) and K link (disposition to know). That is how the initial chaos is organized, and patterns can be discovered, which can be named and whose meaning can now be found. −K (the active disposition to misunderstand) is hostile, full of rivalry, and disorganizes.

The background of the three extensions is the relationship between mental pain and a consciousness, which, as a sixth "sense organ", is capable of being aware, united in a binocular vision with an unconscious, through α function. The combination of the three extensions is what I call the *aesthetic dimension of the mind*.

Mental space is infinite. An infinite number of lines pass through a point. At the beginning of mental life there is no inside–outside differentiation, between mental space and external world, and this non-discriminated space is inhabited by objects, which are experienced as "things in themselves". A differentiation between emotions, sensations, and objects which have been perceived by the senses as sense impressions has not yet been produced. The conscience is still rudimentary.

The evolution of the mind, in the sense of mental growth, is related to:

- a process of generating representations: being able to solve problems in the absence of objects, which implies tolerating doubt, uncertainties, the finite–infinite relationship and that the thought or representation is not the thing.

- a process of maturing, which is associated with becoming in *at-one-ment* with oneself and with a healthy *Establishment* that can separate the finite man from the infinite God and contain catastrophic change;

As psychoanalysts and as human beings we need to make contact again with the Divinity (the unconscious, the mind that is evolving, *the infinite and formless void*, a quotation from Milton that Bion uses as a way to put into words the transformations towards O so as to make possible an evolution towards mental growth and, at the same time, avoid the danger of megalomania.

The aesthetic dimension of the mind is related to the process of differentiating *the thing from the no thing* and to tolerance of the development of a consciousness capable of being aware of the emotional experience that we are experiencing. It implies the generation of a space inhabited by thoughts. The use of points, lines, symbols, and representations is unavoidably related to the tolerance of the differentiation between *the thing and the no thing*, and to the restriction implied in thoughts and thinking. A thought is a definitory hypothesis that includes all that is defined and excludes everything that is left out of the definition. In its characteristic of hypothesis, it contains an unsaturated aspect, which always demands an approach to experience to give it a form and a meaning. It implies tolerance of the unsaturated; that is, it is able to evolve and, at the same time, it can function as an unknown, with the disposition of acquiring new meanings through future experiences.

The aesthetic dimension presupposes attaching space and time co-ordinates to infinite space, which, as such, is transformed in finite, but, at the same time, is open to evolution, as new experiences can bring new meaning.

Speaking of the evolution of the mind means that it is a system open and alive, which, at the same time, accepts limitations. Evolution and growth require an alternation between transformations towards O (the personality becomes in *at-one-ment* with itself, with that which has evolved from the infinite and formless void) and the transformations into K. The transformation in K gives form, which acts as a container for the evolutions from O.

Becoming one with oneself or being in *at-one-ment*, means tolerance of the emotions which are stimulated through the discovery of oneself in an analytic process, or in whatever moment in life in which one is going through a *catastrophic change*. Becoming in *at-one-ment* implies abandoning defences, almost of all of which are due to the archaic super-superego ($-\male\female$), who "promises" omnipotence as a way of dealing with feelings of helplessness and having tolerance for the moments in which there is a loss of known borders, to move towards the discovery of the unknown.

Transformation in K requires accepting the restrictions implied in having thoughts, without the compensation of certainty, as thoughts need thinking and approaching new experiences that might give them new meanings, without losing the characteristics of a pre-conception.

In *Transformations*, Bion reflects on how geometry could evolve towards algebra through the huge step provided when Cartesian axes were invented. Why could mathematics, with its processes of symbolization, become an efficient instrument for the development of sciences that deal with sensorial objects, sciences that could evolve with its help? Why is psychoanalysis still in difficulties and unable to develop a system equivalent to mathematics, which is a system of abstractions, equivalent to that of the Cartesian axes which would make further evolution possible?

One way of thinking about this problem is similar to the aesthetic approach. The psychoanalytical counterpart, as much within the session as in the transmission of psychoanalysis, implies a combination of formulations at the level of models, dream-thoughts, myth (Row C of The Grid) and, at the same time, using them as algebraic unknown or non-saturated preconceptions.

We meet with difficulties in theory (its formulations are easily transformed in jargon) and also in clinical practice. We use conversational language that has its origins in the sensuous world to deal with problems which are not sensorial. We need abstraction, as the equivalent of the algebraic unknown, unknowns as problems that can be "resolved" with new experiences, maintaining, at the same time, the vitality of the experience and a *language of achievement*, with tolerance of the *negative capability*, the doubts and mysteries, without any irritable reaching after the certainties of reason. Bion's investigations show that there is a need for alternation between abstraction and particularization, and between becoming in *at-one-ment* and the inquiry of the meaning of that which one is becoming. It is, thus, that the process of symbolization and its vicissitudes has complex implications from the psychoanalytical point of view.

Mental growth is a process, and psychoanalysis is a method for the development of the mind through the alternation of becoming oneself and knowing oneself. Both processes are related with truth, with tolerance of mental pain, and the reality principle. The turbulence that they generate is inescapable.

The psychoanalytic investigation of the process of symbolization revealed its emotional roots. Bion asks how an atmosphere of turbulence (in the session, in development, in life) can be transformed into a cloud of probabilities, with tolerance of two breasts which disappear, leaving two points, and which are the factors that allow the transformation of these two points into vertices of observation: that is, they can be transformed into signs which can be used to name the "thing", and not be transformed into a "ghost nothing", as in the sensations of a phantom limb.

He also asks if it would be possible to transform the symbolinstruments that were developed for the exploration of outer space, so that they can be used for the inquiries of inner space.

In Chapters Two and Three of this book, I suggest using dreams, myths, and models as algebraic unknowns as well as the fictionalized personification of emotional experiences. The idea of correlating the mathematical level of abstraction of the equations (Row H of the Grid) with complex artistic expressions has been worked through in the artistic field by many music composers and plastic artists. We have only to remember the powerful research of Kandinsky in his book *Punkt und Linie zu Fläche* ("Point and line in front of the plane"), in which he suggests the possibility of the transmission of emotional states through simple forms and their relationship with the sheet of paper that contains them. Something similar happens with the use and management of colours without the representation of the form. What are the implications of considering that it is possible to reach a counterpart of Row H in artistic and psychoanalytical productions? They are of several types, for example:

- the laws that govern the formation of the artistic object could be seen as coming closer to those that regulate the constitution of the psychoanalytical object;

- the aesthetic object and the psychoanalytic object, in acquiring enough complexity so as to be able to be classified in Row H of the Grid, would include a dimension towards the growth of the personality's psychoanalytic function, which could go along with an unexpected development of psychoanalysis.

This book contains the intention of putting forward ideas and thinking about how it is possible to help develop a space for representations in a psychoanalytical process, and, therefore, what mental tools, providing an aesthetic dimension to the psychoanalytic object, allow it to become accessible for thinking. Would we contribute in this way to the development of the personality's psychoanalytic function?

Some final words about Magritte and the picture that illustrates the cover. In the titles of his paintings, and also through those paintings, Magritte tells us about the treason of words and images related to common sense. By treason, this painter means something very similar to what Lewis Carroll makes his character, Humpty Dumpty, say: "I'm the teacher and the words mean what I order them to mean. This is why I pay them." Magritte is showing in his paintings the disarticulation of the pre-established ideas regarding words and images. In his picture "The key of dreams" as in the one on the cover, we see objects painted as the *pipe*, together with words that do not correspond, or that say *this is not a pipe*. As psychoanalysts, we need to understand the patient's personal vocabulary and be able to share it in its evolution. If we take, for example, the word father, we need to understand its singularity, in addition to its commonsense or conventional meaning. What other meanings does it have for the patient, and how do these meanings evolve in the analysis?

The poetry provided by images, dreams, and models must be able to occupy the place of a literal reading. In Magritte's pictures, the objects that unexpectedly imbricate with the written words reveal other meanings besides those that are obvious. That is how *paradoxes* appear, which, used as psychoanalytical instruments, reveal aspects that at first sight could appear as very unlikely. Paradoxes challenge commonsense, showing a very uncommon "commonsense".

In the picture that illustrates the cover, we see written under the image of a pipe, "This is not a pipe". What is obvious is that the image of a pipe is nothing more than a representation and cannot be used for smoking. But, then, if it appears in the dream or in a patient's association, what mystery does it enclose? This pipe is not a pipe in the same way as the word *dog* does not bark.

Magritte is saying that his pictures have been conceived as material signs of the freedom for thinking. That is why they are sensuous images that invite questioning. Enquiring, putting forward questions, is not the same as explaining. The images and the contrast shown in Magritte's pictures are a kind of narrative containing a mystery that can question in such a way that, if considered at the psychoanalytical level, it provides a kind of wrapping container, such as reverie, for mental pain. A psychoanalytic investigation needs to combine a disposition to know with compassion.

Questioning what has been "dreamed" is an invitation to break the mental habits that catalogue or classify the objects in an arbitrary order, but whose arbitrary order is easily forgotten because it falls under the basic assumption agreement (Bion, 1961), through what I call, in this book, the functioning of primitive groupishness.

If the habit is questioned, this is an invitation to thinking. Art reflects what psychoanalysis discovers from its vertex as a scientific discipline: the reality already known, which seems obvious, is related to another reality. The painted "dreamed" pipe that has written under it "This is not a pipe" invites one to perceive it as a mystery that needs to be inquired into.

I want to finish this introduction with a quotation from Kandinsky (1926):

> The geometric point is an invisible entity. Therefore it must be defined as a non-material entity. Considered in material terms, the point resembles a zero. Nevertheless, in this zero are hidden diverse qualities of "human" nature. In our representation, the zero—the geometric point—is associated with an utmost conciseness and temperance that is a strictest reserve, and notwithstanding it expresses itself, it speaks. So the period at the end of a sentence appears to us, in the utmost grade and with great singularity, as the *coming together of silence and speech*. In our perception the period is the essential bridge, unique between word and silence.
>
> And that is why the period found its material form, first of all in the writing: it belongs to the language and means silence. In fluid discourse the period is the symbol for interruption, of not-being (negative element) and at the same time a bridge from one being to the other (positive element). That is its meaning within writing. "From the outside it is not, in this case, more than a functional sign,

destined to a use that carries within it the element of the 'practicum-functional'; it is a sign that we get to know already in our childhood. External signs become a habit covering the interior sound of the symbol with a veil. The inside becomes walled up with what is outside". [Kandinsky, 1926, my translation]

CHAPTER ONE

The psychic birth of emotional experience: the mental equipment for making contact and understanding the psychic reality

"We are such stuff as dreams are made on
and our little life is rounded with a sleep"

(Shakespeare, *The Tempest*)

In this chapter, I am approaching the problems with which we are confronted in psychoanalytical treatments of patients who have serious difficulties in the psychic transformation of their emotional experiences*. Most of these problems are related to failures in the process of symbolic transformation. I am interested in the specific symbolic failure which is related to the obstruction of the development of phantasies, dreams, dream thoughts, etc. I want to focus attention on a frozen area of the mind, which, through immobility and emotional isolation, avoids falling into states of traumatic helplessness. I also want to differentiate bombardment of stimuli, or chaotic states of excitement, from psychically elaborated emotional experiences.

In my clinical experience with severely disturbed patients, I found myself differentiating a pathology that I frame in what Bion (1967, p. 43) calls hypertrophy of the apparatus for projective

identification from another in which a detention of projective identifications and an emotional isolation prevail.

In the first kind of pathology, the failures of the symbolization
process were related with psychotic functioning (ibid.). In transference, they brought problems related to what might be described as
an "excess" (massive projective identifications, catastrophic anxieties, etc.), different from the second ones, in which the most
remarkable features were a lack of emotional resonance and of
affective communication, and also a remarkable absence of dreams,
phantasies, and even of transformations* in hallucinosis (Bion,
1965). The first ones show their manifestations in the analytic relationship as phenomena of a "noisy presence" that were experienced
in the countertransference as disturbing, whereas the second ones
appear as phenomena of "silent absence", which generates a transference–countertransference atmosphere of lack of interest and
vitality and the risk of an endless pseudo-analysis.

Frances Tustin's work with autistic children, and her descriptions of how the autistic shell or encapsulation and the relation with
autistic objects of sensation was a serious impediment for the
construction of a space for playing, imagination, and symbol formation, helped me think about these phenomena that I observed in my
clinical experience. She says that because they cannot be seen,
touched, or handled, psychic experiences are outside the scope of
autistic children. The memories, thoughts, phantasies, imagina-
tions, and play are not within the range of their capacities. Symbolic
transformations are not possible for them (Tustin, 1990). Her deep
understanding of autistic phenomena led her to the hypothesis that
it implies a huge arrest of mental and emotional development and
a defence against the confusion and entanglement of psychosis. She
also stresses the fact that it is a serious responsibility to deprive
such patients of their autistic protections; this means that we need
to help these patients develop something better to replace them.

In this chapter, I put forward the conjecture that a factor in the
arrest of the development is the detention of projective identifications, and that when this primitive form of communication is re-
established it also opens the possibility for the development of a
symbolization process that can replace the pathological "protection". The reader will find a more detailed approach of this conjecture in Chapters Eight and Nine of this book.

Clinical investigation and some theoretical considerations led me to think of *inaccessible* caesuras*, associated with the detention of realistic projective identification (Bion, 1967) and a kind of silent, static, and wide splitting that obstructs any integrative or interactive movement. This kind of caesura and the detention of primitive modes of communication affect in a peculiar way the mental functions that are needed for discovering, for making contact with and understanding psychic reality. So, the personality is left with precarious equipment for dreaming, remembering, and working through mourning, vital life crises, etc. Its consequences are "gaps of representation" (Liberman et al., 1982), "memory holes" (not something forgotten), "identity holes", impeded mourning; these confer a precarious characteristic to the mental functioning that performs a creative transformation of the stimuli which come from the internal and outside world.

The writings of Melanie Klein and her followers (Bion, Rosenfeld, Meltzer, Segal, etc.) contributed to understanding problems that derived from psychotic functioning, characterized by fragmentation, hypertrophy of projective identification, etc., and its consequences in the disturbances of the process of symbolization. Their investigations of realistic and pathological projective identification allowed for understanding its manifestations with growing subtlety.

Frances Tustin's psychoanalytical ideas on autism, and our investigations with Liberman (Liberman et al., 1982) of psychosomatic disturbances, focused attention on another problem: the absence of the formation of symbols, even of symbolic equations, and the development of "facade" symbols or autistic barriers where the absence of emotional communication became obvious. These investigations, and the fact that the symbolization of psychosomatic patients was more an adapted façade (Liberman et al., 1982) that was not at the service of expressing the emotional experience, outlined some questions: specifically, which are the most authentic symbolic formulations for communicating and expressing the facts of psychic reality? How can a psychoanalytical process help the development of this kind of symbolization?

Bion's ideas about disturbances in the process of thinking as obstacles in the development of thoughts and of an apparatus for thinking, combined with Tustin's ideas about the arrest of emotional development in autistic children, helped me to think about the clinical problem of developing potentialities as the psychic birth of emotional experience.

Tustin stresses the fact that autistic children compensate for their early psychological deficiencies over valuating tactile physical contacts and the sensations to which they give rise. These sensations, these autistic sensation objects and autistic forms, are barriers against the development of memories, phantasies, and thoughts, which are intangible. The consequence of this functioning is that mental life cannot follow an adequate development. Without memories and without phantasies, a space for imagination cannot be constructed, and this is essential for the possibility of playing and dreaming. With Liberman (1982), we discovered that certain patients, some with psychosomatic symptoms (see Chapter Nine, my hypothesis about tropisms), had made an over-adaptation to external reality at the price of splitting off their emotional experiences and those that came from their own body. This over-adaptation had the function of a second skin (Bick, 1968), and was based on what seemed to be a kind of pseudo-symbolization acquired through imitation that was useless for dealing with emotional experiences. I think of this phenomena as equivalent to autistic barriers (Tustin, 1986), which impede emotional communication, even in its most primitive form, as projective identifications. They present the problem in a psychoanalytical treatment of how to get through these barriers and create a psychic space for emotional development that is dependant on a capacity for imagination, for playing, etc.

I will postulate that phantasies, dreams, and unconscious dreamthoughts, myths*, and artistic creations are a symbolic womb, which is essential for the psychic birth of the raw, "undigested" emotions and for their transformation as "children of the mind:

> . . . myths themselves are a second womb woven from cultural, interpretive constructions of innate programming of phantasy and external affaires . . . myths and rites, or culture itself, grow from the necessity of sheltering the long-dependent human infant. [Van Buren, 1989, p. 28]

They form the basic equipment of the mental functions for contact, discovery, and understanding of the psychic reality.

Dreams, phantasies, works of art, etc,. can be used as a resistance, or in what Bion called a −K link, in the service of lying, for mental manipulation, and for propaganda. (See Chapter Four.) However, in this chapter, I want to refer to the failures in the formation of this mental uterus.

Then emotional experiences remain as "undigested facts" or pre-natal terrors (Bion, 1977) that are neither unconscious nor conscious; they remain inaccessible because they lack the necessary transformational systems that facilitate their discovery and ulterior understanding. This outlines serious communication problems in an analysis, since analyst and patient have to communicate about experiences whose "psychic birth" is obstructed.

With these patients, we meet with a detained inanimate world without any dramatic character or vitality.

The inability to play or to dream "sleeping or awake" (Bion, 1992) their emotional experiences requires from analysis the construction or restoration of a containing and reverie* function, which will open the possibility of the transformation and evolution of the content. These transformations make them accessible to an approach at a psychic level.

The psychic elaboration of emotional experiences (infantile, vital crises, mourning, etc.) requires mental metabolization. *Phantasies, dreams, dream-thoughts, and myths are instruments for that psychic work.* When the dream work is not possible, as in the traumatic dreams Freud described in *Beyond the Pleasure Principle* (1920g, pp. 22–23), the working through of mourning and any psychic elaboration of emotional experiences is also handicapped.

With these patients we find ourselves neither with Alice's "Wonderland", nor with the dream phantasy world she found behind the looking glass; they seem to inhabit a detained world without dramatics and without vitality. We run into mental blindness, deafness, and muteness, analogous to the sequel that, at an organic level, produced in Helen Keller her very serious illness.

Freud differentiated on several occasions between phenomena related with quantity and with quality, and the possible transition from one situation to another: to mention just a few, the difference he made between actual neuroses and psychoneuroses, or the differentiation between automatic anxiety and signal anxiety, etc.

In the Kleinian thinking of unconscious phantasy as the mental expression of instinct and as the primary content of unconscious mental processes, there is a conception in terms of a dramatic world of internal objects and of a psychic meaning at different levels, which goes from the most primitive to the most evolved. Within this theory, the point of view of the quantitative aspect is mainly given in terms of excess; for example, excessive projective identification, excessive anxiety, etc.

Bion extended the connotations of the term "excessive", giving it the theoretical meaning of excess of omnipotent functioning (Bion, 1967) in the hypertrophy of the use of projective identification, or terming catastrophic a certain type of anxiety associated with psychotic functioning. Many of his formulations, which will be explained throughout the book, opened up new paths for going deeper into the problems of the psychic processing of emotional experiences.

The inability of some patients to dream "sleeping or awake" (Bion, 1992) their emotional experiences requires from analysis the restoration of a containing and reverie function that allows for the transformation and evolution of the content, at levels that make them accessible to an approach at a psychic level. To paraphrase Bion, who said that it is not enough to have thoughts, you need also to be able to think them, I would say that it is not enough to have feelings, there is a need to be able to experience them at a psychological level.

In *Elements of Psycho-analysis* (1963, p. 77 and Chapter Nineteen), Bion suggested that a Grid for feelings could be built as a counterpart, equivalent to the one that he proposed for thoughts. We could speak of and classify pre-emotions as precursors of emotional states, and/or premonitions (*ibid.*, pp.75–76) in analogy with preconceptions, acquiring growing levels of complexity as the fundaments of intuition and empathy. It could also include an axis of columns for the different uses (Bion, 1977), as well as the failures in the development of more complex levels of expression of emotions.

In the following questions that I want now to outline, the reader will find some of the principal axes of this book.

1. If for thinking the thoughts what is required is the dynamic alternation of the two mental functions: PS⇔D (a dynamic oscil-

lation of dispersion and integration) and of a container–contained* ($\male\,\female$) relationship where the point indicates a tolerable emotion, *what is the appropriate equipment for the psychic birth of an embryonic emotion (pre-natal)?*

2. Which are the most adequate means for the transformation of a primitive, violent, extreme pre-emotion into that point-symbol that indicates a detoxified emotion?

3. What happens to the emotion when it cannot have its psychic birth, and what happens in the personality that lacks the equipment for the psychic development of the emotion?

In what follows, I present some theoretical considerations and some aspects of the clinical material from a patient, whom I will call Ana, through which I will try to illustrate the clinical experience from which these hypotheses or conjectures arose.

Reverie, equipment, and mental pain

The human infant has to face the extraordinary adventure of knowing the world, as a central factor of his process of adaptation and survival. Because of the characteristics of our species, its own personality is part of the world to know. The assimilation of the emotional experiences is also a factor of this process.

The neothenia of the human infant—which means being born prematurely—implies the need to develop mental equipment for this adventure. The vicissitudes of this development will be associated for a long time to a link with the capabilities and parental functions for care-giving and reverie.

Bion described the experience of knowledge with its opposite, active ignorance ($-K$), as a complex emotional experience. Mental pain emerges from the implications of the pair knowledge / active ignorance (K and $-K$).

In "The importance of symbol formation in the development of the ego" (1930) Melanie Klein highlights the role of anxiety as a factor that stimulates mental development. The capacity of the self to tolerate anxiety has a direct relationship with its strength, and it is the condition for contact with psychic reality and therefore for emotional growth: "A sufficient quantity of anxiety is a necessary basis for an abundance of symbol-formation and of phantasy . . .", (Klein, 1930, p. 221). She also emphasizes the detention of identifications as a factor of paralysis of mental development, since she thinks identification is a precursor of symbolism: ". . . it is through symbolic equation that things, activities and interests become topics of phantasies . . . next to the libidinous interest, it is anxiety . . . the one that starts the mechanism of the identification" (p. 221).

I discovered that her description of Dick had remarkable similarities with those patients to whom I am referring, mainly in the lack of ego developments and of emotional relationships with the environment. I read with interest the following hypothesis:

> Possibly his development was affected by the fact that, though he had every care, no real love was lavished on him, his mother's attitude to him being from the very beginning over-anxious . . . Dick grew up in an environment rather poor in love. [*ibid.*, p. 222]

Klein describes changes and progress in the boy's mental development when he was in contact with his grandmother and an affectionate nanny. In her description, she speaks of Dick's apparent lack of anxiety, relating the detention of the identifications (that she did not yet name as projective), with a latent excessive anxiety. Observing the description of Dick's changes, from a relationship with a mother with excessive anxiety and an extremely poor atmosphere of love to being in contact with objects with different characteristics, such as the grandmother and the nanny, and his concomitant progress, we can begin to build a bridge to Bion's ideas on maternal reverie and its function in the development of the symbolization process. The modulation of mental pain in a relationship is the central problem for the development of the human mind; especially for being able to tolerate contact with the internal world and the symbolization processes as transformations of primitive emotional experiences that have the function of articulating the internal and external reality.

The methods for dealing with the mental pain of modification or avoidance reflect in the vicissitudes of the mental equipment.

> My experience has led me to the conclusion that insight conveyed by interpretations, lodges in two ways in the mental apparatus, *first*

of all new equipment for the internal objects and secondly as new equipment for the adult self. I call it equipment to distinguish it from the qualities of goodness and badness in their many forms . . . the goodness, strength and beauty of objects are not essentially *useful* although love has implications, transcendental for the personality, as a whole . . . In addition to these qualities the objects must have knowledge, skills, wisdom . . . [Meltzer, 1962, pp. 87–88, my italics]

For the process of discovering and giving meaning to the emotional experience, the infant depends on reverie, that "natural" capability of the mother's mind to accept, house, and transform a pre-verbal primitive form of communication, the realistic projective identification. The infant needs the reverie function for the development of an *evolved consciousness capable of being aware.*

To receive without panic what the baby transmits in an atmosphere of urgency and catastrophe acts as a modulator of pain and for the transformation of that communication into a "dream" or a "dream-thought". In this way, the infant can receive and reintroject a part of his personality wrapped up in a tolerable emotion, similar to a protective atmosphere that favours discovery. If this communication fails at some point, the infant receives in return a nameless dread. This increases its state of helplessness and the precariousness of the equipment to deal with mental pain.

Winnicott, Bion, Money-Kyrle, and Bick, among other psychoanalytic authors, have stressed the mother's function as a thinking object and that maternal mental functioning builds a scaffolding of meaning for infantile primitive experiences. The absence of this scaffolding, especially for pre-verbal experiences, leaves the infant exposed to mental states of empty turbulence devoid of meaning. A long deprivation of the maternal capabilities for holding and give a meaning transforms a relatively benign void into a virulent nothingness, or can degenerate into chaotic states, which, in extreme cases, affect the central nervous system, as described by Spitz in infants with marasmus.

The reverie function undoubtedly depends on the mother's mental state, on her maturity, on her capacity to tolerate pain, to be able to wait and think, which, in turn, depend on her own internal containing space, etc. I think that an important factor in the mother's capacity to help her baby in its first steps towards thinking thoughts and feeling emotions is related to her own mother's same aptitude in the past to help her in that sense when she was a baby. *I propose the conjecture of a transgenerational reverie.*

I propose thinking of reverie not only as a function, but also as a *communication channel* (Bion, 1962, p. 36).

> Leaving aside the physical channels of communication my impression is that her love is expressed by reverie . . . If the feeding mother cannot allow reverie or if the reverie is allowed but is not associated with love for the child or its father this fact will be communicated to the infant even though incomprehensible to the infant. Psychical quality will be imparted to the *channels of communication*, the links with the child. [Bion, 1962, p. 36, my italics]

I propose the conjecture that, in severe failures of the parental equipment for reverie, the direction of the circulation in the *channel of communication* is in reverse: instead of the baby's primitive messages going towards the mother, who transforms them so that the infant receives them already detoxified and made tolerable, the direction is inverted, and the infant receives the undigested emotional messages from the mother, leaving a psychic apparatus overwhelmed by a bombardment of stimuli which overflows the baby's precarious ability to digest it. My clinical experience has shown that we often find, in the psychic functioning of the patient, these undigested facts of the mother as foreign or radioactive elements.

The tasks that the failures of the maternal reverie leave unfinished fall on the infant's rudimentary consciousness and all these tasks are related to the functions of correlation and communication. Projective identification may become hyperbolic or may stop, also causing a detention in the development of the capability to register the emotions and of the capacity for psychic elaboration.

I think that, for this elaboration, the symbolic equation (Segal, 1957, 1981) is a developmental step and not only a pathological modality that produces concrete thought.

> The mechanism of projective identification enables the infant to deal with primitive emotion and so contributes to the development of thoughts. The interplay between the depressive and paranoid–schizoid positions is also related to the development of thoughts

and thinking. . . . The earliest observation I have been able to make seemed to suggest that development of thinking through PS⟷D depended on the production of signs . . . the verbalizations seemed to refer to the objects present . . . the objects were being used as signs to make thinking possible about objects that were *not* present. [Bion, 1963, pp. 37–38]

Through this quotation, I want to draw attention towards the use of objects that are present as signs, not as symbols, as a use of a symbolic equation. I also want to stress the importance that Bion attributes to projective identification in the development of thought when it was transformed in the development of his theory (Bion, 1962) in a container-contained relationship. Projective identification, as a content and a preconception, when it mates with a "realization"* of being received by a breast with reverie (a container), not only enables the infant to deal with primitive emotions, but it allows for the formation of symbolic equations as a primitive mode of establishing relations and correlations.

Mental pain does not belong to the sensorial domain; anxiety does not have shape, odour, sound, or colour. Bion (1970, p. 7) proposes the term "to intuit" as the mental counterpart to what would be to see, hear, smell, etc., in the sensorial domain. I think that this intuition has its proto-mental, prenatal matrix, and its realization and development in the first body experiences of the infant which acquire meaning in the mother–infant relationship, and are thus transformed into communication.

Spitz makes the very interesting observation that the signs and signals received by the infant during his first month of life belong to the categories of equilibrium, tensions (muscular and others), posture, temperature, vibration, contact, rhythm, time, duration, range of tones, and probably many others of which we are not aware in adults. The adults that have the faculty of using one or many of these lost sensitivities are the ones that are specially gifted, such as composers, musicians, and dancers. For the infant, the signs of the affective tone of his mother becomes a means of communication to which he responds and which are perceived in the same way by the mother. Spitz conjectures that during pregnancy and the period that follows, the mother probably finds again these capabilities for kinaesthetic perception that ordinarily she could have lost (Spitz, 1958).

The problem of dealing with mental pain, inherent to life and central in a psychoanalytical treatment, is associated with the development of mental functions and of a consciousness capable of becoming aware as a continuous phenomenon, which depends at the beginning of life fundamentally on parental objects. It sets the foundations for the feelings of existing and feeling real. The reader will find explorations and extensions of these ideas in the other chapters of the book.

The development of these functions is closely correlated with the attitude of the personality towards mental pain. Psychotic, neurotic, or autistic functioning will depend on what defences are erected to avoid mental pain. Maternal reverie is a factor in developing the capability to tolerate pain. Although I do not consider the baby a *tabula rasa* on which the failures of parental functions are inscribed automatically, I think that an infant with more sensibility will develop more inaccessible barriers towards pain if this sensibility remains "naked in the wind" because of the absence of those parental functions that act as modulators of pain.

Mentalization and de-mentalization of pain: different kinds of caesuras

Through the term "mentalization of the pain", I am approaching the problem of the ability to perceive and register emotional states and of their transmission or communication.

When Freud (1926d) makes a difference between automatic anxiety and signal anxiety as a sign, he gives a model* for mentalization of pain. Signal anxiety has psychological meaning and a function: it allows the self to develop defence mechanisms, and that is how the self can avoid the traumatic situation of helplessness. In automatic anxiety, the self remains without bonds and exposed to the threat of the feared situation of helplessness. Automatic anxiety does not have psychic meaning (Pistiner de Cortiñas & Bianchedi, 1988). I think that Bion again takes the topic of automatic anxiety within a relational framework, through the problem of nameless dread. In the context of his theory of thinking, and included in the dynamics of a relationship (mother's mind–infant's mind), the idea of a psychic helplessness gains new meaning. As we have already described, maternal reverie performs a function of mental help. The mother's mind, through her alpha function*, is protecting her infant's mind from the catastrophic experiences of helplessness, transforming panic into a tolerable and thinkable emotion through forging instruments for thinking. (See also Chapters Two and Three.)

The description I offered at the beginning of this chapter, of patients with manifestations of a "noisy presence" and others with a "silent absence", referred to a differentiation of the methods they used for dealing with catastrophic anxieties. I mentioned Bion's ideas of how the psychotic part of the personality faced these catastrophic anxieties. He described fragmentation, the hyperbolic use of projective identification, etc., thus avoiding pain by means of a massive evacuative functioning, which damaged thinking and the mental functions of contact with reality. I found in these investigations of the disturbances of the symbolization processes and of communication when psychotic operations predominate, the conceptual instruments for observing and understanding these phenomena in my clinical practice.

In turn, I discovered that these ideas could not help me to understand the emotional isolation and the lack of vitality and communication I found in the analysis of other patients. I could not observe in Ana attacks on linking, or on the capability to form links, yet neither did I meet with projective identifications, realistic or massive.

Ana would come, she would utter a few words, then she became tense, covering her nose, wringing her hands; she also told me that she had eczema, but nothing she did or said seemed to resonate emotionally in me, or to evoke some image or association. When she missed a session or was late, she seemed not to be aware of it, and if I drew her attention to that point all she could say was that "she had no energy". She did not laugh, and never smiled, nor did she cry or get angry. Everything in our analytic relationship sounded hollow and seemed empty. I also observed these phenomena in other patients, whom I was tempted to describe (as a model) as living in a "world of apathy" or "functioning like a computer", etc. (Frances Tustin's contributions on autistic functioning brought me nearer to the understanding of the phenomena I observed in the clinic, as shall be seen in the last two chapters.)

I associated Meltzer's idea of a two-dimensional psychic spatiality with my hypothesis of the detention of projective identifications. In patients like Ana, the flaws in the container–contained function could be seen reflected in the difficulty of the construction of a three-dimensional psychic space.

The projective identification, as Klein (1946) conceived it, implies an object with an interior, with a three-dimensional space. In *Explorations in Autism* (1975), Meltzer refers to the inability of these patients in the achievement of any degree of projective identification. It would not only be a two-dimensional space, but also an open, flat space, without a sphincter, without closing possibilities. He described these infants as very sensual and emotionally sensitive, with an extreme opening to the emotions and mental states of themselves and of the object. They lack adequate internal equipment, and they also meet with an external object that has a reverie function with serious flaws.

Meltzer described a primary obsessionality as a way of dealing with the initial chaos of stimuli. This obsessionality can be transformed into a pathological splitting with peculiar characteristic. He described it as a *dismantlement* of the perceptive self that reduces experiences to "events" that cannot be considered as mental acts, which means that "they cannot be experienced in a way that allows its integration in a continuum of memories, nor as the base for the anticipation" (Meltzer, 1975, p. 28). In the post-autistic personality, this dismantlement takes the form of an obsessionality that maintains the objects isolated. One of thee models Meltzer uses for this kind of obsessionality is the Chinese boxes: through such isolation, the emotional answer to the complexity of the world is interfered with. The mechanism through which this dismantlement takes place involves a "suspension" of attention. Although babies bring with them, in their innate endowment, the ability to perceive *gestalten*, at the beginning the mother is the one that provides attention as a mental function. The connected mother's behaviour is the one that first "pulls the string" that sustains the baby's attention. "The infant's suspended attention" is related to the inability to sustain a very sensitive baby, so that it may hold on to the mother's attention and thus confront the complexity of the world, which includes their own emotions and sensations.

I could observe the consequences of this dismantlement in Ana in her feeling "lost or as living in a nebula" and through her emotional isolation, based on what seemed to be silent and static splitting that I will attempt to show in the clinical material. This functioning reduces the experiences to meaningless events; it avoids establishing correlations and any kind of transformation that could open access to what she felt would be experienced as a bombardment of the feared emotions.

Dismantlement, bidimensionality, the non-constitution of a containing space in the self and/or in the object, the reduction of the experiences to "events", the emotional isolation and the splitting associated with detention of projective identifications, give a very defective and precarious quality to the self, and produce a lack of communication reflected in the fact that, for the patient, as well as for the analyst, emotional contact has become inaccessible.

Matrixes of the equipment

"El sueño autor de representaciones
en su teatro sobre el viento armado
sombras suele vestir de bulto bello
                              Góngora

The dream, author of representations
in his theatre built on the wind
dresses shades as beautiful bundles".
                              Góngora

I want to develop here the following hypothesis, which I think is a central point for understanding these kinds of failures in the process of symbolic transformation: the primary link between the infant's and the mother's mind is where, through communicational forms that at the beginning are not verbal, the building of a mental equipment takes place. These primitive emotional exchanges are the bases of a profound language, specially designed to express emotional experiences. These experiences need forms of expression to be able to be registered and thought. The unconscious day-dream thoughts, the dreams and myths, have their matrixes in these precursor forms. Their more evolved manifestations will be developed in artistic creations:

> The myth may be regarded as a primitive form of pre-conception and a stage in publication, that is in communication of the individual's private knowledge to his group . . . The dream has a fresh significance if it is regarded as a private myth. [Bion, 1963, p. 63]

I will take as a presupposed hypothesis that there is a continuity between the primitive somatic/emotional manifestations of experiences and the more elaborated at a psychic level. I also have in mind Freud's ideas that the ego is first a body ego, and Bion's suggestion of the need to open the investigation towards a protomental, prenatal spectrum. I suggest the need for the development of an ideo-grammar (in gestures, paralinguistic forms, etc.) in the primary link, as the precursory forms that will be the matrix for the mental tools for expression and communication of the emotional experience. I am referring to the transformation of the primitive experiences as body/emotional manifestations into forms that are thinkable and communicable.

Freud, in the "Project" (1895), describes how the discharge channels acquire the important function of communication. In the primary relationship with another human being, Spitz (1958) describes how, for the infant, the sight of the human face is transformed from a visual sign into a privileged "Gestalt sign" that will stimulate the important response of smiling. So, it becomes for the infant the nucleus of a primary organizer of mental life. A symbol as complex as "no", a factor in mental functions so evolved as discrimination, judgement, and negation, has its origins in the body/emotional movements, when the baby turns away its mouth from the breast, taking the opposite direction of the movements of the baby's head seeking the breast. A grimace of pain can be a discharge reflex, becoming an ideogrammatic expression of pain, and can also develop into the gesture of the mask that symbolizes tragedy, as in the Greek theatre.

I want to include Susan Langer's (1954) philosophic perspective of the differentiation she makes between "presentative symbolism" and "discursive symbolism". Verbal language (discursive) is only one of the symbolic forms; symbols also may be taken from the environment of expressive signs, such as gestures, movements, grimaces, etc., that, in an ulterior transformation, are formalized in such a way that the meaning can be apprehended and stored.

I come back to my initial hypothesis now: the mother with reverie, when modulating the mental pain, can contain and transform it into a meaning. This kind of containment allows the development of forms that we "borrow" from expressions, movements, etc., and that are transformed into proto-symbols, which in turn act as instruments that attenuate the traumatic experiences of helplessness. These "sensorial forms" built in the primary link are part of the matrix of the language apt for expressing a non-sensorial reality: the psychic reality.

The psychoanalysis of adults seems to have privileged verbal communication. However the analysis of children, psychotics, patients with psycho-somatic disturbances, etc., showed the importance of taking into account other forms of communication, such as pre-verbal gestures, ideographic expressions, and so on. This is not new in psychoanalysis, since Freud opened up this perspective with the interpretation of dreams (thoughts expressed mainly in visual images) as the "royal road" of access to the unconscious (1900a).

I will also take an idea developed by Bion in his posthumous book, *Cogitations*: that of "dream-work-alpha" (later on transformed into alpha function), the name he gave to a function that is going on continuously in the human being, not only while he is asleep. (See Chapter Three.)

He suggests that the transformation (Bion, 1991, p. 180) of sensuous impressions into visual images is part of the process of mental assimilation, transforming the entire experience into an appropriate form for its storage in the mind: "the impressions of . . . any event are transformed in a personal visual image becoming an appropriate form for its storage in the mind". This transformational function uses the sensuous impressions of the experience so these impressions are given durability. This is the process that transforms them into images that can be stored and evoked.

The impression has to be ideogrammized. That is, if the experience is a pain, the psyche has to have the image of rubbing an elbow, a face full of tears, or something like that. [Bion, 1991, p.180]

The dream-work-alpha*, later called alpha function, is that which effects the transformation necessary to store the emotional experience in a communicable form.

Dreams, dream-thoughts, myths, and models express the stored and communicable version of an emotional experience. This transforming function is vital, so that the experience can be presented to the conscious in such a way that it can be discovered, thought, and given a meaning. I suggest that, with "dream-work-alpha", each of us builds its "alphabet images, formed through the conjunction of the sensuous impression with the emotional experience, and that this alphabet of images combines in different forms, able to be evocative of past, present, and future experiences, forming "the eyes of the mind" that are needed for imagination and insight.

In Row C of The Grid*, Bion places dream thoughts, dreams, and myths, and he puts them before the preconceptions of Row D. These dream thoughts can, in turn, be transformed into preconceptions which have an unsaturated element and can mate with new experiences. I think that when used at the service of the reality principle, this category of thoughts is the "royal road" of contact with, and understanding of, psychic reality. They are part of the preconceptual apparatus.

Our mind needs thoughts and feelings to be expressed by forms that are "borrowed" from the sensuous world; presented through these forms, they may then be matter for thinking. Jorge Luis Borges, with his artist's intuition, has expressed this idea like this:

> We can feel oppression and we look for an explanation. Then I absurdly, but vividly, dream that a sphinx is seated on my chest. The sphinx is not the cause of the terror; it is an explanation of the felt oppression. [Borges, 1980, p. 47, my translation]

The transformation in images linked by a narrative, sensorial form of a non-sensuous reality are a vital part of the mental equipment and necessary for thoughts and feelings to be thought and experienced without losing their vitality. They are some of the necessary conditions for the development of the process of "becoming aware"; so the experiences can be forgotten, repressed, remembered, can become conscious or unconscious, not inaccessible. This point has special interest for me, because I have been able to observe in my clinical experience with Ana and with other patients this characteristic of inaccessibility, and that it was related to a failure in this cognitive emotional grammar's development, in the primary link.

The failure is manifested as much in these patients' emotional isolation in the analytic relation as in the relationship with their own psychic reality, and in their inability to "dream" their emotional experiences, which would reveal a meaning. These experiences are lived, therefore, as a bombardment of stimuli that overflows them. They become inaccessible, only showing under somatic and very primitive forms, such as crying, which lack psychic meaning; it is a very concrete overflow which causes panic.

I suggest that those primary links where an absence, or failures, of parental functions of understanding and containment predominate, together with my conjecture of a defective *transgenerational reverie*, is precarious equipment for the development of expressive modes, of an "ideo-grammar", through which it is possible "to play" the conflicts of hate and love. Here is the ground where pathologies that are related to a kind of sterile apathy can develop, because of the impossibility of elaborating appropriate mental instruments to process the emotional experiences psychically.

The inborn and the acquired equipment

I will take as presupposed Bion's hypotheses (1979) about prenatal preconceptions as an innate endowment that has its phylogenetic and ontogenetic inscription in the human being, and Money-Kyrle's hypotheses (1968) about innate cognitive structures.

Bion refers to the mating of a preconception with a positive or negative "realization", giving birth to a conception or a thought. The word "realization" means materialization, and also becoming aware of an experience. The capacity to realize, and the tolerance of the realization, is a central factor for the development of conceptions and thoughts. The development of this capacity is part of the mental equipment for thinking.

Money-Kyrle's (1968) hypothesis is that the human being has an innate disposition to discover the truth. Ethology makes a contribution to psychoanalysis with elements that allow thinking of an innate cognitive structure, which has remained as a phylogenetic inheritance of the species, through mutations and selection processes. The first steps in the development of concepts are related to what is known in ethology as "imprinting". The obstructions in the development of notions of class and of concepts are of an emotional nature. The role of maternal reverie is fundamental for the transformation it can offer the infant towards a cognitive development.

> Failure to conceive and internalize a breast that converts chaos into meaning (β elements into α elements and higher forms of thought) may in part result from a defect of the environment. The mother may be too anxious or be too narcissistic to be receptive of distress, or she may be intolerant of certain kinds of it . . . In other words baby may find no adequate realization to mate with his innate preconception . . . [Money Kyrle, 1968, p. 402]

Also interesting is what Money-Kyrle thinks about three stages in cognitive development:

> three stages in the development of representational thought, that is, the use of "concepts" to represent separate and absent objects. In the first, what later will become a representation of an absent and separate object is experienced in a concrete way as introjective or projective identification with the object . . . Presumably it operates by the same primitive mechanism by which an emotional or kinaesthetic state spreads through a group of any social animal. The second stage is that of the "*ideographic representation*" predominantly in terms of *visual metaphors*. Dream thinking, as explored by Freud, is largely of this kind, and some of the difficulties in understanding dreams would seem to stem, not only from resistance, but from the fact that they had become unfamiliar because replaced by the third stage . . . of verbal thought which dominates our conscious activity. [Money-Kyrle, 1968, p.400, author's italics]

I propose, as a hypothesis, that this second stage, that of the ideographic representations, have their roots in the first symbolic equations (Segal, 1981) and are part of the basic equipment for the construction of an internal world, in which the object relations acquire their characteristics of dramatization and personification (Klein, 1930). This is an unavoidable transformation for intrapsychic and intersubjective (that is, private and public) communication and for the psychic birth of the emotional experience.

Pathologies such as autism, or the psychosomatic disturbances, show evidence that the construction of these "dramatic" character-istics might not have been achieved, with serious consequences for mental life and for the capacity of being aware of psychic reality. From the point of view of the developmental process, the symbolic equations built through projective identifications are a first stage of the process of symbolization; they are used as concrete signs, not symbols. However, later on, they might also provide the elements for analogy and for building authentic symbols, when depressive elaboration by means of the differentiation between self and non-self is achieved. The arrest of the projective identifications obstructs the development of symbolic equations; this also means that the transition towards analogy and metaphor, as well as the depressive elaboration involved in this transition, is also being hindered.

To develop the idea about the importance for the cognitive–emotional development of this analogical language, I will introduce some of Gregory Bateson's hypotheses. This author, through his investigations of ethology and the theory of communication, con-tributes to the understanding of the matrix of cognitive–emotional communication. Bateson (1972) maintains that communication of mammals takes place through rules about the relationship; so their communications are mainly about the rules and vicissitudes of the relationship. It is an iconic–analogical pre-verbal communication that is carried out through kinetic and paralinguistic means, such as body movements, the tensions of the voluntary muscles, changes in facial expression, hesitations, alterations in the rhythm of sounds or of movement, overtones of the voice, and irregularities in breath-ing. And these expressions are the ones that "transmit" emotion, and to what objects it is referred; they communicate the rules of the relationship with the object. In all mammals, the sense organs also become the organs for the transmission of messages about the rela-tionship. The pre-verbal, kinetic, and paralinguistic language is specially designed for the communication of the emotional relation and of the rules of relationship among members of the same species. This language can only express something about the relationship, and in this it differs from the verbal language that can express something about things. A kitten that meows is not saying "milk"; it is expressing a relationship of "dependence": to meow is his way of expressing the relationship rule with its mother.

In the human species, our mammal condition and this kind of communication is evident in spite of the verbal linguistics that we have acquired recently. We have evidence of this in the fact that the paralinguistic and kinetic language of people from different cultures, and even the paralinguistic expressions of other terrestrial mammals, are still intelligible to us. On the other hand, we find verbal languages of other cultures to be completely opaque. Verbal language is almost purely digital (but not entirely so). A name has a conventional or arbitrary connection with the class that it designates. On the other hand, kinetic and paralinguistic communication are analogical.

Bateson (1972) maintains that verbal language is not an evolutionary substitute for kinetic communication. If this were so, the oldest systems, predominantly iconic, would have disappeared. Yet, observation shows that, in the human being, kinetics have become richer and more complex and the paralinguistic language has also flourished, parallel to the evolution of verbal language, developing elaborated forms of art: music, dance, poetry, etc. These ideas agree with those formulated by Langer about "presentative symbolism" as another "symbolic form", and the importance given by Meltzer (1983) to what he calls music and dance in the elaboration of a deep emotional grammar. It can also be correlated with Bion's idea, regarding Row C of the Grid and "dream-work-alpha".

This evolution of the kinetic and paralinguistic language indicates that our iconic–analogical communication is at the service of functions different from those of the verbal language, and those functions are related to emotions in the relationships or links of love, hate, respect, fear, dependence, etc. Bateson also says that dreaming and human myths is a connection area between the iconic code of the animals and the digital code of verbal language.

> I arrive at the conclusion—I do not know if it is a scientific one— that dreams are the most ancient aesthetic activity . . . very curious, as it is of a dramatic order . . . in dreams we are the theatre, the audience, the actors, the plot, the words we hear. [Borges, 1980, author's translation]

This strongly evokes Winnicott's transitional space.

In the next section, I approach the problem of differentiating different kinds of symbolization. Taking into account Langer's ideas, I propose the hypothesis of presentative symbolism as being especially capable of formulating emotional experiences, psychic reality, and the most unconscious phenomena. I think this without leaving aside the importance of verbalization, provided it is used in the aspects that I am highlighting, to name and to express emotional experience.

The mental equipment: the function of presentative symbolism, fantasy, "dream-work-alpha"

Freud in "Formulations on the two principles of mental functioning" (1911b) says that

> With the introduction of the reality principle one species of thought-activity was split off; it was kept free from reality testing . . . this activity is *phantasizing*, which begins already in children's play and later continued as *daydreaming* . . .. [p. 222]

In a footnote, he makes an analogy between phantasy remaining outside of reality testing, and the way in which some nations leave aside certain areas of reservation in their original state to protect them from the changes brought about by civilization (*ibid.*).

And, although he says that in the realm of phantasy repression remains all-powerful, and that this is the weak point in our psychical organization, Freud also refers to art as a "reconciliation" between "the two principles" in a peculiar way.

> An artist is originally a man who turns away from reality, because he cannot come to terms with the renunciation of instinctual satisfaction, which it at first demands, and who allows his erotic and ambitious desires full play in the life of phantasy. He finds the way back to reality . . . from this world of phantasy by making use of special gifts to mould his phantasies into truths of a new kind, which are valued by men as precious reflections of reality. [*ibid.*, p. 224]

What kind of reality finds its reflection in art? What are these new truths? Freud describes the fantasy like a thought activity that can—I emphasize can—remain outside the reality principle, but not necessarily always, and we can find evidence of Freud' s argument in the artistic creations that nurture fantasies, but how do we find the way to return to reality? By using them as representations of desires and frustrations in psychic reality, by transforming them through the works of art through which those fantasies are captured into symbols of emotional experiences, so that other men might feel identified. Thus, they can share the destiny of desires and their necessary frustration, as well as help them to find ways to tolerate frustration and to mitigate it.

I want to draw the reader's attention to what Freud says about the function of fantasies as "ecological reserves". I think that Bion express this idea as "thoughts without a thinker", wild intuitions prior to becoming prematurely domesticated. "If psycho-analytic intuition does not provide stamping ground for wild asses, where is a zoo to be found to preserve the species?" (Bion, 1991, p. 5). The "wild asses" are those untamed thoughts (Bion, 1997), which are received and stored in the artist's mind. By giving them expressive form, he develops a reverie function for humanity.

This idea would give man's neothenia, coexisting with its symbolic capability, of which phantasy is a part, a meaning of resources that have survived because they are useful tools for evolution of mental growth. This hypothesis coincides with Bateson's (1972) argument about the survival of paralinguistic language.

Segal, in "Phantasy and other psychic processes" (1981), outlines the interesting idea that thought is a modification of the unconscious phantasy, owing to the need for a further examination of reality. The wealth, depth, and accuracy of the thought of an individual, will depend on the quality and malleability of his unconscious phantasy life and of his capacity to subject it to the examination of reality. An infant approaches reality "equipped" with its phantasies; that is, with the expectations that his unconscious phantasy has forged.

Thus, for Segal, phantasy has a similar function to the one that later on will correspond to thought, of allowing the infant's immature self to tolerate the tensions without an immediate discharge that could have a disintegrating effect. It works as a preconception, similar to the hypotheses that a scientist uses for approaching a "realization", to the encounter and confrontation with facts. The

result of this confrontation depends on the infant's capacity to tolerate doubt, waiting, and frustration, and this has a correlation with
the mother's capability to maintain the frustration within limits
tolerable for that infant. (I will leave aside the differences between
the Freudian and the Kleinian conception of the term fantasy, since
I think it is not relevant for the question I am outlining.)

I will take some of Langer's ideas, which include the notion of
phantasy and symbolism as *a new key* in philosophy, combining
them with my psychoanalytical perspective. The sensuous image
is a subjective testimony of the experience; it is not a copy. Just
as words (of discursive symbolism) evolve from sounds to combinations of sounds, into words, and then to a grammatical combination, images, too, evolve. With the "eyes of the mind" we have
pictorial representations, associated with experiences. Presentative
symbolism develops from an image that "presents" a simple concept
towards combinations of images, which establish reciprocal references, such as changing scenes through which we perceive the
course of the events.

It is these combinations, which, in addition to having visual
components, have kinaesthetic, auditory, etc., patterns that Langer
calls phantasies. She thinks that, if an experience needs to remain in
the memory, the processes that we perceive must be registered as a
phantasy, through which it can be evoked in the imagination and
experienced again. For this author, presentative symbolism is the
most appropriate for expressing the emotional experiences as
symbols and not as emotive symptoms, provided that certain
conditions occur, among which she gives a relevant position to
"psychological distance". This means that, at the symbolic level, the
symbol expresses the interpretation of the experience and does not
have a cathartic function. These ideas undoubtedly have much in
common with the psychoanalytical hypotheses of alpha function
and the contact barrier* (Bion, 1962). For Langer, phantasy, at the
symbolic level, is a *metaphor of cognition without words*, and *metaphor
is the basic law for development of all semantics*.

In presentative symbolism, the fundamental experiences of
human existence are symbolized; this would be the way to enun-
ciate, register, and, I would add, contain, man's emotional reactions
to such experiences.

My conjecture is that the presentative symbolism, because of its characteristics similar to the primary process (although the feature of symbol already implies the reality principle) can be considered the most appropriate language for expressing emotional experiences and for storage in a kind of dream-like memory. This conjecture agrees with Bateson's hypothesis that the paralinguistic analogical language is neither archaic nor obsolete. I also relate this conjecture with Money-Kyrle's ideas, which I have already mentioned, and with the function Bion ascribes to "dream-work-alpha", the category of thoughts of Row C of the Grid that correspond, in my opinion, to presentative symbolism.

I have already referred to the use of thoughts of Row C as preconceptions. Bion goes one step further when he suggests that the function of "dream work-alpha" could be used in a similar way to the one that mathematicians use in algebraic formulations. (See also Chapter Two.) In this way, phantasies, myths, dreams, and dream-thoughts can be conceived also as the artists' creations, as psychic formulations necessary for carrying out "psychic operations". Some of these operations, such as the psychic birth of emotional experience and its mental assimilation, would require an appropriate formulation. The static caesuras and the detention of the realistic projective identifications are obstacles for the formulation in dream thoughts, dreams, phantasies, etc., of the experience, obstructing the possibility of transforming it through thought.

In patients like Ana, flaws take place in the formulation of the emotional experience about which they need to think. They lack the instruments to be able to think and to communicate. The course of an analysis under these conditions requires the development of these tools.

Considerations of the clinical material

During a psychoanalytical treatment, it is supposed that emotional situations and crises are displayed in the relationship between patient and analyst and between the patient and himself. Analyses of patients like Ana seem to develop without turbulence, presenting a different kind of problem, associated with the absence of manifestations of pain or its appearance as very primitive manifestations, more at a somatic than at a psychological level. To these, we may add those peculiar difficulties in communication I attempt to describe, due to the "development" of "instruments" for avoiding contact with pain, through the detention of projective identifications, static splitting, and emotional isolation.

> The nature of the functions which excite the patient's curiosity he explores by projective identification. His own feelings too powerful to be contained within his personality are amongst these functions. Projective identification makes it possible for him to investigate his own feelings in a personality powerful enough to contain them. Denial of the use of this mechanism . . . leads to a destruction of the link between infant and breast and consequently to a severe disturbance of the impulse to be curious on which all learning depends. [Bion, 1967, pp. 106–107]

The emotions fulfil a similar function for the psyche to that of the senses in relation to objects in space and time (ibid., p. 119).

Through the clinical material, I will follow three lines that show a pattern: emotional experiences that are "not digested", and their manifestations at:

1. The somatic level, as an unborn, prenatal area, which, through its embryonic manifestations, try to make themselves "heard". The appearance of the somatic symptom during the analytic treatment, in this case, indicates that the detained projective identifications are starting. The fact that these somatic manifestations are followed by the first dreams in the analysis, a communication of emotional experiences at a more psychic level, and Ana's concern for not being able to remember important aspects of her life story, is also, in my opinion, evidence of the beginning of the development in the analysis of a symbiotic container–contained function (Bion, 1962).

2. The static splitting of great amplitude, together with emotional isolation that avoids contact with the emotional facts, about which the patient can neither dream nor think and whose emergence threatens as a "chaos of stimuli". It is an illustration of these problems to see, as I will show in the clinical material, that

any progress towards a possible integration is followed by catastrophic feelings of being overwhelmed and different levels of
retraction.

3. The non-assimilation of experiences also shows as " holes of
    the memory" (Ana felt that facts of her life were "missing";
    they were felt as if they had disappeared, which had a different
    quality than repressed memories), and this was associated with
    an inability to establish relations and to put together a story of
    her life. Different situations remained isolated from each other.
    All this reflected in holes in her identity, and through an almost
    permanent feeling of being "lost" to herself during a long period
    of time.

I will try to show the transformations from these precarious
operations towards the development of mental functions more
capable of communicating and containing experiences. My hypothesis is that, as "a dream-work-alpha" was settling in the analytic
process between patient and analyst, the direction of analysis
changed for Ana. The psychoanalytic function of the personality
was acting as a powerful factor in the analyst in order to tolerate
this process. The change of direction showed through a change in
functioning in which prevailed an oscillation between isolation and
a very concrete search for me to organize her as to what to do, also
in a very concrete way; towards finding in the analysis, in the
analyst's mind, and in her own mind, through her dreams, a space
where she would be able to feel, to imagine, and, for moments, to
think her experiences.

Through the evolution of the somatic symptom, I will try to
illustrate the hypothesis of the formation of an "ideo-grammar" in
the analytic relation that later acquired growing levels of symbolization, with the formation of a contact barrier, as is also evidenced
by her first parapraxis.

The importance of images as containers and forms of communication was seen in the role played by the photographs for Ana, and
from the evolution of a capacity to dream, used in the service of
discovering and communicating her experiences. These changes,
together with the transformation of the splitting from static into
dynamic, were facilitated by the onset of the oscillation of the
operation PS⇔D function and a change in the container–contained

($\male\female$) relationship. They allowed Ana to begin looking for elements of her "life story"; first, very concretely, and often through geographical references to her native city, and then through photographs, images, and dreams, in which a representation of her experiences already appears. Later on, it also showed through dreams as the symbolization of a dissociation, in the service of a discrimination between "good–bad", "those that love me and those that don't love me", which also used to be located in geographical places and at levels that belong more to the neurotic part of the personality.

In this process, she likewise goes towards encountering an identity, when she starts the mourning until then detained in her evolution, with the appearance in the analysis of those emotional crises and turbulence, absent for so long, that I described at the beginning.

Ana was twenty-four when we met for the first time, and had an adolescent and careless look that showed in the way she dressed and in her hair. I was surprised to find out that she had a baby that she was breastfeeding.

I could get that information as "data"—not as emotional experiences—through questions I asked and that Ana answered in a tone devoid of vitality or emotion, regardless of the emotional significance that I could presume they had.

In her first interview, Ana could not tell me why she needed to be analysed. All she could say was that she was not feeling well, she wanted analysis, but she could not refer this requirement to any psychological suffering. I could observe that she seemed to live as if in a cloudy state of mind; my observation was corroborated when Ana's treatment began: she repeated over and again that she felt lost. Indeed, she seemed lost to herself, as if something serious had damaged her capacity to hear, to see, her interior communication, damaged her consciousness as the "sensorial organ for the apprehension of psychic qualities", as Helen Keller's (1954) sensuous organs had been damaged because of her very serious illness.

In the course of her analysis, Ana told me of her almost deaf and "mentally weak" mother, in such a mental state of permanent panic that she even could not tell her husband—Ana's father—of the serious risks their son ran. I thought then of the failure of the maternal reverie, incapable of transforming the panic, of thinking it, of evaluating the real circumstances of the danger, and to act in accordance with it. The mother herself acted like a frightened child without resources: when Ana felt lost and without knowing what to do with her own emotional experiences, she waited for the arrival of her mother, only to meet over and over again with somebody that in turn functioned as a little child, afraid of taking a taxi, unable to find an address, etc. So, when the expected meeting happened, the failure of the maternal reverie, and the "excessive anxiety" of the mother was an emotional experience that Ana could not digest.

These "encounters", in turn, were reflected in her not coming to session, of falling asleep, of being without "energy", according to her own expression, without being able to make a phone call, as if she did not exist. She could not confront the "overdose" of stimuli that came from the analytic relation. She was left without resources to face pain and she had "to put to sleep her pain" in the same way as she attempted "to put to sleep" the realization of the weaning of her baby and its implications. She had weaned her with the "help" of a paediatrician when the baby's teeth began to come through and she in turn was very afraid of that situation.

She would give the baby, during entire nights, one bottle after another, watching for the moment in which the rubber nipple escaped from her mouth in order to introduce it again. Years later, she herself could describe this mental state as "drooping like a vegetable", a description that we related to her phantasy that vegetables do not bite, do not cry, and they seem not to suffer.

In the analytic relationship, I was alerted by my lack of interest in the patient and because, if I allowed myself to be taken in by the atmosphere of the session, I was also dragged into "falling asleep" in this analysis and "to put to sleep" my psychoanalytical function.

Ana used to come or not to come in a way that I found erratic. When she did not come "she disappeared", she did not give me any warning and, when I drew her attention to this fact, she said that it had not occurred to her that she could call; she could not imagine that there was somebody, me, waiting for her. She also frequently arrived late, apparently without realizing the time, as if she lived in a dimension without time. She used to remain in lingering silences, silences that had the quality of not transmitting anything. When she spoke, besides the tone without vitality, the beginnings did not seem to be beginnings, but the continuation of something. The content was practical problems: how could you get a maid? How could you get a job? The baby cried at night; Ana did not know what to do, nor how to. She did not bring dreams (she said that she did not dream), nor did she remember anything of her childhood, nor of the family, nor important circumstances of her life. She did not remember anything about the childbirth, nor the circumstances that surrounded her brother's disappearance, in spite of the fact that she was then twelve years old.

The emotional relationship with the husband seemed also lost. In synthesis, all these facts made me think of "black holes" more than of experiences. They seemed events through which she moved, "lost" and with a latent terror. I thought then that Ana was oppressed by the facts of her past and the circumstances of her present, and I was suspecting a strong deficit in her symbolization processes that seemed to impede some form of psychological processing.

The level (so concrete) in which she referred to her life and in which she received the interpretations, together with her emotional isolation, led me to think of important post-autistic nuclei. The lack of emotional resonance, the difficulties in communication, alerted me to the risks, those to which I have already referred, of becoming a deaf analyst, or performing an analysis based on "giving recipes on what to do".

The sprouted hand

In the middle of the first year of analysis a symptom appeared: "the sprouted hand". Ana told me that her right hand was inflamed; it was reddened, the cracked skin was open, it burned, etc. She referred to the symptom as the hand that had "sprouted". No medical consultation could give a diagnosis as to its origin.

During the analysis, Ana evoked the sexual relationships of her parents, to which she referred as something that overflowed her, since there was no "door" that separated her from those exciting and frightening stimuli. She remembered that she resorted to a compulsive masturbation without pleasure, which she could not stop, as the only means of "calming". This exposure to massive stimuli that she was not able to elaborate, again threatened her in current situations: she panicked about the possibility of getting pregnant again. She was equipped with notably precarious resources for these situations, since she had been able only to close up, to isolate herself, to get disconnected from her terror.

In the course of the analysis, we began to link the symptom of the hand with an excess of stimuli that overwhelmed her, represented by that memory of the sexuality "without doors" of her parents. The patient then said, "Without at least a curtain" (which was her way of bringing to the transference that excess of stimuli related to the analyst's name). In the past, when she was a small child, she tried to deal with "that", which was what she felt could drive her mad, with the hand ("compulsive masturbation"), and now, the "curtain" at times seemed not to be enough for the containment of her feelings, and so Ana would miss the sessions, because she remained asleep, "without energy." The analyst's name, Cortiñas, is similar to "cortinas", which means curtains, in Spanish.

Later on, she began to describe that her hurt hand bothered her; she felt it as an obstacle for the contact with her baby daughter, with her husband, with the analyst, whom she greeted by shaking hands. Later on, that hand was the "main character" of the first parapraxis: in the last session of the week, at the end of her third year of analysis, Ana told me that her hand had worsened, it had swollen, etc. Immediately, when she was speaking about her husband's (John) first trip, and meaning to say, "I wanted to speak of my hand with him", she said, "I wanted to speak of him with my hand," With this material, I try to illustrate how a transformation took place, starting with the beginning of projective identifications and of a containing function in the analysis. I am describing the transformation of the hand as a somatic part of her body into a hand as a "gesture", containing feelings (of shame, of pain, of awareness of an obstacle to communication), and then into a "hand" as a character that begins to personify a "dramatic" dynamic of absence and presence.

I think that the hand was, in the first place, a corporeal container, in which to place something sick, something that hurts, like an amplification of her capacity for consciousness. It had a different and more evolved quality, compared with the moment in which Ana first consulted because she was "feeling bad", as a diffuse uneasiness of which she could specify nothing. A more extended form of registration was when she felt her sick hand as an obstacle, because it awakened—I emphasize awakened—feelings of shame.

With the parapraxis, the hand is already on its way to becoming a symbol, my conjecture is, of the absent object. She can try to deny the absence, "speaking of him with the hand", but the negation implies the development of the function of judgement (Freud, 1925h), which has a high symbolic level and is a defence mechanism, with less damage to mental functions than splitting, emotional isolation, and the detention of realistic projective identifications.

Visual images and dreams

I am going to include the capacity for storing visual images among the alpha function's factors; visual images, if they are differentiated from sense impressions, are a kind of registration of the emotional experience.

I illustrate the development of an "ideo-grammar" and the beginning of a containing space and a dream-work-alpha function through the importance that visual images were beginning to have for Ana. At the end of her first year of analysis, one day she brought two pictures: one was of her brother, the other of her husband. She said that she wanted to show them to me, she did not know why, because she always carried them in her wallet. Through my alpha-function, with the capability of making correlations, I saw that they were both very alike. I thought that with these photographs, in a very concrete way, Ana was trying to tell me something.

Some time after this episode, for the first time in her analysis, she spoke of a dream. First she told me that when she was staying in Cañada (her home town), at her mother's house, she was "searching in the wardrobes". "I like to search in those wardrobes . . . there I found and I took this jacket that I sometimes wear [it had belonged to her brother] and I gave John a shirt that belonged to my brother . . . I also like to look at photograph albums."

When I told her that in those wardrobes (I thought of them as the beginning of the formation of a container, in a very concrete sense), she seemed to be trying to understand something about herself, about her mother, her father, her brother; for the first time she associated with a dream, expressing concern for having forgotten almost everything: "There was that image of a woman that I knew, but later on it was erased and I no longer knew who she was, and that woman spoke of something that had disappeared." I thought that, in the dream, the loss of a function seemed to begin to be represented, through the "erasing", and also that that function was being incarnated in the woman (the analyst) that spoke of what disappeared.

But, also, that dream, still very "raw", the same as those more elaborated ones that followed, provided us with "models" (Bion, 1962) to begin to speak of the emotional experiences: through these models we could speak of an Ana that "erased herself" when she missed her sessions, and, as it came up in another dream, of an Ana that felt that "her furniture" (mental) was very precarious, and that it could not resist without being damaged by those vital "jumps" of a baby that was growing.

Splitting and emotional isolation

Bion refers to the oscillation of the positions in the operation that he named PS⟺D (oscillation between states of dispersion and of integration) that enables the discovery of the selected fact* that harmonizes and gives coherence to, until then, disconnected facts. This oscillation, together with a container–contained ($\male \female$) relationship, where the point represents a tolerable emotion, are factors of alpha function and of the development of the process of thinking.

I shall describe these mental functions as a principal innovative "theme", and as one of the contributions that Bion introduced in psychoanalysis, with my own variations, through the different chapters of this book.

With this clinical material, I attempt to show a static modality of splitting which is related to the impediment of the PS⟺D oscillation*.

This splitting modality, together with the emotional isolation and the detention of the realistic projective identifications (all in the service of nothing "happening"), isolate the links* that establish relationships, also going against integration processes. They are isolation phenomena that make emotional experience *inaccessible*, and, as long as they are not detected in the analytic process, they continue silently.

I will refer now to another aspect of Ana's clinical material. During the second year of analysis, I realized that the patient referred in such different ways to the same people that this did not allow me to be aware of the fact that she was speaking of the same person; sometimes, even, I could not know of whom she was speaking. Sometimes they appeared with their names, sometimes as "the mother" (one did not know whose mother it was), sometimes "the father's wife", etc.

It made me think that if a meta-communicational context of a play existed (Bateson, 1972), the names could be those of the actors and the characters, without any specification, an actor sometimes representing one character, sometimes another. But the way Ana brought them into analysis: the "mother", the "father's wife", the "sister", the "daughter", they appeared to be interchangeable roles, played by different persons or the same one, but without anyone knowing who they were, and who was who.

I thought that this modality evidenced a very wide dissociation, a static splitting, where the gap was produced by isolation. It seemed to be in the service of maintaining a barrier against the emotional experience and its consequences, which would emerge if these divisions disappeared.

In a session in which Ana was referring to the amnesty for the militaries of the dictatorial Military Process in Argentina, during which her brother "disappeared" (he continues to be one of the 30,000 "missing" people), she said that, watching the news on television, her mother and her sister seemed not to be aware of what was happening, remaining inexpressive. "I don't understand: if I go to a park and I see the daughter or the sister of a military officer, I leave the park in haste; I would run away."

When I pointed out to her that she was the daughter of a military officer and the sister of a missing person, this correlation released the first crisis in analysis. She began to cry—it was the first time in a session—with a great deal of emotion. Some time later, she told me that she had made a discovery: while seeing photographs of her brother, she thought that her mother was somebody very disconnected and she, Ana, cried a lot "because of pains that she felt inside"; she had been a long time without being able to cry. Then, looking at her hand, she discovered that the swelling had gone down. At that same session she said that she was impressed by the way in which I could put together different parts of her life story.

I thought that a container–contained relationship was being formed inside Ana; she could speak of an "inside", and of somebody, the analyst, that could put together parts of her story. At the same time, the disconnected and "disconnecting" part of her self was projected and identified in the mother (with a great deal of reality).

I will show, through a dream, how a more appropriate, more dynamic dissociation and a capacity for consciousness and representation about what made her sick was settling in.

> I was in some place in Cañada and I was lying on the ground. There some girls, high school classmates, found me. At that time, there was one, the one that knew everything, the intelligent one, and I was the idiot, the fool. In the dream I was sick, but only on my right side. Some classmates helped me, they helped me to stand up.

This dream already has associations for Ana: "I thought of this, about being sick on one side. My dad had hypertension, he had many hypertensive episodes and, well, he had a stroke, which left him in the same state of paralysis as I saw myself in the dream, with a side that he could not move . . . Ah, in the dream I also saw like cuts in the skin . . . from where blood gushed out . . . I thought of a blood effusion."

This dream shows more appropriate and dynamic dissociations, which herald the possibility, maybe still distant, of an integration: the intelligent part of the self and the stupid, silly part, one helping the other one. A sick side, through which hypertension and effusion (emotional, confusions?) flow, that has an immobilizing effect, but that can receive help from an intelligent partner. The dream appears on one side as container of the sick self that appears also as silly, as long as she seemed to be confused with a deaf mother, mentally weak, disconnected. Now, at this "time", she seems to be able to allow herself to be helped by an intelligent aspect that, in turn, will give her the opportunity, as is happening now in analysis, to have instruments to deal with her Oedipal conflicts and her identity problems. The fear of the intensity of emotions also appears represented as the brain effusion and the cuts (splitting?) from where the blood (vitality) gushes out.

History, memory, mourning and identity

> . . . the capacity to mourn, or pine for a loss, and the capacity to remember the lost object are inseparably linked. Without memory there can be no mourning, and without the mourning there can be no memory. And if the development is to be unfavourable, this is what seems to happen: there is no concept and no capacity to mourn. [Money-Kyrle, 1971, p. 444]

From the beginning of the analysis, Ana had some recognition of the fact that she had almost no memories. Her past, when she did not feel it as lost, was present in her as disconnected facts. Her mother, whom she sometimes asked, seemed also to have her mental functions damaged. Ana felt lost in everything she did: at the faculty she forgot things, she did not write down data she needed, and because of that she had to miss assignments. When she started to show concern for this " forgetfulness", she began asking, in analysis, why this happened to her. I thought that this question implied the possibility to express, for the first time, her fears about having something damaged in her head to somebody who was not deaf, and who could listen to what she said in a different way from her mother. For a long time, I listened with astonishment, and wondered how this girl, with such a precarious mental state, could study and be doing well in her university studies. Years later, after having twice failed an assignment, she forgot that she could not attend that course for a third time: when she realized that she had forgotten that, she asks herself, "Where did I bury it?" (referring to the memory).

However, some threads began to be knitted together in her head. The main factor seemed to be the dreams "knitting" associations where before were "holes". A dream, for example, that had as scenario her paternal grandfather's house, surprised her: on the roof she saw a boy, whom some men wanted to kidnap or to kill.

This dream brought her a memory that astonished her: in that house her brother was born. Regardless of the content of the dream, it is my impression and my conjecture that the dream functions as a private myth (Bion, 1963) that provides the possibility of investigating what it means for Ana to remember.

To remember seems to be related with the re-presentation of something painful, e.g., that she had already studied the assignment twice and that she could not take the course again; or also representing in her dream the traumatic "disappearance" of her brother. However, remembering gives her the chance to get out of a dilemma and to think about what to do realistically: she needs to take the course again. Burial is not the same as forgetting. Burial means to erase relationships and to erase herself. I think of it as the burial at Ur (Bion, 1977), not as a mourning ceremony, but like a drug, as a radical forgetfulness (oblivion) for her mental functions.

With such a damaged mental apparatus (because of the static dissociations and the autistic mechanisms of isolation, the autistic barriers took the form of a burial and also of the compulsive masturbation) there cannot be memories. On the other hand, my observations in the analysis made me think that, when the evolution of the process allows moments of integration, it seems to be that the mourning and the feelings of guilt are too much for that precarious apparatus to bear, and these are critical moments for the analysis. That is why, for example, Ana still was not able to carry out her purpose of investigating (a purpose that arose during an interruption for vacations) what had happened to her brother.

The same thing happened when, in the analysis, she began to transform "events" into experiences. For example, because of the very strange way of paying that she had (she counted an arbitrary number of sessions, without reference to what month, or to how many days, etc.; that is, isolated numbers [similar to the little girl, Jane, in Chapter Eight]), Ana had made a mistake that she could not understand: she said that she had paid me for five sessions and not four, and, clinging concretely to this way of counting, she insisted that she could not understand.

When, after a time, she began to realize her mistake, she insisted now she did not understand why such things happened to her, why she had counted four instead of five. This was followed by a deep emotional disconnection. I made an imaginative conjecture and I decided to tell her about it: "I have a conjecture: the mistake is related to a family of five, before your brother disappeared, now you are four." Ana cried when listening to this, for the second or third time in he analysis. She cried with emotion, she seemed very moved, and after a while she said: "I cannot remember us five as a family, neither can I remember four, I remember us three as a family, after my brother disappeared . . . the life of the family of five is like a dream." (I understood that, by "dream", she meant that she did not feel it as real, as something that actually happened.)

Emotional experiences, from which there seemed to be left only "holes" in the memory and in the identity, are beginning to appear through the dreams. During the fourth year of analysis, she relates the following dream:

> I was in a place that was like this office, the consulting room, but it was a house and there was a patio, and there was you [the analyst] with a grown-up son, and a daughter also grown up, and your husband. I was seated on a bench and had a baby on my lap. Before me, in front, there was a stage, a lot of people and a woman that sang with a microphone.

In the dream, the analyst or somebody said to Ana that the baby she had on her lap was the analyst's baby. This dream was associated with becoming aware that now her "dramas" were internal, and she did not know what to do with them.

She was recovering, or constructing, functions, the equivalent of opening her eyes and seeing her "internal dramas" of being part of, and living in, a family, but this in turn woke up" the "internal dramas" of jealousy, of rivalry, and also a baby-part of hers. This made her oscillate between her autistic barriers: closing her eyes again, and isolating, and her desire to grow: to open her mental eyes and meet with a pain that she felt as unbearable, and also realize that she lived, feeling exposed again to a quantity of stimuli that she could not assimilate.

Something in her stimulates her tendency towards mental growth, which implies the search for who she is, to leave that painful state of "feeling lost". But, when functions and memories and real achievements begin to emerge, represented, for example, by finishing her studies, she withdraws again; although, now that she is repairing her functions and no longer can stay isolated in the session, a more neurotic conflict seems to show up: she wants to come to two sessions instead of three, or she misses sessions, or comes late, but with awareness that this is not due to external circumstances.

I will finish this clinical illustration stressing again the importance of visual images and the role that the photographs, as pictures, and the dreams play here in starting up functions, such as evocative memory, not of data, but of emotional experiences. A final example of this was Ana's decision to investigate her father's origins, to be able to get the same citizenship that he had through her paternal grandparents. First, she said that she could not apply for this citizenship (part of her identity), nor could her mother remember where the relevant documents were. Then Ana found some old photographs, pictures, and she began to identify her relatives there. At the same time, some memories of her childhood appeared, with clear transferential implications: "One night, when I had taken my medicine, suddenly I remembered that when I was a little girl I had warts on my hands. I was treated by a woman, one of those that 'cure through sympathy and empathy'." (I think that this was a real insight.) After this episode she made some references about her mother; because of Ana's insistence, her mother went to the Civil Registration Office to obtain her father's ID documents. Ana also said that her sister found an old box, with all the data they needed. I think of this whole process as the development of instruments apt for the investigation of the father's functions inside the mother (Meltzer, 1973), and also about her own identity.

The arduous process of achieving an identity and of recovering her mental functions implies for Ana a very painful process. In that sense, the problem of the elaboration of mourning is complex: for example, finishing her studies, having the opportunity of an analysis, means as well a process of differentiation from her brother, who will never be able to have these achievements, and also means making contact with the damage to her mental functions, as a consequence of dissociations and isolation.

Reverie, psychoanalytical function of the personality, and the equipment of the analyst

Although Freud referred to the development of attention as a function that was designed for periodically searching the external world, so that when an urgent internal need arose its data could already be familiar, he also described free-floating attention as the necessary mental attitude of the analyst for his inquiry into the patient's internal world. As analysts, we know that we need the same floating attention for apprehending our own emotional experiences and our countertransference.

My question is: what are the peculiarities of that free-floating attention that marks the difference from the characteristics required for attention to the data of the outside world? I think that it has a receptive quality, not directed, related to maternal reverie, and that it is especially apt for the intuitive reception of the selected fact. The models the analyst constructs with his alpha function are, for the psychic reality, what recordings are for the attention, constructed in relation to the outside world. (See Chapter Three.)

The other question refers to Bion's well-known technical advice: that analysts need a discipline of "no memory, no desire, no understanding". What is the memory that we have to avoid? As analysts, while analysing our patients, we seem to work with a prodigious memory that usually astonishes and that is not based on the gathering of data, but rather, in my opinion, is in fact linked with the free-floating attention. This memory, which I will call an *evocative or dream-like memory*, is based on free association, *and, in this kind of memory, any screen memory, just as for dream-thoughts, dreams used as models, or personal myths, acts as an instrument for discovery because of the associations and transformations* that it is able to stimulate, if the conditions for inquiry are given. I think that functions with these characteristics are part of the capacity of becoming aware, of the capacity for discovery and making contact with emotional experiences. Together with the modulation and tolerance of mental pain that are fundamental for the understanding and development of the psychoanalytical function of the personality, they are part of the basic equipment.

Patients with Ana's characteristics present obstacles that seem to impede, or to turn useless, as much the free-floating attention as the evocative memory of the analyst. Their verbal expressions and their silences have a peculiar lack of "resonance", lacking shades and meaning. The analyst who is listening, even trying to "listen to the silences", wonders what he can do to make contact with something that seems to evoke nothing.

Thinking of how to establish contact with Ana, I remembered Helen Keller and her governess, and also Melanie Klein and her patient Dick, as models (Row C of The Grid). Both had found a way of solving the obstacle of establishing contact. Melanie Klein, observing the indifference and lack of affect in Dick, proposed the trains, which she also named, and found an instrument for establishing contact; Helen Keller's governess discovered a way of transforming sensuous contact into a symbol and found a key to access thought and communication. In her autobiography, Helen Keller (1954) records the moment of this discovery: becoming aware of the relationship between the tactile sensation of the water and the signs that the governess drew on her hand, which, until then, had lacked meaning. What I call my preconceptual equipment—my models, such as Helen Keller, and Bion's (1965) and other authors' theories, used in the way of hypotheses—helped me to think of obstructions or paralysis in the development of phantasies, dreams, and dream-thoughts.

If, in Ana, there was a lack of phantasies, dreams, etc., together with her silent isolation, how could I establish with her an analytically significant contact? The difficulties in reaching an authentic communication with her and with other patients stimulated my investigations of the function of dreams, myths, and phantasies for the mind as organizing instruments of the chaos of primary experiences. I tried to go deeper into the concept of reverie, extending it towards a hypothesis of a *transgenerational reverie* as a conjecture about symbolic failures as failures in primary relationships.

The challenge that these patients present to us as analysts is, in my opinion, to be able to maintain our technique as analysts and, at the same time, to develop the means to establish contact with the needy and suffering aspects of the patient.

As I was putting the accent on the function of maternal reverie, I think that now I have to specify some differences between the primary relationships and the analytic situation. Can reverie, as a transformational capacity, receptive of emotional experiences which generate alpha elements*, be extended to the "psychoanalytical function of the personality"? I think that it can be a factor, as a "capacity for dreaming", but the psychoanalytical function of the personality, besides being, perhaps, a mysterious gift of the great creative artists (often called experts of the human soul), might perhaps be developed only in an analysis, through the discipline and the courage required for a mind observing itself.

The capacity for reverie is a factor of the mother's alpha function, but the psychoanalytical function of the personality, which is developed in a psychoanalysis, also has to be maintained over time. It requires the willingness and courage of the analyst to deepen the analysis, to follow the evolution and contact with his own self as the analysis evolves. Using Bion's ideas, the analyst needs tolerance of the development of the container–contained factor in a K link (of disposition to know) and of the PS⟷D function, also in a K link (of knowledge). The deepening of his own analysis and this link of disposition to know, taking arrival points as starting points as well, has to be in the service of observing a mind in evolution, of observing its transformations. For the analyst it implies, simultaneously, the observation of what happens in his own personality to go on becoming in at-one-ment, becoming oneself. This implies facing the obstacles that we find in our own mind, in that of the patient's, and in the relation, because that is where the pain resides, as do all the emotions that require transformation and psychic processing.

CHAPTER TWO

Dreams and lies: the discovery of psychic reality and the aesthetic dimension of the mind

"El sueño, autor de representaciones
en su teatro sobre el viento armado
sombras suele vestir de bulto bello"

Góngora

"The dream, author of representations
in its theatre built on the wind,
dresses up shadows as a beautiful bundle"

Góngora (author's translation)

". . . If somites could write, the book would be
Interpretations of Reality and the theories would
all be what we call dreams"

(Bion, 1991, p. 470)

The Interpretation of Dreams (1900a) was a landmark in the development of tools for understanding and dealing with "reasons" that "THE REASON" does not understand and tries to ignore, classifying them as "crazy", "primitive", etc. The discovery of *resistance*, as the point that marks a crisis, a conflict that could not follow its evolution, was the other fundamental milestone. In analysis, the process of getting to know our personality, of becoming aware, of becoming "oneself", can be carried out only through obstacles. The narcissistic injuries that psychoanalytic discoveries added to the human being, and that Freud describes, draw our attention to some of the difficulties we meet in the process of becoming aware of what it means to be only a human being.

People born in the West in the twentieth century met with a culture in which psychoanalysis, more or less accepted, was already becoming a part. The fact that dreams, jokes, slips of tongue, etc., have meaning has been incorporated to the body of Western culture. Now, in the twenty-first century, it seems that psychoanalysis has become assimilated by this culture, but its disruptive ideas remain still undigested. In contrast with this apparent incorporation, we meet with not only an open criticism, but we can also see a frequent resistential and/or distorted use of the psychoanalytic theories. This should not surprise us, because, in our psychoanalytical practice, we have the opportunity to witness the obstacles that appear in our own minds and in those of our patients, while going through the process of knowing and becoming "oneself".

We cannot know what the future of our discipline will be, but I think that psychoanalytic investigation will be able to develop, as long as the tools we use to discover the realm of psychic reality continue developing and deepening. At the same time, these instruments should offer the possibility of removing the obstacles that oppose this discovery, obstacles which are related mostly to conscious and unconscious lies. The development of such instruments through the evolution of the psychoanalytic method is fundamental for clinical practice.

In this chapter, I wish to stress the significance in theory, and above all in psychoanalytic practice, of the use of dreams in their function as tools for discovering and understanding psychic reality. Dreams and "dreaming"—in the extended sense I shall develop—not only need to be interpreted, but also to function as interpreters of both psychic and external reality. A "fact in itself", a thing, is not interpretable, it has no meaning; for this reason it needs to be transformed into a "dream". At the same time, it is necessary to pursue our research into the different modalities of lies as the manifestation of the development of a capacity for deceit and self-deception, since the process of becoming aware is associated with emotional turbulence, and, as contact with mental pain is generated, emotional forces that try to avoid it are stimulated.

Steps in the discovery of psychic reality

Freud's clinical investigations, together with a mind open to new discoveries, led him to doubt the truth of the scenes of seduction he heard from his patients. In letter 69 to Fliess, he writes,

> . . . I no longer believe in my Neurotica [SE V.1 p. 259, letter 69] [this was one of the first steps towards the discovery of a new dimension: psychic reality].

> If it is true that hysterics carry their symptoms towards fictitious traumas, the new fact is that they fantasize those scenes; therefore it is necessary to take psychic reality into account next to a factual reality. [SE XIX pp. 17–18]

Thus, a path for exploring this new dimension develops, beginning with the theory of traumatic events and evolving towards the interpretation of dreams, slips of the tongue, screen memories, jokes, etc. There is no doubt that dreams and their interpretation constitute a decisive step in this direction.

Klein's contributions revealed different ways of expressing this psychic reality. She thus discovered a relationship between them:

> In their play children represent symbolically phantasies, wishes and experiences. Here they are employing the same language the same archaic, phylogenetically acquired road of expression as mwe are familar with from dreams . . . if want rightly to comprehend children's play in connection with their whole behaviour during the analytic hour, we must take into account not only the symbolism which often appears so clearly in their games, but also all the means of representation and the mechanisms employed in the dream-work . . . [Klein, M. V.1 1926, p. 134]

This quotation also shows how the achievements in exploring this new territory runs parallel to the development of new tools of investigation. Her concept of an inner world extends the discoveries in this new domain; the development of the technique of using toys and playing for child analysis reveals itself to be an efficient instrument for research into very primitive mental states and the function of unconscious fantasy.

The next step was taken by Bion, transcending the caesura from the Freudian theory of dreams as disguises of psychic conflict that could unveil the hidden unconscious towards considering dreams as instruments that represent marks or formulations of an emotional experience that "rescue from the void and formless infinity" (a quote from Milton's *Paradise Lost* that Bion uses frequently), a form that thus can be thought and investigated.

Meltzer, in turn, expands this contribution with the idea that the external world has no meaning. Meaning, instead, is created in the internal world and essentially through dreams, which he considers the theatre and stage where meaning is generated. Meaning is not an event of the external reality that has to be grasped, but rather one that has to be generated and developed. This point of view places symbol formation and the generation of meaning, and, thus, the construction of meaning, as the essential objective of an epistemological investigation. (See also Chapter 3.)

Bion developed these ideas when he began treating severely disturbed patients with the psychoanalytic method. He was trying to solve the technical problems that arose in the analysis with patients who showed disturbances in their ability to think and communicate.

Meltzer, in his explorations on autism and dementalization and in his developments on aesthetic conflict and dream life, contributes with formulations that expand the instruments for the discovery of psychic reality and the disturbances generated by the different modalities of avoiding contact with it.

Binocular vision, multiple vertices: dreams and lies as vertices

The theory of transformations (Bion, 1965) takes the following perspective or vertex*: O*, the origin, the ultimate reality of emotional experience is unknowable and we can only have access to its transformations. If "beauty is truth, truth beauty" (Keats), the aesthetic conflict (Meltzer, 1990) is a formulation of the contrast between the outside of the object, apprehensible by the senses, and the inside, which can only be conjectured. From this epistemological perspective I think of dreams and lies as transformations of O and as contrasting interpreters or observational vertices. While dreams are potential generators of meaning in the internal world and favour the development of the aesthetic dimension of the mind, the vertex of lies leads to its deterioration. (See also Chapter Four, the description of the difference between being in at-one-ment with O and being in rivalry with O.)

Awareness of psychic reality is inevitably associated with the workings of an instrument that offers at least two vertices of observation, whether as binocular vision—conscious–unconscious—or as one that offers multiple vertices, as when one changes different observational lenses, without losing the perspective of either the differences or the relationship. Dreams, myths, play, etc., are transformational systems that contain that possibility of multiple vertices, which are obviously lacking in lies.

The evolution of the rudimentary consciousness, a sensorial organ for the perception of psychic qualities towards a consciousness aware of internal and external facts, is always premature in dealing with the emotional experience with which it is connecting. (See also Chapter Eight.) Lies are born together with the development of consciousness, and aim at its destruction. The narrative of the burial at Ur (see Bion, 1977, *Caesura*) is an illustration of this relationship between lies, becoming aware, and mental pain: burying the dead and funeral rites mean awareness of death and its implications. The burying alive of the entire court when a king died, accompanied by the sound of songs and dances, shows the burial of such awareness. It is necessary to take a drug in order to carry out this second burial, because awareness has already developed.

One of the aims of psychoanalysis is self-knowledge, and this implies adequate equipment. Meltzer says;

> I mean by equipment something essentially *useful*, a *content* of mind rather than a *quality* of mind . . . But the goodness strength and beauty of objects are not essentially *useful* . . . In addition to these qualities the objects must have knowledge, skills, wisdom, the

form and content of which must necessarily be a reflection of the external culture, of which the science of psychoanalysis has become a part. [Meltzer, 1967, p. 88]

The pre-conceptual apparatus (Bion, 1977) holds a prominent place in this equipment. This apparatus includes dream thoughts, dreams, and myths as unsaturated formulations ready to match emotional experiences that have to be thought out and investigated. In our practice, we are constantly faced with the problem of how to help the patient to be aware that he/she has an inner world, that he/she needs to get to know his/her personality and to respect his/her psychic reality.

Freud considered dreams the "royal road" to the unconscious, and Klein extended this consideration to play. From the perspective of Bion's and Meltzer's contributions, we can also consider them to be privileged tools for discovering the meaning of emotional experiences, and for the development of consciousness as a capacity of "becoming aware"; that is, of an evolved consciousness.

The human baby's ability to become aware and give meaning to the emotional experience depends on reverie, that "natural" ability of the mother's mind to accept, contain, and transform into meaning a primitive pre-verbal form of communication (realistic projective identification). The capacity of reverie is a necessary condition for the development of a consciousness capable of tolerating facts and becoming aware. To receive without panic what the baby communicates as urgent and catastrophic acts as a modulator of mental pain and as a necessary condition for transforming that communication into a "dream" or a "dream thought". Thus, the baby receives and reintrojects a part of his personality wrapped up in a tolerable emotion, similar to a protective atmosphere, an atmosphere suitable for discovery. If, at some point, this communication fails, then the baby receives a "nameless dread" (Bion, 1962), and this increases its feelings of helplessness and the precariousness of the equipment to deal with mental pain. Meltzer and Bion emphasized the significance of the mother's function as a thinking object and that this maternal function builds a scaffolding of meaning for the infant's primitive experiences. Absence of this scaffolding, most of all for the pre-verbal experiences, leaves the infant open to mental states that remain in the empty turmoil of a world of no meaning. Spitz (1958) described this chaotic turbulence as marasmus: by this, he meant that a long deprivation of maternal detoxifying capacities, transforms a relatively benign emptiness into a virulent vacuum, which could deteriorate into chaotic states and, in extreme circumstances, become malignant.

One of the consequences of the failure of maternal reverie is a premature development of consciousness, which is transformed into a moral conscience (super-superego), which substitutes discrimination between what is true and false for what is morally good or wrong. This is illustrated in the relationship between Galileo and the Cardinal, as described by Brecht in his play *Galileo Galilei* (1943): while Galileo invites the Cardinal to look through the telescope, the latter answers that first they have to discuss whether the use of the instrument is right or wrong.

Another of the consequences of the failure of reverie is the one described in autistic children (see Chapters Eight and Nine): the coming together of a very sensitive child and a mother who is not able to help him/her develop attention and interest and to traverse the aesthetic conflict, transforming the flood of stimuli into experiences from which he/she can learn. Attention is the helm that guides the organ of consciousness in the prolific world of psychic qualities. The mechanism through which dismantling occurs in the autistic states involves "suspending" attention (Meltzer, 1975). Even though babies have as an innate endowment the power to perceive a "gestalt", at the beginning they need the mother's reverie, which includes attention as a mental function. The behaviour of the connected mother is the first one that sustains and provides a holding for the infant's attention. "Suspended" attention seems to be related to the failure of holding a very sensitive infant; in contrast, if the infant feels that it is held in its mother's mind, it also can "hold on to" its mother's attention and face the complexity of the world, including its own emotions and sensations.

The other point we have to consider is that emotional experience is ineffable. How is it expressed? How is this experience communicated in the private relation that the person has with himself/herself and in the public one he/she has with others? Dreams, play, poetry, and art all seem to be the most suitable languages, not for talking *about* the emotional experience but rather to allow for the emotional experience to *talk* through those languages. (See Chapters Three and Eight.) Thus, these "languages", which include "let's pretend" in their formulation, have at least two observational vertices: indicating that they are not "the thing in itself".

Bion (1970) thought about the relationship between lies and the thinker, considering that a liar knows very well where the truth is in order to avoid it. Bion often compared lies to drugs, or poison for the mind, used out of intolerance to waiting, or to mental pain, and he observed that everything that is falsely used as a substitute for what is real is thus transformed into poison for the mind. When he stated that lies are a substitute that cannot satisfy without destroying the ability to discriminate real from false, he included a wide range of situations, which he thought could be investigated psychoanalytically, differentiating himself from Klein on this point.

It is interesting, I think, to discriminate between mythifying and mystifying. It is also useful to differentiate between the resistential use of a dream and the use of the dream at the service of untruth. As a famous clinical example of dreams used at the service of untruth, I would like to mention the hypocritical dreams of the young homosexual patient, whose deceitful use Freud so intuitively perceived (1920a, 164–166).

We find another kind of obstacle, as well, in the inability to dream related to proto-mental or dementalized functioning. One difference is that the resistential use marks a point of conflict; the lie, instead, and also dementalization, systematically avoids crisis and becomes a barrier against catastrophic change* (Bion, 1965). The dictionary defines mystifying as a means for creating perplexity or confusion, and this is the problem which we have to deal with when lies appear in our practice. In the liar, we can also find an ambiguity mounted on a splitting, contrasting with the polysemy of dreams. What is sought is not only to avoid consciousness "becoming aware", but also to destroy it. (See Chapter Four.)

Meltzer, in turn, describes how intolerance to aesthetic conflict can lead to a meaningless world, one of automatic functioning, to the empty world illustrated so well by Beckett in *Waiting for Godot*.

Psychic reality, dreams, and sensuous reality

In psychoanalysis, we use conventional verbal language derived from sensuous experience, originally created to refer to events of the external world. The psychoanalyst has to use the same language for communicating non-sensuous experiences of the inner world. The patient needs to be able to communicate to the analyst his mental states, and, in turn, the analyst needs to be able to find a way of communicating his intuitions and observations. The polysemy of language and the predisposition towards concretization observed in the way many people use language, etc., immediately raises, among other things, the issue of misunderstanding, misinterpretations, etc.

Another problem is the use of language in a computer-like fashion, to report data, or to reduce emotional events to trivial anecdotes. Meltzer discriminates between contractual, conventional, and intimate relationships. Language, in psychoanalysis, refers to intimate relationships. Thus, one of the problems in psychoanalytical communication is the need to construct, together with the patient, over and again, a language which analyst and patient can share.

In 1957, referring to the attacks of the ego functions and of the matrix of thought in certain patients, Bion observes: "The consequences for the patient are that he now moves, not in a world of dreams, but in a world of objects which are ordinarily the furniture of dreams" (Bion, 1967, p. 51). These are patients who "dream awake" without knowing that they are "dreaming". In Chapter Nine of the same book, *Second Thoughts*, where Bion reproduces his paper "A theory of thinking", he mentions for the first time alpha function and the mother's capacity of reverie as the receptor and transformer for the infant's harvest of self-sensation gained by its consciousness. The infant personality by itself is unable to make use of the sense-data, but has to evacuate these elements into the mother, relying on her to do whatever has to be done to convert them into a form suitable for employment as alpha elements by the infant (Bion, 1967, p. 116).

He will, thereafter, consider that the personality, in order to be able to think and develop a process of knowledge of itself and of the external world, requires a function for the digestion of emotional experiences, equivalent to the digestive function for food. He will call it alpha-function. Those patients in which this function has severe impairments do not differentiate the mental state of being awake from the state of being asleep and, thus, either do not dream or fragment and evacuate their dreams. Living in a world not of dreams, but of "furniture of dreams" that he does not discriminate from "the thing in itself", leads to not recognizing dreams as such. These people are opposite to a Magritte, who makes the problem obvious when he draws a pipe and writes on the same picture: "This is not a pipe". To have a dream while asleep leads in some way to an inscription similar to that of Magritte: "This is not an event that belongs to the external world". What does it mean to say that they dream while awake?

It is necessary to discriminate between a rudimentary consciousness as a sense organ to perceive psychic qualities, and consciousness as becoming aware of emotions and perceptions. This distinction is fundamental, because consciousness, in the sense of becoming aware, implies the operation of alpha function, while consciousness as a rudimentary sense organ can be lacking the operation of alpha function, as in an infant or a psychotic, whose consciousness is rudimentary, has no shades, has not achieved, or has destroyed, discrimination between conscious and unconscious elements. The patient can be conscious, but cannot become aware of what is required in psychoanalytic treatment for the development of a process of "awareness", which is the transformation and formulation of thoughts so that they can be thought. It is here that the hierarchy of the function of dreams and myths arises, since not only can they be used to reveal unconscious aspects, but can also, through alpha function that "produces" alpha elements, generate unconsciousness, and thus offer the possibility of observation from two vertices. What is "dreamed" in this broad sense can be forgotten and recalled. The "thing in itself" cannot.

Dreams belong to the process of thinking about emotional experience. Naming the constant conjunction* (Bion, 1963) (which implies the rescue of an infinite and formless void) is not a sensorial process, and its beginning is related to objects for which it is necessary to create forms or borrow them from sensuous reality. Emotional links are at the heart of this process of symbolization. The psychoanalytic object, psychic reality, and emotions are a-sensorial.

The dreamer is the thinker who, through his dream-work-alpha, gives a form to the emotion (trans-forms it), and the analyst operates on this transformation thinking the thought: what is involved is not only discovering the meaning of the dream's scenes, but also the meaning of the interaction of the mental states that it depicts.

In psychoanalysis, theories tend to multiply and become dogmatic, and language becomes quickly covered by a penumbra of associations that saturates it, there frequently being a tendency to transform it into jargon.

Mathematics, with the invention of algebra, produced enormous progress in the scientific research of the "hard" sciences. Might there exist something equivalent in psychoanalysis that would allow furthering its development? Where can we find a way to formulate a problem from a scientific vertex, and yet also from an artistic one, both for communication between colleagues and for communication with the patient?

The function of myths and dreams

Bion has an innovative approach to the function of dreams: not only can they be used to "unveil what is concealed", as Freud conceived, but they also can be used to formulate and investigate the emotional experiences that unfold in the course of analysis. They also can be used as models to explore emotional experiences that have not yet taken place. In this sense, dreams are not only the "royal road" to gaining access to the unconscious, but "the royal road" for contact, discovery, and understanding of psychic reality. This does not refer only to dreams in the mental state of being asleep; Bion thinks that "dreaming" is an activity, related with alpha function, that takes place continuously, also while one is awake. There are people who are deeply incapable of achieving this; others, such as artists, have this transforming possibility to a high degree.

An emotional experience can be a digested or an undigested fact. In order to be digested, this experience has to undergo a process of metabolization, a process that occurs, as I said, through alpha function (Bion, 1962), which transforms sense and emotional impressions into alpha elements, apt to be stored and thought, because they are not confused with sense-data. Alpha elements are a representation and a registration of the experience. In his posthumous book, *Cogitations*, Bion called the alpha function dreamwork-alpha, and, although he did not make it explicit, it seems to me that this work, by means of condensation, displacement, etc., creates ideograms (visual, olfactory, sonorous, tactile, etc., patterns) that contain the registration of the experience.

The act of dreaming is a "digestive" act. In Freud's view, constructing a dream allows the access to consciousness of an unconscious wish with the distortion of censorship. For Bion, dreams have the function of metabolizing undigested facts, transforming them into alpha elements by means of the dream-work-alpha (Bion, 1991), and thus they can become unconscious. The dream-work-alpha is a transformational system for digestion of facts.

Dreams at an individual level, and myths at a group level, have a digestive function, producing alpha elements and at the same time binding these elements into a narrative. The narrative is one way of binding a constant conjunction of experiences*, like a net that "catches" the selected fact that gives it coherence. Thus, dreams constitute a reservoir of symbols, or, better, of ideograms that, as we shall see, can be used to have an approximation to future emotional experiences.

As I have already stated (in Chapter One), a sense impression, to be able to be stored, needs to be transformed into an ideogram. For example, if the experience is of pain, the psyche must have a visual image of rubbing an elbow, of a tearful face, etc. That image is like a small box, a container that stores not only that particular experience of pain, but also this form, as a preconception, will give the opportunity for approaching new contents of pain, thereby constituting equipment to metabolize new experiences.

At this point, I will consider, in the light of Bion's contributions, the function of myths and dreams as instruments for investigating psychic reality, comparable to the function of mathematics in the hard sciences. Bion considered that dreams and myths could occupy the place that algebra does in the "hard" sciences, as variables or unknowns. The psychoanalyst can take the visual images of dreams or myths and use them as models to represent an emotional problem; this model (which contains an incognita), thus constructed, has the potentiality to be examined and thought, but, at the same time, if it is not saturated, it can be used as an "unknown variable" (incognita) to approximate to new experiences that have not yet happened. In analysis, the image of a dream, as will be seen in the clinical vignette of the coat, can be used once again to approximate to new experiences which had not yet occurred when the dream took place. The incognita is once again cleared up and takes on new "values", in the mathematical sense.

Thus, for example, if we are investigating the relationship in the link of knowledge, Tiresias, in the Oedipus myth, can be an element for approaching the issue of inner vision that has as its condition to be blind to the senses, or may be an element to formulate an obstruction to research, when he tells Oedipus not to investigate. The element Oedipus can, as well, be seen in the aspect of its arrogance of going on questioning at any price or in its aspect of curiosity, etc. *Tiresias and Oedipus are the names of variables to be cleared in the clinical situation with each patient and in the different moments in analysis.*

Bion thus assigns to the construction of models, myths, and dreams the function of tools for investigating present and future emotional problems of the mental life of individuals and of groups. He suggests using them in a way analogous to a scientist's using an already existent mathematical formula to solve a new problem. *This implies not interpreting the dream or the myth but, rather, using it as a tool to interpret a problem.*

The dream operates, therefore, as a container seeking for contents. The contents are the emotional problems that the dream can formulate, just as the Oedipus myth provides models for the emotional problems of incest and parricide, for example, but also can provide models for problems of knowledge, as Bion used it, etc. The dream is a private myth, because it formulates the very particular problems of a person, while myths contain more the universal problems of a culture. *We cannot borrow dreams from others, except in the case of artists, who have a capacity for reverie for humanity.*

The analogy with the algebraic formula derives from the fact that the images of dreams or of the various components of a myth can be taken apart from their narrative and be used as variables or unknowns (incognita), whose value will be given by the elements of the problem we are investigating.

In what follows I will try to illustrate these functions with some clinical vignettes.

The use of images of the dream as algebra

A patient dreams that she meets her former analyst, who is wearing a grey overcoat. She associates the coat with one she had bought, and which she thought was very feminine, like a Christian Dior coat of the 1940s. But when her husband saw it he said, "It looks like a Nazi soldier's overcoat from the Second World War". This image of the coat constitutes an ideogram (in the sense that the image of the coat can be transformed into an abstract variable) that, when unfolding in the course of the analysis, contains the element "coat" (*in Spanish, the word for coat,* tapado, *also means something hidden, covered up*), not only as a cover for what is concealed, but also as the unknown that allows for investigating what in theory would be called the problem of bisexuality. Used as an algebraic formula, two variables can be obtained: *feminine* = Christian Dior, elegant, 1940s, and *masculine* = Second World War Nazi soldier.

In turn, these two images can be transformed again into an unknown variable, to approximate new investigations of the masculine–feminine problem in the personality of the patient as they unfold. Why does feminine equate with Christian Dior, the 1940s? Why does masculine equate with Second World War Nazi soldier? Why grey, which is neither black nor white, but instead indefinite?

A symptom allows for going further in the investigation: a pain in her right arm makes her feel that it is rigid and "welded" (*in Spanish,* welded, *or* soldado *also means* soldier). The unknown variable "Nazi soldier" can be approximated now to this new experience. But welded (*soldado* in Spanish) also means fused, united without discrimination. This implies taking a further step to formulating and investigating the masculine–feminine problem.

Another dream offers a new formulation of the problem: in the image of the dream the patient is looking at herself in a full-length mirror: she is wearing a dress and a green jacket which, when awake, she thinks do not match, but which instead, in the dream, match really well. The jacket, too, is like a Christian Dior model of the 1940s.

With another clinical vignette, I want to illustrate the idea of the *"digestive" function* of dreams and the creation of ideograms that signify the emotional experience.

This is a clinical experience where I think one can observe the transformation of a somatic–emotional experience into a "dream picture", or "image"; the experience then can be stored and presented as a problem that can be thought about. A patient, on arriving at her session, says that she cannot shake my hand because hers is injured. When she lies down on the couch she tells me that on Sunday she "made a hole" in her hand; she was terrified, all the family seemed frightened, she thought it would not stop bleeding. While saying this she was trembling as if she were experiencing the event in her body all over again. I call your attention to the word "hole", which appears to have catastrophic connotations and corresponds not to the injury she sustained, but to the terrifying personal experience.

Then she said that instead of doing the usual, that is, telling herself, "Don't think about that", she recalled a Dali painting that had holes like bleeding eyes. Then other pictures came to her mind. On Sunday, she went to see a Frida Kahlo exhibition, and she remembered a painting: it was a self-portrait, with Kahlo's husband on her lap as if he were her son; he had an eye in his forehead; there was also the sun, the night, and a big breast from which milk surged, and a smaller one, bleeding. While this picture came to her mind she forgot the hole and her fears, and the "dreamed" pictures allowed for the possibility of thinking about the experience.

With this vignette I would like to show, as I said, the transformation of a somatic experience that became manifest by her trembling in the session, an experience that she was tempted to evacuate by saying, "Don't think about that". The painting, or paintings, can be considered "a dream" that form a container holding a constant conjunction, a pattern of emotional experiences. In this way, she could start to think and attempt to investigate their meaning. Thus, she was able to find another method of resolving her emotional problems, a method different from evacuation. I want to make a special point of the digestive and detoxifying function of this "dream": the patient was no longer paralysed or overwhelmed by this experience. She now was capable of thinking about it.

From very early on in her analysis, this patient appeared very interested in her dream life. I think that this is a factor of the psychoanalytic function of the personality that she is developing at this moment and that becomes evident by her ability to pay attention and show interest and courage in the task of the mind observing itself. Dreams and the ability to "dream" experiences constitute factors of that function.

With another vignette, I will try to illustrate the *evacuative use* of dreams related with the persistence of the operation of very primitive methods of swallowing and spitting out in order to deal with complex emotional problems. Here, the clinical problem consists at first of how to draw the patient's attention to the nature of this evacuative method, and then try to revert its relationship to dreams so as to be able to transform them into instruments in the sense I have already described.

It was often very difficult for Z to speak about her dreams in the session; she remembered them but she felt they were either terrifying or disgusting, with a strongly sensorial quality. This evacuative direction could be reverted once we were able to put a name to the experience. The patient said in that session that she had had a terrifying dream: she was seeing a ball of red flesh on the couch, as if it were without skin. After many difficulties, because she felt very terrified and was looking concretely towards the place where the ball of flesh seemed to "be", she finally could put a name to it: it was the head of a foetus.

It was very interesting to observe how, from that moment onwards, the patient started to classify her dreams: some dreams were disgusting, experienced concretely as faeces to be evacuated; others were nice dreams that contained a mystery that she agreed to investigate. In order to be able to examine the content of the disgusting dreams, we had to undertake a previous discerning task about how she dealt with them.

One of those disgusting dreams dealt with the very complex problem of separation. It was dreamed on a Sunday night, and on Monday she had a session. It terrified her so much that she had to stay awake with the light on. Two men kidnapped her and put her in the back of a car, like one of those Ford Falcons from the times of the Military Process Government; she was terrified. With great difficulty, she came to associate the dream with the cabs she took after her sessions. She said that in the back of those cars there are two handles, or ashtrays, to hang on to. In the dream the patient was terrified, and also in the session, and she could not talk about it. She finally said that, in the dream, she did not know where she was, or what was happening, everything was black, as if charred. She was very frightened of being raped. She hung on to something, and this something turned out to be two penises. In the dream images, the patient evacuates intolerable emotional experiences and, while operating so concretely, feeling disgust, she was unable to investigate the dream, and could not realize that she had been thinking in a peculiar, dreamlike, way.

I want now to refer to another clinical problem: the *lack of dreams*, an issue raised by those patients who live in a very concrete, factual world, and thus cannot enter into an "as if" play. They cannot gain access to their psychic reality because they do not discover it, and they do not succeed in discovering it because they do not "dream" it. It could be said that, for them, even their dreams are sensuous experiences that they cannot narrate, or, if they do, they cannot produce any kind of associations, not even in the analyst.

This issue is related to the clinical problem of how to help the patient traverse the caesura between sensuous reality and psychic reality, or, in other words, between "anecdote" and "dream".

Meltzer (1983) mentions frequently that the analyst needs to "dream" the session, "dream" the patient that cannot "dream". In this sense, it is not necessary for the patient to tell about a dream in the session; the analyst can attempt to transform the patient's associations into a "dream"; that is, "imagine it" in the form of visual images, a story, a narrative, a film, etc. To put this another way, he or she can construct models.

Dreams and myths are particularly suitable as a language for communicating psychic reality, because they have a strong sensorial impression and, at the same time, they convey a playful wink to the reader (Eco, 1994), the "let's pretend that . . ." of the game, the "as if" level. By "dreaming" the session, the analyst attempts to create that playful wink between him and his patient.

Dreams and poetry both share aesthetic devices: metaphors, oxymoron, similitude, alliterations, etc., resources that contribute to the transformation of the external object with sense qualities into a symbol with emotional meaning. The lack of dreams indicates poverty of imagination and avoidance of the turmoil of emotional life.

One of Bion's contributions to the clinical practice was his reflection that analysts need to enrich their equipment for the investigation of psychic realities with stories, dreams, myths, narratives, etc., to form a "verbal picture gallery", which can provide models that can be used for approaching different aspects of emotional situations. This kind of approach belongs to the realm where the practice of psychoanalysis intersects with psychoanalytic theories; in *Elements of Psychoanalysis* (Bion, 1963, p. 85) gave it the name of negative growth, by which he meant the need of combining, in a binocular vision, Row C (dreams, myths, models) and Row H (algebraic abstraction) of The Grid (Bion, 1977).

Bion calls this kind of equipment the apparatus for intuitive awareness of one's self, which also includes the preconceptual apparatus that permits getting in contact with the "realizations". The private Oedipus myth, which means the particular configuration it has for each person, is part of this preconceptual apparatus; this preconception allows establishing contact with the real parents and the relationship with them. So, through multiple realizations, the growing child or the patient in analysis can have a conception of the parents and of the relationship between them and with them. Damage to this preconceptual apparatus is a serious obstacle for the investigation and understanding of these relationships.

Myths and dreams become part of this preconceptual apparatus, and are the modality of thinking with certain qualities that makes them especially suitable for the discovery and understanding of psychic reality in contrast to lies.

It also gives a new value to the function of "constructions" in psychoanalysis, as the construction of a model, by using symmetry and analogy, makes the relationship more evident than if we use only the related objects (for example: breast, penis) which are the anchors of the relationship.

I would like to bring, as a clinical illustration of the "not playing, not dreaming" issue, the description of a patient whom I will call Adriana, who remembered two groups of childhood friends, neither of which she belonged to. She only "observed" their games and their fights from the outside, without participating.

Adriana seemed to live in a museum, she being, in turn, an object in it. Her perception of analysis was that of a mechanic's workshop where she could leave her car and the analyst/mechanic would repair it; the problem the car had was that it did not start. That is to say, that the problem of immobility was present even in the mechanical world. The systematic answer to interpretations was, "How is it done?" Some light was thrown on the mystery of that question when she said that she did not know what would happen with the car should she press the accelerator and the brakes at the same time.

I think that, for its development, psychoanalysis has to get rid of the medical model of healing and adopt the model of psychic change, crisis, turmoil, and growth in a process of constant evolvement.

Those patients in whom the failure of symbolization of their emotional experiences is evident need to generate elements and equipment to carry out the task of transformation that will allow them to think/dream their emotional states.

Adriana mentioned a film that would become a model for thinking of her isolation and the latent turbulence in her analysis. In the film *The Collector*, a vital young woman, a student of the arts, is kidnapped by a man who wants only to have her locked up. If she escaped, he would murder her.

This model allowed us to think about what it was that stayed locked up, and what was the danger of getting out of the locked-up, isolated situation. Then I "dreamed/thought" another model to approach the problem about the dreaded turmoil should the isolation disappear. I also used a film, *Jurassic Park*, and formulated the problem we were exploring through the following model: what happened when what was locked in the amber drop was taken out of its enclosure? We can consider this as a model for Adriana's autistic functioning of isolation and disconnection.

The film shows the uncontrolled violence and terror attacking the "scientific mind" that set them free.

This was one of the problems we had to consider with Adriana, who not only slept during the sessions, even though she made great efforts to stay awake, but had all her life got by with sleeping with a "resting plate" in her mouth, like the one the dentist had prepared for her, to avoid the wearing down of her teeth. Already having a certain possibility of playing/dreaming the model of the Tyrannosaurus with horrible teeth, she preferred to use that of the cannibal, to become aware of her difficulties to "take hold of" the psychoanalytic breast.

Lies and psychic reality

Under this last heading, I would like, via a clinical illustration, to talk of how lies—in this case conscious ones—compete with dreams in two obviously opposite tendencies: one towards becoming aware of, the other towards destruction of, awareness. Truth is a nutrient for the mind, and lies are a toxic (Bion, 1970).

I will present a vignette with the intention of illustrating the conflict between the emotional forces that push towards the discovery of psychic reality and mental growth, and the ones that tend towards lies, so as to retain omnipotent beliefs and avoid feelings of helplessness, need, and dependency. The interesting thing in this material is that parapraxis and dreams appeared, and were those that informed the patient of his lies and the consequences they had for his mind.

A patient who, at that moment of his analysis, was dealing with the problem of leaving behind adolescence, which meant growing and becoming responsible, used to lie, asking for schedule changes for the session, changes he did not need. Or he would arrive late, adducing that he had been held up at work; or he would ask for a day off at work because he had an exam, then would not go to the exam, but all the same he missed work, saying he had taken the exam and had failed, etc. After a one-week trip, during which he took the vacation he had not taken in the summer, he paid my fees, deducting the week without making it explicit. When confronted, he had to admit that that was not our agreement. He argued that he had not left in the summer and that those were *his* vacations, although he also realized the fact that it had crossed his mind to ask for a schedule change before the trip, taking into account the sessions he was not going to have, but later, not knowing why, he did not do it, letting the chance slip away.

When he came back, he said that he had felt tempted to call me several days after his arrival, miss those sessions, and say he had just arrived. He could not explain, not even to himself, why he had wanted to do that. He finally, under protest, accepted paying for those sessions.

Although he continued to smoke marijuana at weekends, he started to feel that there was too much time between the last session of the week and the first one of the next. The marijuana starts to appear in his dreams: in one he sees a bookshelf that has, instead of books, compact discs in disarray. The day he tells this dream, he can only associate it with the bookshelf in the house of A, one of the "guys" that provides him with marijuana.

In another session he tells the following dream.

> He was sitting with the bunch on a low wall smoking pot; they had their backs to their primary school, whose white wall appeared in the dream. [This time he associates the position in which he was sitting in the dream, low and with his back to the school, which was higher, with his position on the couch and my sitting higher. We knew from other dreams that the school was associated with his grandmother and that many times she represented me.] He had just broken off the relationship with a girl and he said, "Had she been crazy about me then we would be together." "I was pissed off by the conversation with A because I couldn't tell what side he was on, mine or S's [the girl]" "A quit smoking cigarettes . . ."

At that moment, he associates with the first dream, the bookshelf one. "When he has marijuana, A always says, 'I have compact, I got a compact.' I like to always have marijuana available."

It is obvious that the analyst is not always available. The unnecessary demands for schedule changes for the sessions tend to maintain the belief of my being always available to him. But when he again tries to make a schedule change to maintain the belief that I am always available to his demands, he wants to adduce that he cannot come to the session because he has to be at the faculty at 6:45 p.m., the time he finishes his session. The truth comes out through a parapraxis, because he says that the time he has to be there is 7:45 p.m., which is the real time.

He feels bad and is annoyed: from the ambiguity of a lie mounted on splitting, he turns to the polysemy of the parapraxis and to the dream, which show the disarray or the confusion that is caused by trying to keep two value systems separated. It becomes obvious that he uses my "unfaithfulness", the frustrations in the transference situation, to turn to deceit/marijuana always and thus avoid entering into the crisis or the catastrophic change implicit in dealing with the shattering of the belief of an always-available object.

An absolute truth does not exist. The term "truth or lie" depicts a conjunction. Using an operational definition of truth, it could be said that the truth or falseness of a statement becomes manifest when a correlation with action is required, a step that in turn needs an adjustment to reality. As we see with this patient, the phenomena linked to beliefs tend to manifest themselves persistently. These beliefs are convictions that maintain an impenetrable barrier to facts. The questions are: why do they continue operating despite the evidence, and what is pushing in an opposite direction, as I attempt to show with the vignette? These barriers are built to avoid mental pain, but it seems that the patient also needs the nourishment of truth.

In analysis, we depend on the patient's informing us truthfully. In the case of lies, we need to have the tools to be able to detect them. In his paper "The Grid", Bion wanted to design an instrument that psychoanalysts could use outside the session to exercise their analytic function, in the same way a pianist needs to exercise before and after a concert. I will take on the proposal he made about Row C (which covers the category of dreams, myths, etc.): that it would merit the construction of its own Grid. This extension is useful for classifying statements both from the patient and from the analyst, considering the different uses of these statements. It is useful so as to take into account when a use is at the service of discovery of psychic reality or when it is used for covering up lies.

The extension of the vertical axis of The Grid (with an upwards direction ↑), allows for classifying thoughts in an increasing grade of deterioration or degeneration (dream thoughts in this case, for example, with a direction towards hallucinations or towards pseudo-symbols); the direction downwards (↓) indicates an increasing degree of complexity. The extension of the horizontal axis to the left (←) gives the possibility of covering the untruthful uses, or those at the service of un-knowing. Column 2 (with a direction to the right →) of The Grid includes what I call "unconscious lies" or "misconceptions", that is the resistential use. If we use The

Grid as an instrument, we can classify the statements that operate as substitutes (lies), ←↑ (leftwards and upwards) in opposition to the progressively abstract statements capable of becoming operative ↓→ (downwards and to the right). We can compare a scientific statement (in the sense of its respect for the facts) with a lie.

We will observe in the latter a great degree of incoherence, as was obvious in the patient when he discussed payment of the fees. But should we examine it from the observer's vertex, that of my patient, we will see that he will consider his statements as coherent: he considered that it was unfair to pay me because he had not had his summer vacations. It was difficult for him to recognize his incoherence: if he felt it was so unfair, why had he avoided communicating his not intending to pay? Why had he not stated his disagreement (not made explicit until that moment) with our explicit agreement?

Undigested facts generate dread, and an immature apparatus cannot help to digest them. In the case of the patient that associates with a picture by Dali, the "dream" appears as a successful attempt at digestion; it produces alpha and also develops alpha function in a terrified personality, but with tolerance to frustration and without a high degree of envy. The seemingly threatening mental catastrophe can be turned into catastrophic change. Dali's and Frida Kahlo's paintings lend now a form to emotional experiences that can thus be investigated, signified, and thought.

In Verdi's *Othello* (the opera version of *Othello*), there is a duet in which Othello says to Desdemona that she loved him because of his misfortunes and he loved her because of her compassion. This pair represents the world of emotions, of emotional links (L, H, and K) that imply tolerance to mental pain, respect and consideration for others, and this is what Othello murders.

The world of lies is also an emotionality-divesting one. In *Othello*, Iago represents the rival and an envious attack on one aspect of Othello's personality that blinds him and pushes him to a murderous catastrophe. The blindness is produced by the anti-emotions: $-K$, $-H$ and $-L$ (in Bion's terms). The pair Desdemona–Othello is murdered by the pair Othello–Iago. This world was well depicted by George Orwell in *1984*, and by Aldous Huxley in *Brave New World*. I find it very important in my practice to be able to discriminate the lack of development from an attack;

nameless dread as a consequence of envious looting discriminated from nameless dread because of lack of development of the digestive alpha function. The co-operation towards growth or the lack of it is a strong indicator.

Dreams, the capacity of "dreaming", are central factors in the development of a capability of being aware. Untruthful functioning is related to a predatory, cannibalistic activity, as *Othello* very clearly shows: Iago exacerbates the worst in Othello. It may be said that, with his intrigues, he cannibalizes Othello's mind, and Othello plunges into the furious waters of not thinking. What would have happened if Othello had been able to dream Iago, just as Shakespeare dreamed both of them?

As for the social aspect, group blindness seems to be instrumented and reinforced by the use of pseudo-symbols in the service of inoculation and manipulation, characteristic of all totalitarian regimes, which—what a coincidence!—are always associated with generating terror. The powerful emotional forces present in Ur that Bion used as a model are still alive, as are those incarnated in the "gods" hostile to the possibility of becoming aware of our own predatory nature. At the end of *A Memoir of the Future*, Bion says that if we do not succeed in moving towards wisdom instead of shrewdness: Happy Holocaust.

Meltzer refers to the deep truth in Prospero's phrase: "we are such stuff as dreams are made on", to suggest that dream life *is* our imagination, constituting the antidote for excursions into the world of lies and/or dementalization.

CHAPTER THREE

Prenatal aspects of the mind: science and fiction in the psychoanalytical game

"... with Kant, I hold that the thing-in-itself is unknowable. Falstaff, a known artefact, is more 'real' in Shakespeare's verbal formulations than countless millions of people who are dim, invisible, lifeless, unreal, whose births, deaths-alas—even marriages we are called to believe in, though certification of their existence is vouched for by the said official certification . . . If psychoanalytic intuition does not provide a stamping ground for wild asses, where is a zoo to be found to preserve the species?"

(Bion, 1991, pp. 4–5)

"I would make a distinction between existence—the capacity to exist—and the ambition or aspiration to have an existence which is worth having—the quality of the existence, not the quantity; not the length of one's life, but the quality of that life"

(Bion 1979, p. 249)

In this chapter, I intend to extend the imaginative conjecture of prenatal aspects of the mind to include in it thoughts without a thinker and wild intuitions, or untamed thoughts. This extension has the purpose of providing elements for psychoanalytical investigation from the vertex of mental growth.

These thoughts cannot be known and investigated until they evolve and meet at a point of intersection with a thinker who has the possibility of lodging them. The term *thinker* in this context has the meaning of the mental functions developed for using the thoughts. Bion (1977) placed these functions in the columns, the vertical axis of The Grid.

Bion's revolutionary idea that thoughts are prior to thinking, and that they stimulate the development of an apparatus or functions to think them, is the starting point of many evolutions, of which the postulation of prenatal aspects of the mind is one of the most fertile.

In *Learning from Experience*, Bion formulates a ". . . supposition in which the patient is a foetus to whom the mother's emotions are communicated but the stimulus for the emotions and its source, is ignored" (Bion, 1962, p. 41).

This is a model for the difficulties of communication between patient and analyst, and between prenatal and postnatal parts of the personality. In this model the prenatal parts are not aware where the emotions come from or what stimulates them. Awareness needs the development of alpha function (Bion, 1962).

The model of the foetus can be extended to "foetal thoughts", thoughts that have not yet had a psychic birth, and it implies the idea of an embryonic mind, neothenic and in evolution.

I have developed the idea of "psychic birth" in Chapter One, and by this expression, here I mean a model that does not refer to an origin but to a point of intersection, that is to say, a junction between psychic reality and the sensorial aesthetic forms in which it can be expressed. There can be points of approximation and of distancing with these prenatal "thought-feelings", without a thinker.

I wish to put forward the idea that there is an optimum method for a creative transformation that has possibilities of evolving to generate that point of intersection, which is the dream thought when it acquires the condition of preconceptual in the mental state of being awake.

Science and *fiction*, linked with psychoanalysis, contain a reflection about tools whose combination provides a binocular vision for observation of the domain of psychic reality. Binocular vision provides depth, using the model of the difference between seeing with two eyes that converge on a point and seeing with just one eye.

"Psychoanalytical game" has an allusion to the implications of the extension of psychoanalytical method to child analysis, providing, through toys, a means for communicating emotional experiences.

Clinical experience, combined with Bion's innovative ideas, opened up a new perspective in my approach towards dreams and the use of models and personification as analytical tools, equivalent to the "toys" which figure in the psychoanalysis of small children. These tools possess a modulating function for mental pain and act as metabolizing mediators in a communication where there is a need to find the appropriate point of intersection between psychic reality and the forms rooted in sense-impressions in which it can be expressed.

In this context, the point of intersection is a transformation into a kind of fiction, which gives *embodiment* to objects of the internal world and lends forms to prenatal aspects of the mind. Transformation into fiction, in this specialized sense, has also the quality of evoking vividly the emotional experience and of providing the psychoanalytical object with one of its dimensions. An ulterior step, transforming this fiction into a question without an answer, provides a level of non-saturation characteristic of preconceptual thought especially well suited to psychoanalytical investigation.

Through this preconceptual use, scientific fiction becomes a tool for extending psychic space. In this way, the prenatal aspects that contain the capacity to evolve towards mental growth can be housed and given a form.

In this regard, Bion mentions Leonardo's drawings of hair as the achievement of a container able to capture and communicate turbulence in an artistic transformation (Bion, 1976). (See Figure 1.)

In what follows, I will attempt to explore the development of tools for psychoanalytical treatment which could make it possible to anchor such turbulences without removing their vital character.

Exoskeletons or mental prosthesis

"Most people experience a mental death if they live enough. It is not necessary to live a lot to have this experience—all that is necessary is to remain mentally alive" (Bion, 1977, p. 178).

In our practice, with increasing frequency, we meet patients who have developed some form of "pseudo-adapted prosthesis" at the cost of splitting off vital emotional forces. (I would say that it is also a characteristic of our "postmodern culture", which privileges shallowness, adaptation at any cost, the pretended effectiveness of the "machine", and the splitting of the emotional experience.) These split-off elements sometimes reappear as an alarming somatic manifestation, or they precipitate crises in emotional relationships, and on these occasions it is often possible, in analytic treatment, to discern evidence revealing the precariousness and poverty of the emotional links.

When the problem is facing developmental crisis implied in metal growth, or situations of emotional turbulence, this "exoskeleton" that takes the place of an endoskeleton (Bion, 1991) shows its shortcomings for "digesting" emotional experiences. Real emotional contact is a vital nutrient of the mind, and this is prevented by a sclerotic, non-living structure intended as a replacement for an "endoskeleton", which sustains from inside.

The presence of an "exoskeleton" may also manifest in feelings of emptiness or as a lack of a sense of identity, or the assumption of a false, "as-if" identity. In short, one could say that these are persons who do not manage to find themselves. This usually coexists with precariousness in sustaining lively and meaningful vital projects, and a lack of awareness of mental pain as something coming from the inside, all signs that something very wrong is going on in the development of their personality.

Such a prosthesis represents a strong obstacle for establishing contact with the true self, and for being able to face the emotional conflicts that are inherent in life and mental growth. It is a saturated functioning, one that is incapable of absorbing new emotional experiences, and it prevents, in particular, the possibility of housing the prenatal aspects of the personality as new thoughts that strike the mind. They contrast with the disposition and potentiality of an infant's mind.

Often, in these cases, we meet with people very attached to concrete and factual aspects of life. They do not dream, or, if they do, theirs are dreams without associations. Little or no value is placed on dream-life, and frequently there are serious difficulties when there is an attempt in analysis to move in a "let's pretend" world, a world where the word "cat" has no hair nor nails, it has a meaning.

I think that this imaginative conjecture—of prenatal functioning, vital and with developmental potentialities—is a fertile one with which to approach many problems in clinical practice.

To develop what I called science-fiction in the psychoanalytical game, I will refer to the technical implications of the idea of an *aesthetic dimension of the mind*, which I develop through the different chapters of this book, together with the notion of the transformation of the consulting room in the counterpart of an "atelier".

Art, in its diverse manifestations, has found powerful forms capable of articulation with vital emotional experiences and of harbouring them. These forms, with a lasting but not saturated meaning, retain a capacity for casting their shadows into the future and a flexibility for subtle variation and evolution. It thus makes possible a form of language that grows among the possibilities of new articulations, and this is why it always contains developmental potentialities.

Prenatal functioning

". . . can we catch the germ of an idea and plant it where it can begin to be developed until it acquires the necessary maturity to be born?" (Bion, Seminars of Sao Paulo, 1980).

The ideas about prenatal functioning emerge in Bion's work long before this imaginative conjecture was formulated, under different names such as: "nameless terror", proto- mental, somato–psychotic, sub-thalamic terrors", etc. The clinical implications of this conjecture, complemented with the metaphor of a psychic birth, is related to the construction, due to α function, of a semi permeable membrane, the contact barrier that separates conscious from unconscious.

Clinical practice brings evidence that alpha function might have important deficiencies: the contact barrier can be damaged, and this implies clinical work of helping the patient in the task of building and repairing equipment for thinking and for becoming oneself (be in at-one-ment), rather then that of lifting repressions. An idea in germ form, an untamed thought, an intuition, should not be expelled, but be helped to find a container where it can be lodged until it is able to be communicated. Once it can be formulated and published, we can investigate it and decide whether or not it is something with the potential for growth, or even if it is a sick germ.

Any factor that inhibits psychic birth is likely to function as an obstacle to discernment and investigation. The development of psycho-analytical trained intuition is related to the idea of at-one-ment (Bion, 1970), of becoming one with oneself. The Copernican turn of the implications of this idea can be synthesized as being the passage from learning towards mental growth.

At-one-ment is an expression, probably derived from playing with the word atonement, which means sacrifice, expiation. I think that Bion opposed at-one-ment to atonement. This idea contrasts becoming one with oneself with powerful omnipotent and omni-scient emotional forces that oppose and inhibit investigation of the self, which is the essence of a psychoanalytical treatment. These ideas are related with the idea of "becoming", of "evolution" and with transformation in O.

These powerful omnipotent and omniscient emotional forces are also prenatal aspects of the mind that take the place of reverie when and where it fails. They are "embodied" in a primitive "super"ego, as a moral conscience without morals that only toler-ates relationships of superiority–inferiority. This means, on the one hand, the usurpation by this primitive superego of the position that should be occupied by the ego functions and involves imperfect development of the reality principle, which is an exaltation of a "moral" outlook and lack of respect for truth (Bion, 1965, p. 38).

This moral, primitive, arrogant superego that usurps the ego functions can be observed in clinical practice as a persecutory critic: feelings of guilt, reproofs, all of them sharing inhibitory character-istics. In *Transformations* (Bion, 1965), these characteristics of the primitive superego are presented as a rivalry between the psycho-analytic method and the method of transformation in hallucinosis. Bion describes this rivalry as:

> . . . the analysis has been changed into a contest between a) thought against action, b) therapeutic use of insight against insight used to exacerbate, c) pairing and dependant group against flight-fight group, d) individual against group. [Bion, 1965, p. 166]

To transform criticism, feelings of guilt, reproofs, inhibitions, etc., into characters that are able to begin a dialogue with each other and with those that are criticized has been, in my experience, a very useful instrument. Because of its transformation in a psychoanalytical game, it helps the patient develop an observational vertex regarding those problems instead of being crushed by them. I can attempt to create a play zone with a patient who does not know how to play, "playing at having sit down" in a chair the guilty and/or critical character, and engaging in a dialogue in which other parts of the personality, the accused, can manifest their fears and discomfort.

The usurpation of ego functions by a precocious development of a primitive superego is also linked to the primitive group functioning. Personification, with its characteristics of fiction and dramatic play, can establish a dialogue between, say, "Miss guilt", "Miss patience", and "Mr reproof", and so helps to develop a separate mind that is able to think the primitive group functioning instead of transforming it into action. This "group mentality" is present in every human being, even if isolated, because it is inherent to our condition of being a herd animal.

In *Experiences in Groups*, Bion says that the three basic assumptions (BAs)* coexist. When one prevails in connection with the work group, the other two BAs are relegated to a hypothetical proto-mental apparatus, at humoral and neuropsychological levels. The idea of this hypothetical proto-mental apparatus contains the seed of the prenatal conjecture. It is also an epistemological posture towards the body–mind relationship. The posture is monist: it depends on the observational vertex: psychosomatic or somato–psychotic. (See also Chapter Five.)

In analysis, group mentality ("groupishness") manifests itself as a preference to avoid mental pain through crossed projective identifications and collusions between analyst and patient. The idea of "cure" stimulates the operations of basic assumptions (Bion, 1961) and contrasts with that of mental development.

Another manifestation of these prenatal aspects of the mind is Bion's idea of "thoughts without a thinker", complex and powerful in its potentiality as much in theory as in the clinical practice. One perspective of this idea is that of unborn thoughts, and we can think of them as thoughts with the capacity for evolution that, at some

point, intersect with the thinker. Evolution depends on transformations towards O and on the two functions that are the matrix of
thought and thinking: oscillation PS⇔D (states of dispersion and of
harmonization) and ♂♀.

In a psychoanalytical treatment, this idea implies the conception
of a mind as an open system that evolves, with developmental
potentialities. This idea is different from one of a closed psychic
apparatus, in which the clinical task is that of lifting repressions or
closing gaps opened by dissociation. It also implies that a personality can be helped to develop a more appropriate container–
contained relationship for housing these thoughts when they
emerge. The emotional turbulence generated through the threatened emergence of thoughts without a thinker cannot be contained
and managed within a mental structure having the qualities I have
described as prosthetic, which provide only limited, false, and
fragile foundations.

In this chapter, I try to approach some of these queries:

How can we build, in a psychoanalysis, screens as receptive
possibilities for emotional prenatal forces, for wild intuitions, for
thoughts without thinker, in a similar way as the poet, the sculptor,
the painter, etc., do when they build forms that catch the light,
generating more light than heat?

Psychic space and mental growth

The space of psychic reality can be conceived (Bion, 1965) as a space
occupied by "no things". Liberating this space from its penumbra
of associations with the perceptual world opens a place for
thoughts and thinking. Psychoanalysis deals with the relationship
between the "thing" and the "no-thing".

> Intolerance of a no-thing, taken together with the conviction that
> any object capable of a representative function is, by virtue of what
> the sane personality regards as its representative function, not a
> representation at all but a no-thing in itself, precludes the possibil-
> ity of words, circles, points and lines being used in the furtherance
> of learning from experience. [Bion, 1965, p. 82]

Emotions and ideas are "no things". If the patient is able to differentiate the map from the territory, it demolishes a strong obstacle to a psychoanalytical inquiry. Bion describes this problem by quoting Shelley, from the poem "Hellas":

> that state of mind in which ideas may be supposed to assume the force of sensations through the confusion of thought with the objects of thought, and the excess of passion animating the creations of imagination. [Bion, 1965, p. 133]

Mental growth is a parameter of development of the capacity for insight, and of maturity to confront emotional conflicts. It is associated with tolerance of the development of thoughts and of their use to solve problems in the absence of objects. When, in the clinical practice, we deal with prenatal aspects, in the wide sense in which I have defined them, we meet with situations that go beyond the area of thinking. These ideas imply an extension of the mind towards spaces not conceived previously as mental.

The classical theory of transference did not include the notion of projective identification in its different characteristics. An extension of this theory is required to take into account the clinical reality of projective identification and what I am referring to here as the way in which projective identifications become "crossed". The classical theory considers that the analyst is the person on to whom the patient transfers internal images. The notion requires extension to take account of the operations of primitive group functioning and of projective identifications as they appear in the clinical manifestations of the session. By crossed projective identifications, I mean what happens between analyst and patient or in a group at the level of "primitive group mentality". Bion refers to this problem in *Elements of Psycho-analysis* (1963, p. 16) when he describes the difficulties of developing a separate mind.

In the multi-dimensional space of the analytic session, the patient projects and communicates across a wider field than that which encompasses the analyst, his/her own personality, and even the relationship between them. In one direction, it extends into a somatic dimension, and, in another, fragments of it can be lodged in institutions, friends, relatives, since what is experienced by the patient as the personality is not limited to the anatomical boundaries.

A psychic space with discrimination between inside–outside, which includes time as a fourth dimension, is the outcome of a complex developmental process. In many patients, this process has not been achieved through the digestion of emotional experiences. This implies operations adapted to some of the circumstances of external reality, but, because of their rigidity, they are not appropriate for confronting emotional turbulences. Experiences in clinical practice often lead us to encounter patients who live in a time that has stopped and/or in claustrophobic or agoraphobic spaces.

These problems not only refer to patients with a part of their emotional life immobilized, as in the tea party of the Mad Hatter in *Alice in Wonderland*, where it is always five o'clock and the tea, when served, instead of going into the cup, returns to the teapot. A patient with these characteristics evoked in me a model of analysis as a game in which he played with dice that always fell in the square "Return to the Starting Point".

There are also people that live in a literal world, unable to tolerate the coexistence of a dream-world with an external reality of commonsense. They have serious flaws in their contact barrier, and they fear the invasion of powerful emotional aspects into their mental state of being awake, because they feel that would be tantamount to allowing themselves to be totally invaded by madness. This happened with the patient whom I described in the previous chapter as having felt disgusted by her dreams.

By way of a brief clinical illustration, I will refer to a patient A, who observed that the bookcase of the office was bent, which indeed it was. She expressed a warning that there was a danger that it could break and the books would be scattered. The analyst's conjecture that she was expressing a fear that the analyst's mind or her own could break up and be at risk of spreading or disorganizing was met by an explosion of fury. Miss A said that the bookcase was bent, and that she only described what she saw. This literality is not a clinical manifestation of a resistance in the classic sense, but an evidence of a world where the absurdity that a verbalization can have more than one meaning is felt as a menace to her sanity.

The intolerance of conjugating the intersection of an imaginary and a real point also showed through the intolerance of the paradox, expressed in the reproach to the analyst about interpreting her statements as if they were a dream, and, on the other hand, finishing the session exactly on schedule according to the clock. This patient was very successful in her professional life, and had turned to analysis following the traumatic failure of a sentimental relationship. Her intellectual growth and development had not been in harmony with her emotional development. A small and frightened little girl was entrenched behind an exoskeleton, which she felt to be her only safe anchoring point in life.

Mental growth is a-temporal and catastrophic (Bion, 1965). The elaboration of the notions of catastrophic change and of caesura seem to require the introduction of space and time categories in psychoanalysis, following models that bear a strong analogy with the discovery of the theory of relativity in physics.

Time and space are notions that are achieved when a process of tolerance to the place and the time where the "breast" used to be and is no more. Bion supposes that that "emotional" place and time are transformed through tolerance to the "no thing", that is, the thought, in non-saturated observation vertexes.

If the emotion remains in a state of "non digestion", "space" and "time" will be invaded by projective identifications of β elements, "things" which have the characteristic of "ghosts". By occupying this space, they turn it into a claustrophobic or agoraphobic space. The place that would potentially be available as an observational vertex then becomes occupied by a one-directional evacuation, rendering it unfit for housing prenatal aspects of the mind that are evolving.

Time can also be saturated, immobile, reversible, or circular (Meltzer, 1975) and also be a scenario of catastrophic anxieties instead of being a vertex suited for observation. If past and future are profound experiences of the present, the psychoanalytical problem is the character of those experiences and their different transformations. Our clinical experience shows us patients that "live" in a frozen time, a time that is an eternal "present", blocked in their capacity to work through mourning and develop psychic change.

In his profound investigation of the function of thinking and its disabilities, Bion made remarkable developments that are an important contribution to psychoanalytical technique. He conceives the idea of a realistic projective identification that works as a communication in a container–contained relationship.

In that context we can consider prenatal emotions not only as archaic vestiges, but as preconceptions or pre-emotions, as seeds in an evolutionary process of growth on their way to becoming a tree. They are expectations that act as a search for a container through realistic projective identification. The problem is how to move caesuras from "foetal ideas" towards forms, metaphors of creative thought disarticulating defensive jargons, empty shells, to give birth to a contained thought in a flexible containing form. (See also Chapter Five.)

If there is a conjunction of tolerance of frustration modulated by a reverie function, projective identification can operate as a searcher, a probe thrown into space. If the search finds an appropriate container, the experience of the discovery of elements perceived in outer space will be the way in which preconceptions and pre-emotions acquire meaning by experience. The matching of preconceptions or premonitions—intuitions with realizations (negative and positive) with tolerance of frustration and reverie— are factors for creating a conception of space as the place where the "breast" used to be. Then points, lines, and circles can mark that place and be conceived as "no-things".

What I am trying to express is a conjectural idea about how an "alpha space" is generated as a place that houses or contains the "no thing" that marks the place where the "thing" used to be and is no longer, and how this contrasts with a concrete space inhabited by "things" that work as "ghosts of departed quantities" (Bion, 1965, p. 157) and which may be experienced as nameless terrors. Our clinical experience shows us then what we call "claustrophobia or agoraphobia". Said more simply, a "thing in itself" functions as "stones" in one's head; one cannot think with stones. Alpha space is a representative space, equivalent to that of geometry, where relationships can be represented.

In psychoanalytical practice, the development of a capacity for thought to capture "non-sensorial realities" belonging to the domain of the psychic reality is, in my opinion, associated to the possibility of tolerating the preconceptual quality of the thought.

This means tolerating the "seeds", the prenatal aspects not yet evolved, which include "communications" of a very primitive, even somatic, level, that are more authentic than what I described earlier as the postnatal "prosthesis".

"Preconceptual" also implies a use where a somatic symptom, an expression, can be transformed into a dream-thought element, etc., and in a question without an answer, in an unknown, in the algebraic sense. (In The Grid, Bion uses the term preconception as a stage in the evolution of thought [Row D] and as a use in columns 4 [attention] and 5 [inquiry].)

This means that a psychoanalytic vertex implies an approach that tolerates mystery, doubt, uncertainties, and unknown variables of non-saturated elements. A question without a closed answer, with unsaturated elements, contains the possibility of evolution in which new meanings appear or a somatic symptom can acquire a psychic meaning as a "dream". This was illustrated in relation to "dreaming" in Chapter Two.

In psychoanalytical practice, the development of a capacity for thought to capture "non-sensorial realities" as those that belong to the domain of the psychic reality is, in my opinion, associated to the possibility of tolerating the preconceptual quality of the thought. This means tolerating the "seeds", the prenatal aspects not yet evolved, which include "communications" of a very primitive, even somatic, level, that are more authentic than the post-natal "prosthesis". Pre-conceptual also implies a use where a somatic symptom, an expression, can be transformed into a dream-thought element etc. and in a question without an answer, in an incognito, in the algebraic sense.

A furious beating of the heart can have no meaning for a patient; the analyst can "dream" it, transform it into a pictorial representation, verbally expressed, and give it a name. The patient can also try to explain it as a heart disease, because he is intolerant of the unknown and strives instantaneously to feel that it is explicable, familiar. The following dialogues, from A Memoir of the Future, intend to illustrate the idea.

> Heart: If the cap fit—wear it. Let you and your damn silly mind go back to the Front, but why drag me in? I didn't enlist "for the duration". I was furious when you told me to stop thumping.

> Seventy-five years: You were always thumping—if not with fury, then with fear. Later it was love. Rabbits always "thump"; it's like trying to interpret a motor horn—it tells you nothing and leaves you to imagine something is going to happen to someone, somewhere, sometime.

Heart: If only you listened to me and learnt my language . . . [Bion, 1991, p.452]

Body: It is the meaning of pain that I'm sending to you; the words get through—which I have not sent—but the meaning is lost.

Mind: What is that amusing little affair sticking out? I like it. It has a mind of its own—just like me.

Body: It's just like me—has a body of its own. That's why it is so erect. Your mind—no evidence for it at all.

Mind: Don't be ridiculous. I suffer anxiety as much as you have pain. In fact I have pain about which you know nothing: I suffered intensely when we were rejected. I asked you to call me Psyche and promised to call you Soma.

Soma: All right Psyche; I don't admit that there is any such person than a figment of my digestion. [Bion, 1991, p. 434]

Externalization → transferential space

In the psychoanalytical relationship, realistic projective identification communicates to the analyst prenatal emotions, which the patient has not been able to "dream" or name. From this vertex, projective identification is not only a phantasy of a mind related to an object, but, rather, it becomes an operation that occupies a "space" in common of two minds which are linked by an emotion in a container–contained relationship.

But when two personalities meet, emotional turbulence is stimulated (Bion, 1987), and this refers as much to the meeting of the patient's pre and postnatal aspects as for the analyst–patient encounter. What tools has the analyst for developing and maintaining his capacity for preconceptual thought and also for helping the patient develop a separated mind?

Bion's ideas inspired in his *Experiences in Groups* (1961) and developed through his approach of the psychotic and non-psychotic aspects of personality, made a contribution to an as yet very little investigated notion: "the group or social component" of mental perturbations. (See also Chapter Five.)

The conception that parts of the personality can be split off and lodged outside of its anatomical limits enlarges the observational area of "emotional space". It also makes a differentiation between the analyst's unconscious countertransference and the loss of insight due to the powerful emotional forces that move inside the session, because of the contribution of this primitive group mentality.

The analyst is exposed to this "group mentality component" not only because of the primitive group mentality inherent in all human beings, but also because he needs to develop his intuition to be able to put his mind in at-one-ment with the "O" (Bion, 1965) of the patient. This exposes him to a functioning that goes beyond the area of thought, to prenatal terrors, evacuative operations through projective identification, and to the primitive group component of the members of the analytic couple.

The technical postulation of a negative capability* is well known (Bion, 1970, p.125, defined by Bion with a quotation from Keats:

> . . . and at once it struck me what quality went to form a man of Achievement, especially in Literature, and which Shakespeare possessed so enormously—I mean Negative Capability, that is when a man is capable of being in uncertainties, mysteries, doubts without any irritable searching after facts and reason.

It means a capability to develop tolerance of uncertainties, disciplining the mind in an attitude of "no memory, no desire, no understanding". This attitude harmonizes with preconceptual thinking and is complementary with the idea of free-floating attention. It implies avoiding meanings already saturated, because even an analytically trained mind still runs the risk of being pulled in by the emotional turbulences inevitably agitated in a psychoanalytical session, when the analyst is in contact with the O of the patient.

Detoxification of emotions

> The geometric transformation may be regarded as a representation, "detoxicated" (that is with the painful emotions made bearable), of the same realization as that represented (but with painful emotions expressed) by the intuitive psycho-analytical theory. [Bion, 1965, p. 125]

How can we think about the means for "detoxifying" primitive emotions, a necessary precondition for creating a mental space (an alpha space?) in which meanings and conflict can be tolerated, a space of psychic reality?

Bion took Klein's idea of the positions and transformed it into a mental function: the PS⇔D oscillation. This function, when operating at mature levels as shifting observation vertices, implies that a process of detoxification of primitive emotions took place, and offers the possibility that the powerful primitive emotions, characteristic of what Klein called the paranoid–schizoid and depressive positions, can be transformed and rendered less overwhelming to the developing psyche.

The PS⇔D oscillation has the function of delineating the field of psychoanalytical investigation because it implies a tolerance of feelings of uncertainty and dispersion at moments of "not understanding", and also to emotions associated with the discovery of the selected fact. This function is complemented with a container–contained symbiotic relationship, from which meaning arises.

PS and D are the ways in which the mind assembles facts; in its primitive or primary operations they correspond with the configurations and anxieties that Klein described for the schizo–paranoid and depressive positions. When detoxified, they become functions at the service of thinking.

Detoxifying is a process of transformation that implies non-violent emotions, allowing for a tolerance of the uncertainty of facts still not articulated, and the disarticulation of the previously articulated conjunction, without feeling it equal to fragmentation. By violence, I mean not only a destructive characteristic, but also an explosive or implosive quantitative characteristic. In contrast with this violence, the English poet Shelley speaks of emotions recollected in tranquillity.

In the psychoanalytical process, detoxification makes possible discovering the relationship and the reversible perspective. The well-known gestalt experiences can be an illustration of the idea of reversible perspective and the need to change and relate different vertices: you cannot see at the same time the two profiles and the vase, or the old and the young women.

In the session, we are faced with what we do not know; we are in contact with phenomena that we have not yet observed. This is associated to the observation of a series of seemingly unconnected facts that arouse feelings akin to the anxieties of PS, an emotional experience of uncertainty. Bion observed that the capacity for patience helps the analyst to manage the hazards implicit in this similarity.

In the mental state of D, the feeling of security (Bion, 1970) in the analyst makes a difference to a mental state akin to the depressive position, but that is not identical. When the analyst finds the selected fact and makes an interpretation, he has to make a decision and a choice. This implies a restriction and a tolerance to the relationship *finite–infinite*: he has to recognize limits and to give up other possible interpretations. This decision means also a tolerance of what had been harmonized, knowing that it is only a point in a process, that any point of arrival is also a point of departure. This means perhaps dealing with some depressive anxiety at a mature level and not at the primitive levels which Melanie Klein described.

Bion takes the idea from the mathematician Poincaré of the discovery of the selected fact as the harmonizing fact of elements seen previously as dispersed. *The process of discovery of the harmonizing fact cannot be started and maintained without the mobilization of the mental processes of "dreaming".* The analyst needs to cultivate that capacity "to dream" while he is awake, and that capability needs to combine with what is generally conceived as the ability for logical thought of mathematical character. This implies the establishing of correlations and tolerance of the preconceptual use of the "dream" as a variable, or incognito in the algebraic sense, whose "value" has to be found. (See also Chapter Two.)

Clinical experience has helped me to consider "dreaming" and personification as methods appropriate for the discovery of the selected fact, indispensable for the generation of meaning, and as good, detoxifying resources because of their quality as mediators and as "instruments" for playing that harmonize well with a mental state of non-saturation. They are good assistants in giving form to pre-emotions, to "wild intuitions", taming them without depriving them of vitality and the capacity of evolution. "To play" in a domain of "let's pretend" contributes to the creation of a space of psychic reality, a "scenario" shared by patient and analyst in the dimension of "myth". It implies the generation of a common space for observation. (For clinical illustration, see Chapters Two and Eight.)

Dream-thoughts and generation of meaning

Bion's investigation of the disturbances of thinking enabled a deeper understanding of the complex operations of this function, in both its unconscious and conscious aspects. His contributions offered some foundations for a psychoanalytical epistemology, which takes into account the emotional forces as factors in the generation of thoughts, of mental functions that facilitate thinking, and the capacity for self-reflection.

Taking these developments as a starting point, I will try to show that their deep implications introduce changes in the psycho-analytical technique, without modifying its fundamental structure.

Bion extended Freud's ideas about dream work to what he called, in *Cogitations*, dream-work-α*, and then alpha function. (See also Chapter Two.) He took as a basis for his investigation Freud's and Klein's ideas.

1. From the "Formulation of the two principles of mental func-tioning" (1911b), he took the idea that the "bitter experiences of life" stimulate the development of consciousness, as the sense organ for the apprehension of psychic qualities, towards linking it to impressions of the sense organs and not only to the percep-tion of pleasure and pain. This process leads from a rudimentary consciousness that perceives without understanding to an evolved agency capable of awareness, with such functions as thinking, memory, attention, etc. These functions are able to deal with stimuli in a more complex way than the immediate discharge of them.

    The postulation of alpha function opened up the possibility of construing a new relationship between unconscious and conscious processes, as complementary operations that provide a binocular vision.

2. From Klein, he took her hypotheses of splitting and projective identification related to the ideas of the construction of an inter-nal and external world based on the processes of projective and introjective identification.

    The postulation of maternal reverie introduced a funda-mental function of the human environment in the emotional development of the personality.

3. The relationship between reverie function, alpha function, and
    the mechanisms of dream work not only produced very impor-
    tant innovations in the theory of dreaming and dreams, but also
    led to unsuspected theoretical and clinical openings.

Why did Bion add alpha to "dream work"? The mechanisms of
dream work, described by Freud as condensation and displacement, are not only at the service of censure; my conjecture is that
certain innate capacities of the species as those for producing
synthesis, as the Gestalt's research demonstrated for perception,
also act for unconscious thinking, have much in common with the
sources of poetry, and are processes of synthesis that establish relationships or associations.

Bion extends the idea of dream work to dream work alpha, or
alpha function, as a form of a continuous processing of emotional
experiences: "dreaming" the reality works as a process of "digesting" emotional experiences. "Dreaming" is the way through which
the mind records and assimilates emotional experiences.

"Dreaming" has the function of creating a contact barrier
between the domains of the conscious and the unconscious. It transforms and organizes the continuous flow of our experiences with
ourselves and with others.

"To dream" is a kind of thinking that does not happen only at
night; it is continuous in vigil and in sleeping mental states. This
modality of thinking transforms an incoherent mass of stimuli of
sensorial impressions into ideograms that are used to register
present and future experiences.

These ideograms, or alpha elements, can be articulated or
disarticulated, giving form and synthesizing a mass of incoherent
stimuli. They are sensorial forms: visual, auditory, olfactory, tactile,
patterns, etc., that house non-sensorial experiences. We can find
a noteworthy example in literature, when Marcel Proust (1913)
describes the sudden revelation of lost emotional experiences
through the taste of a madeleine dipped in tea.

Alpha function operates on the awareness of the experiences.
Projective identification becomes hyperbolic and with a strong dose
of omnipotence when this function has severe flaws. In my clinical
experience, I can observe other phenomena also, such as detentions
of realistic projective identifications or evacuations at somatic

levels. (See also Chapters One, Eight, and Nine.) In all these situations, the process of assimilation of emotional experiences is disturbed. There is no "dreaming" and no space of "psychic reality". And without phantasies and dreams, there are no means for thinking a problem.

The use in reverse of the sense organs, to evacuate instead of receiving sensorial impressions that could intersect with emotional experiences, impedes the formation of a space for psychic reality.

The idea of O as an ultimate reality, that cannot be known but that one can "become", and from which something evolves that intersects with a thinker, leads to the postulation of alpha function as an emotional and sensorial function with an *aesthetic dimension* that is receptive to the evolutions of O (Bion, 1965). Starting from this intersection, an evolution takes place from O towards K: that is, the way of formulating a problem so that it can be thought. The "dream" allows assimilation and communication of the pre-communicable material, as much at the level of private as of public communication. This process facilitates learning from the emotional experience.

> O does not fall in the domain of knowledge or learning . . . It is darkness and formlessness but it enters in the domain K when it has evolved to a point where it can be known through knowledge gained by experience, and formulated in terms derived from sensuous experience. [Bion, 1970]

The inability to "dream" implies that the person cannot transform his/her emotional experiences to be able to store them and to use them for introjective processes. He/she remains with the concreteness and lack of meaning of facts that fail to become internalized experiences. These experiences remain as undigested facts. My investigations with patients that live attached to the literality and concreteness of the facts of the external world made me realize that their contact with the world is not based on the digestion of emotional experiences.

So, some of these patients might seem to live a life without turbulences, because of their prosthetic adaptation. But, in a psychoanalytical treatment, we find out that they move in a shallow world which hides untransformed prenatal terrors. Therefore, they lack instruments to understand and to confront the conflicts inherent to emotional development.

Contrary to the chaotic and indiscriminate stimuli of the raw emotional experience (beta elements*), the ideograms (alpha elements) can be assimilated and introjected by the personality, constructing a system of notation which is the base of evocative memory, whose laws are those of free association in consonance with emotional vicissitudes.

One of the functions of "dream" thoughts is the creation of these ideograms that facilitate the functioning of evocative memory and free-floating attention, open to meet with new experiences.

This function is also essential for a process of transforming experience into a "myth", a process that could also be seen as a transformation into a fiction.

This process embodies in characters and dramatic actions the prenatal emotional experiences. "Dream" thoughts are used to produce "myths" that are communicable. Bion suggests that the "dream" has some of the qualities of commonsense, as the establishment of correlations, and it is also a kind of a "not common" commonsense. This means, in my opinion, that "dream" thoughts allow "non common" correlations, the "absurdity" that seemed so intolerable to the patient in the clinical vignette of the bookcase. These correlations show new vertices not discovered until then. It is equivalent to such articulations as that of the oxymoron in literature.

"Dreaming" has the function of finding the selected fact that harmonizes a series of dispersed elements and it is the way of forming constant conjunctions and of generating meaning.

The failures that can be observed in the capability "to dream" in some patients led Bion to suggest that the analyst should cultivate a capacity to "dream" while he is awake. This "dreaming" can no longer be relegated to an archaic category. Because of its ability to make evident non-common correlations, and also, in the vigil states of mind, to provide a means of tolerating the unknown, its function is complementary and at a similar level to that of logical and mathematical thought.

Dream work alpha, combined with the oscillation of the mental states of the positions (PS⇔D), achieves the transformation through "mythmaking" of that which evolves from O and facilitates the mentalization of the emotional experience.

The oscillation of the positions opens the possibility of alternation of vertices that allows the apprehension of the reversible perspective. You cannot see at the same time the two faces and the vase (Gestalt). *Binocular vision, alternation of vertices, and reversible perspective are the operations necessary for apprehending totalities, which are always partial if we frame them in the relationship finite–infinite.* The developing of these instruments is indispensable for mental growth.

The contact barrier works as a semi-permeable protective membrane, which functions as contact and as a barrier. It facilitates in the patient the process of differentiating the internal world from external reality and to move in a world where he/she can recognize analogies, symmetries, and metaphors.

The failure in establishing this caesura leads to a series of dysfunctions that can go from something equivalent to a mental state in which the patient lives in a world that should be the "furniture of dreams" to a concrete and two-dimensional world, where there is no space for imagination. This last alternative was described by Borges (1944) in his masterful tale: "Funes el memorioso", where Funes, immobilized by an accident (we can imagine it as an equivalent of a mental damage), wants to make an infinite dictionary, because he cannot tolerate, for example, that the dog seen from the profile angle should have the same name as the dog seen from the front.

The analyst can *build an artificially constructed dream*, in a way similar to what Borges did in the narrative of his tale. The fact that the analyst can "dream" in an awake state of mind, that he can "dream" the patient, provides the possibility of repairing and developing the patient's alpha function. Therefore, it opens a perspective for the patient for developing thoughts and the capacity of using them to make contact with himself.

Bion suggests that the manifest content of the dream must be considered as an enunciation that certain alpha elements are constantly conjugated. Here, conjugated elements means establishing a relationship between them, a relationship that contains an incognita, and whose meaning can be investigated in psychoanalysis. It can be seen as quite similar to the selected fact.

As was explained in Chapter Two, I suggest the possibility of using, in one's waking life, images of this contained manifest (a set of visual images presented in a narrative) as the equivalent of a mathematical formula, as an algebraic calculation acting as an incognita to be cleared. *This pre-conceptual use of dream-thought implies a mind open to discovery, which constructs a net with which to approach emotional experiences that have not yet happened.*

"To dream" the session

The idea that the analyst has "to dream" the patient and what evolves from the O of the patient in those situations in which the patient's alpha function is damaged *is harnessed to a different technical approach in the psychoanalytical practice.* This "dreaming" not only generates a contact barrier; using dream images as unknowns can also develop the patient's capacity for abstract thought for correlation and private and public communication. This contrasts with the patient's use of an empty or literal speech that avoids contact with the emotional experience. *This kind of approach creates instruments for mental growth, starting from a relational model of container–contained, in which both maternal reverie for the baby and the analyst's dream-work-alpha for the patient, are of central significance for emotional development.* For Bion, abstraction has a characteristic different from the usual meaning. The idea is not to "take" something from something, but rather to go finding synthesis via the finding of the selected fact, in each turn of the screw of the PS⇔D oscillation. Its characteristic is to unite constant conjunctions, establishing increasing degrees of synthesis by way of expanding correlations (Bion, 1962). This is different from arriving at abstraction by a stripping away of meanings as a way of eluding paranoid anxieties, so that "table" can mean that, and nothing more.

In *Cogitations,* Bion describes his dream of a Negro. He wonders if the facts captured as sensorial impressions are used for "digesting" or assimilate emotional experiences. Are they a container for an eroding liquid that could in itself resist the erosion produced by the emotional contents?

In relation to his dream, Bion says it can be that the Negro has been thought as a real person, a fact, not assimilated. But also, the

Negro in the dream is an ideogram that condenses and contains the emotional experiences that Bion discovers when they are revealed by his associations. Before falling asleep, Bion was thinking about negative, and the dream-work, as a complex representation, and includes this abstract problem that he was thinking when awake. [Bion, 1992]

The image of the Negro is, at the same time, an element with sensorial qualities which also contains the word Negro, where emotional experiences not digested, which, in my opinion, could be considered as non-resolved problems or ill-resolved ones, have been housed by condensation. *The first associations arise in the waking mental state, but the dream thoughts already produced an association process through condensation in the image of the Negro. Negro is the image and the name of a constant conjugated conjunction.*

This example of the dream of the Negro is interesting, and it evoked in me, as a contrast, the clinical material of the "black glasses" that Bion describes in the paper "Differentiation between the psychotic and nonpsychotic part of the personality".

Bion could dream the Negro and develop a mental process; the patient, on the other hand, had had the need of the concrete presence of the black glasses to house there, in a compact and agglomerated form, primitive emotional experiences such as his relationship with the bottle, the paranoid anxieties aroused by the experience of feeling that he was spying on the primary scene, etc.

Bion draws attention, in this clinical material, to his patient's inability "to dream"; he did not have available ideograms, so he depended on the existence of an external object, the black glasses, and on the analyst's presence to be able to "dream". The glasses provided him with the equivalent of an ideogram, and the analyst could help to build a dream artificially, approximating him to the world of analogy and symmetry.

"Dreaming", combined with preconceptual thought, provides a binocular vision and allows location in space and time; emotions, the "eroding liquid" needed to find, through externalization, a container resistant to the erosion of the content. It is a necessary step for the evolution of prenatal aspects from the formless and infinite void (O). Through externalization in a container–contained relationship of mutual benefit, these prenatal aspects acquire a form and can be thought.

Reverie function is the condition that makes reintrojection possible, because it transforms prenatal thought into a "dream". When this function fails, the projected material comes back transformed into a "nightmare", a terror without image, without name, without container that contains the erosion. It leads to confusion between sensorial objects and emotional experiences.

In the projective–introjective movement, a strong interference takes place.

"Dreaming" facilitates the process of reintrojection because, using a digestive model, one can say that it transforms heteronymous "proteins" into "proteins" akin, or tolerable, to the personality that will then be able to assimilate them. As Shakespeare tells us:

> We are such stuff
> As dreams are made on and our little life
> Is rounded with a sleep . . .
> [Shakespeare: *The Tempest*, IV: 156–157]

The work that Bion does sleeping and when he is awake with his dream of the Negro, the patient of the black glasses is unable to do.

Maternal reverie, or the analyst's alpha function, is the receptive organ for the infant's or the patient's harvest of self sensations. The process of containing them, toleration of not understanding without intense states of anxiety and without denial, opens the way to find the selected fact that confers on them coherence and meaning.

Meaning is a psychological need, the lack of meaning is felt at primitive levels as destruction and not as a stage of something that has not evolved yet, or has not been discovered yet (Bion, 1965). *Meaning arises from a correlation equivalent to the discovery of reversible perspective.* If the baby projects his fear of dying, the mother gives it a meaning: a fear of dying means a desire to live. *In turn, the preconceptual thought implies training in the tolerance of uncertainties and of the lack of meaning, indispensable in a psychoanalytical investigation.*

The failure of alpha function prevents "dreaming". The patient of the black glasses was attempting a "scribble"; he could not make a "drawing"; he needed the analyst's help to repair his equipment for thinking and understanding psychic reality.

The tasks that the breakdown in maternal reverie leaves unfinished are imposed on the infant's rudimentary consciousness. They are all related with the function of correlation. Psychic qualities are perceived by a premature and fragile consciousness and the place of reverie is occupied by a primitive, prenatal superego which usurps the functions of the ego. This usurpation has an inhibitory function towards thinking. Bion suggests that, in psychoanalysis, the relevant developmental criterion is whether an activity promotes or interferes with mental growth.

"Dreaming" as a relational process

The patient establishes a connection not only with the contents of interpretations, but also with the analyst's mind and how it works, and this opens for him opportunities to repair his equipment for understanding and being in connection with his psychic reality. As the infant introjects, together with the alpha elements, the maternal reverie function, so the patient receives and introjects the analyst's alpha function.

The conjecture of prenatal thoughts as germs with the potential for evolution towards mental growth changes the psychoanalytical vertex from "cure" towards the development of thoughts and of mental functions for thinking them. This also implies a different position towards externalization processes.

If projective identification has a function of communication, and if the generation of thoughts depends at the beginning of life on the functioning of another's mind, the development of thoughts and the process of symbolization becomes a relational process. What is relevant from this point of view, then, is that there are two minds in at-one-ment, generating new meanings, new relationships, and new possibilities.

Transference is a field of translation, of externalization. This implies an intense emotional experience for both participants, with the challenge of being and becoming oneself and not of "seeming" to be. When in an analysis, the patient can establish contact with his true self; a process of growth seems to start that involves the analyst, who, far from being a neutral mirror, is also exposed to the turbulence of catastrophic change.

Bion puts forward a crucial question for clinical practice that, in my opinion, is related to the construction of the instruments to which I am referring: is externalization to be considered only an escape stimulated by intense paranoid and/or depressive anxieties, or is it also a movement that, under certain conditions, facilitates the construction of a tool for investigating the same emotional experiences that stimulated the externalization? If it is not viewed as a mere defensive escape, then the projection will not only be impregnated with archaic aspects that must be revealed through interpretation, but also it can be considered as a potentiality with the capacity of evolution.

The following question that Bion formulates is: if the discovery of the selected fact (SF) has only a reassuring function that modulates the internal tensions derived from anxieties of the depressive position, by virtue of being a creative and reparatory intent, or is this SF also, in itself, an instrument that allows the evolution of the personality, because it is important to start the dynamic oscillation of the positions (PS⇔D function), and it provides the possibility of the development of a capacity to "see" totalities and to possibly to discover new meanings?

I share Bion's viewpoint that externalization in a container–contained relationship of mutual benefit and the discovery of the SF offers the possibility of building new instruments, which have their roots in the transformation of primitive anxieties, perhaps subthalamic terrors, but that in turn can become tools for the investigation of that same archaic or prenatal functioning.

When emotions become detoxified due to a container–contained relationship, they become emotions associated to images and thoughts, which can be used as elements for thinking, and the oscillation PS⇔D becomes dynamic, which implies more tolerance of mental pain.

In my opinion, this process also provides appropriate conditions for housing thoughts without a thinker and for taming wild intuitions, for traversing the turbulences of catastrophic change without a transformation into a psychic or psychosomatic catastrophe.

Psychoanalytical observation brings us evidence of what I denominated prenatal emotions. Often, they arise as corporeal states, sometimes noisy and sometimes subtle: we hear that the patient says "my stomach makes noises", "my legs tremble", "my head aches", "I feel a burning in my stomach", etc. A patient, referring to her elbows, where the skin was dry and bled, said, "My elbows cry." Here, the externalization field seems to be the body.

Sometimes, these externalizations appear as actions or as "dreams" that could not be dreamt because, as the Argentinian author Macedonio Fernandez said, not all vigil states mean being awake. Sometimes we meet with detained projective identifications, in personalities in which no communication has emotional resonance, as in some functioning with autistic nuclei. It is in the analytic work and in the space of the session where these prenatal states can find a container, a form of externalization that is an element that can be "dreamt" and therefore assimilated, digested.

The central hypothesis of this chapter is that the development of a capacity "to dream" in the session, of patient and analyst as well as "the play of personifications", starts an externalization process into more appropriate containers because, obviously, they are not "the thing". They are, in a certain way, the equivalent to what Melanie Klein did with Dick when she investigated what were the boy's interests, and then she took the trains as a selected fact, and, through naming them, helped to start a process of playing and of symbolic transformation.

In *Cogitations*, Bion brings a very interesting model for some clinical situations, in which the patient is unable to find the selected fact and he has externalized a terrifying experience through the enunciation "blood everywhere". Bion says to the patient that he has attacked his commonsense, and now he sees it spread as blood everywhere.

The patient's pattern is that of a mirror reflecting a murder, but the analyst's construction works as a mirror that does not reflect, but, rather, reabsorbs and unites the spread fragments and formalizes them in a scene. When the patient speaks, the analyst receives as if it were the end of a film in which a murder has been committed. It is not known what was murdered, but "blood everywhere" is the remains. When the analyst says to the patient that he attacked his commonsense and now he sees its fragments spread as blood everywhere, he is "reconstructing" the murder (as a detective). We could also say that he is painting a picture. With this formulation, which has the function of a selected fact, he contains the patient's dispersion in what is felt as a mental space without limits, equivalent to an astronomical space. It is a saturated space, where there is, in a very concrete shape, the debris of the "murder". We could say that Bion could "dream" the murder of the commonsense, and in that way he built a scenario or a representation space.

Constructions: analogy and symmetry

... And if the analogical direction is a continuous and inalienable force in all men? Wouldn't it be time to descend from only a poetic consideration of the image and look for its roots, to that that is subjacent and rises to life together with our eye colour and our blood group? ... It is necessary to wonder if the analogical direction would not be much more than an instinctive assistant, a luxury coexisting with the reasoning reason, and throwing her a cable to help her conceptualize and judge. Answering this question, the poet proposes himself as the man that recognizes in the analogical direction ... an effective instrumental medium ... something such as eyes and ears and touch projected outside of the sensuous, *apprehending relationships and constants*, browsers of a world constant in essence to all reason. [Cortázar, 1996, p. 515, my translation, my italics]

The artificially constructed dream is a construction in terms of Row C of The Grid, which corresponds to myths and dream thoughts. This construction shares analogy and symmetry at a metaphorical level, with artistic forms. The language of achievement* and the negative capability share the same characteristics. The "dream" is a step in the formulation of a problem to be investigated, and its different characters can be considered as much an unknown as an observation vertex.

Bion deals with the analogy in the article "The Grid" and considers it, together with construction and symmetry, to be a polyvalent weapon that contrasts with interpretation, which he considers monovalent. Analogy draws attention to the relationship. Psychoanalysis is a science of relationships, not of the related objects. The related objects are the anchorages of a relationship. In psychoanalysis, "mouth" "breast", "penis", "container", "contained" are analogies that express relationships.

In analysis, we are investigating the relationship, transference being one of those powerful relationships. Analogy and symmetry are powerful instruments for providing a binocular vision when the problems are those of combination of a real with an imaginary point (complex conjugated), as those that obviously are presented in psychoanalytical practice.

The problem, the object of the curiosity, has to be approached symmetrically. 'Too good' and 'too bad' is not the formulation of a conflict; it is the formulation of a *symmetrical relationship* . . . Real and imaginary only supplement each other when they do not meet, when it is known that two parallel lines in the domain of the sensuous experience meet, but in the domain of personality they become symmetrical . . . for some purposes for which analysts use interpretations they require constructions, and that these constructions are essential instruments for the demonstration of symmetry. A sensuous component of this apparatus is the visual image. The C elements . . . differ from the interpretation which is usually monovalent, whereas the construction (C element) is polyvalent and faster than the F or G formulations. . . . This is a matter of great practical consequence when the psychoanalyst has to cope with primitive material. [Bion, 1977 [1989], p. 25]

Paraphrasing Freud, in *The Future of An Illusion* (1927c), Bion asks about the future of an analogy. Meltzer gives priority to an exploratory attitude, in which the combination of the analyst's attention and interest and a co-operative disposition to play of the patient contributes to the formation of a container with qualities of flexibility and firmness.

Personification and vertices of observation

While, in Freud's and Klein's views, the analytic work implies an investigation of elements that have their "reality" in a remote or a very early past, an imaginable history that has an archaic and "forgotten" logic, for Bion, the analyst investigates fragments of a personality conceived sometimes as a palimpsest, and, in other circumstances, as the result of a remote explosion with the model of the Big Bang. *The analyst meets with the debris of that explosion; if he can visualize these remains as potential germs or vestiges, as related to aspects that have not had yet a psychic birth and that lacked a psychic space in which to exist, this vertex transforms the analytic task into something more difficult and turbulent, in which the analyst's personality is more deeply involved.*

Klein (1929) discovered that toys can be used in child analysis, "personifying" internal objects. Bion uses this personification to investigate the relationship between different aspects of the personality (Bion, 1967).

The theory of transformations is elaborated for observation in the clinical practice. It introduces the idea of a transformational process that goes on between patient and analyst. The analyst makes a transformation of the transformation that he receives from the patient that in turn will make another transformation, in different transformational cycles.

Bion uses the model of the painter, who transforms his emotional experience in relation to a field of poppies into a painting. He differentiates this transformation from that of the gardener, who works directly and transforms the garden.

When, in the field of the analytic session, the clinical problem that is presented is related to prenatal aspects of the mind, and/or with projective identifications that cross the anatomical limits of personality, or with detained projective identifications, analyst and patient move along different transformational systems. The analyst is in a similar position as somebody who listens the description of a work of art, carried out with a material and in a scale that he ignores (Bion, 1965). In these situations, it is necessary to build a common field, to find the means to intersect the evolution of the "O" of the patient.

Meltzer says that the analyst needs to modulate his interventions on the patient's transformational register.

What does this modulation mean and how can we operate in the analytic field in such a way that we also respect what is central to the analytic attitude, the rule of abstinence? To answer this query, I will take a quotation from Bion and relate it to Meltzer's idea of the aesthetic conflict.

> The analyst's position is akin to that of the painter who by his art adds to his public's experience. Since psycho-analysts do not aim to run the patient's life, but to enable him to run it according to his lights and therefore to know what his lights are . . . a healthy mental growth depends on truth as the living organism depends on the food. If it is lacking or deficient the personality deteriorates. I cannot support this conviction by evidence regarded as scientific. It may be that the formulation belongs to the domain of Aesthetics. [Bion, 1965, pp. 37–38]

According to Meltzer (1990), the aesthetic conflict outlines the problem of the contrast between what is apprehensible by the senses, and the interior of the object, which is only conjecturable. In relation to problems of clinical practice, which stimulate intense anxieties, the imaginative conjecture can be a powerful tool in analytic work, especially when we deal with an evolution towards "O" and from "O" towards K, with catastrophic changes and with "sub-thalamic" terrors.

I have been interested in combining the idea of personification of the emotions and parts of the personality with Bion's ideas of vertices. (In the clinical material of Chapter Eight, there is an illustration of this technical idea.)

Personification, through creating characters that "incarnate" emotional experiences, thoughts without a thinker, etc., has the function of generating a container where emotional turbulences can be contained in an atmosphere of investigative playing. (See also Chapter Eight.) The transformation of a rivalizing superego into a third character, an "evil monster" that, with ferocious criticism, interfered in the analytic dialogue with a patient and also that of the patient with himself, allowed us, for example, a greater degree of mediation and co-operation for investigating that aspect of the patient's personality. The "evil monster" that would not permit dialogue was transformed into a third point of view, or vertex, assisting, thus, an escape from an enclosure situation in which there was only one way of seeing things.

Clinical experience shows us that the internal world works with a dramatic quality. But with some patients, especially those with autistic enclaves, it seems that we find ourselves with a frozen desert, as I describe in Chapter Eight, and also with those patients with a prosthetic adaptation to this lack of dramatic quality, who live in a literal, "practical" world in which it seems impossible to find a second point of view. By approaching certain clinical problems of the patient's communication, as mentioned above, I have found, through the perspective of "dramatic forms" that a kind of "personification" of aspects of the internal world becomes possible. Personification creates different characters, as we can see in the representation of prenatal parts, as the "somites" of *A Memoir of the Future*. Such personification may also occur of abstractions, or of different observation vertices, and of scientific hypotheses that, through this device, can start an interesting dialogue.

In my clinical practice, in a context of playing, I transform feelings of guilt or criticism, resentment, reproofs, etc., that the patient experiences as "things in themselves" into characters, and create an imaginary space: I play "let's pretend" that these characters are seated on chairs, for example, and imagine a dialogue with them, including the patient in this "conversation".

It is a kind of construction that is polyvalent and opens the way for new associations. It does not mean a change in the substantial aspects of the psychoanalytical technique, but a way of trying to make contact with emotional experiences of the patient and find means for communicating. In *A Memoir of the Future*, Bion creates dialogues between the "characters" *"psyche"*, *"soma"*, *"body"*, or between *stegosaurus* and *tyrannosaurus*, or between different ages of the same person, *the boy of eight, the man of twenty, the old man of seventy-five*. *The heart* (as we have seen) can be a character; also abstract concepts, such as the schizo–paranoid and depressive positions, are transformed into characters. Each character represents a vertex, which can also change, as we see with Rosemary and Alice, for example. These different characters and points of view try sometimes to have a dialogue with another character or point of view. So, some agreements, disagreements, and correlations can be established.

Through this technique of personification, the character "guilt", "hate", or "envy" speaks from "his/her" point of view.

The concept of vertex, defined as the "angle", or perspective, from where a problem is approached, understood, and communicated, confers scientific character to formulations, and facilitates a correlation, or at least an interaction or dialogue, between different vertexes. One can understand that an aesthetic vertex illuminates a different aspect of a problem than that of a religious, financial, or psychoanalytical vertex. Absolute truth is unknowable; we "see" only from one or more aspects or vertices. With this concept, Bion puts the analyst in a position of modesty. The interpretation is given as a "second opinion", a point of view, or an imaginative conjecture that never has the characteristic of certainty, which is related to omnipotence and omniscience. Personification, here, means playing, and also defining a vertex from which a problem is visualized, in contrast with omnipotent and omniscient statements. It helps the patient to develop a capacity for observation of his emotional experiences and to be able to approach a problem from more than one perspective.

The definition of the vertex makes evident the points of disagreement and of agreement. To be able to sustain disagreements between the patient's and the analyst's vertex is a good container for primitive groupishness functioning and helps, in my clinical experience, to understand the psychoanalytical communication as a dialogue between feelings and ideas. With the "evil monster" transformed into a character always irritated and critical, it is possible to attempt a "conversation" which, until this personification, was impossible.

When, instead of vertices, we have closed worlds, inhabited by different aspects of the personality isolated and without communication, divided by impenetrable caesuras, the personification of different kinds of functioning, including those that appear as somatic, makes it possible to transform them into vertices and useful instruments of observation. It also allows the possibility of giving up a tenacious search for certainty and meaning, and of developing a disposition for curiosity and knowledge.

The "personification game", combined with the idea of the characters as multiple vertices, where each character plays its role as an observation vertex that can be alternated, allows the development of a capacity to receive influence and understanding from another point of view. This increases the capacity for tolerating mental pain associated with doubt, ignorance, a sense of infinity, frustration, and also opens up the possibility of transforming mental pain that derives from lack of meaning and of waiting until some understanding is achieved. The primitive infant's mind does not have a notion of time, and does not conceive the absence of meaning and the need to wait with patience until you find the "selected fact" that harmonizes what was seen before as dispersed or fragmented. The primitive mind feels that the lack of meaning is the evidence that the meaning, and the breast as the source of meaning, have been destroyed.

The dialogue of characters in the form of a game brings us close to the "let's pretend" of child's play, attenuating anxieties and facilitating an approach to the K link, the disposition to know, and also to become in at-one-ment with oneself.

These considerations led me to think of giving the interpretation the form of a *psychoanalytical conjectural game of science fiction*, as a "personification" of the patient's raw emotions: to give the form of a character to guilt, accusations, intuition, to tears, skin, belly, mistrust, etc. Paraphrasing Pirandello (1921), instead of characters in search of an author, *to propose feelings in search of characters in which they can be incarnated. Playing is a crucial step in distinguishing between map and territory, in which both are identified and discriminated at the same time. In this context, I consider playing an activity that is the continuation in the waking state of one's dream life.*

We can create the experience of "having a conversation" with the inflamed skin, with the bellyache, or with the headache, or with the guilt, or the accusation, etc. When the patient can take a vertex of playing, interesting and fruitful "conversations" can be developed.

Conclusions/openings

My clinical experience, elaborated through the ideas developed in this chapter, brought me evidence of the potentialities of technical tools such as the personification game, the use of dreams, myths, and dream thoughts for the generation of a space for playing that offers a possibility of modification of intense anxieties through transformation of the claustrophobic or agoraphobic spaces (which are "inhabited" by beta elements, concrete things in themselves, terrifying "ghosts" of no-things) into a space of psychic reality.

As I said before, when Klein (1929) developed the technique of playing for child analysis, she realized that children personified their conflicts in their play. She conceived a dramatic interior world where different objects were constantly on stage and in interrelation, and were expressed through personification. But, in that same line of thinking and creativity, believing that toys were the instruments of communication for child analysis, when faced with Dick's characteristics of not playing (which we can understand today as an autistic functioning), she did not hesitate to give him the trains and to name them as a means of providing him with tools for expressing himself.

The patients whom I described as living in a literal, factual world, as my patient Miss A from my clinical vignette of the library, need to find a ground for playing in the session. The models or "dreams" that the analyst constructs are a way of providing him/her with tools for expressing his/her emotional experiences in a context of psychic reality. Personification allows an interpretation; the concrete statement of Miss A did not. She could not accept my interpretation as I formulated it. I then learnt to try to reach her, saying that I knew that she was not telling me a dream, but if it were a dream, I would interpret it as . . . Or I can take the fact of being late as "the dream the patient could not dream", and so we can find a meaning that also modulates the anxiety. I can also transform the interference that too often appears in the communication between this patient and the analyst, with the characteristics of an "evil monster", into a third character that appears whenever our dialogue seems to reach a fruitful point. In my experience, this is an excellent tool for showing how envy is ruining any good relationship or dialogue, without "inviting" also the primitive super-super-ego.

Bion's ideas of the mind as an animated and growing object imply new technical approaches, in which first it is necessary to develop or repair functions of the personality, when and where there are flaws, in order to build up the necessary tools as conditions for mental development.

In trying to synthesize the central ideas of this chapter, I would say that Bion and Meltzer developed the idea that the analyst has to "dream" the session and to "dream" the patient for those patients whose alpha function is seriously disturbed and cannot "dream or play". "Dreaming", in this context, means that the analyst has to use his alpha function for developing constant conjunctions of alpha elements that will allow for the possibility of finding the selected fact and a meaning. This "dreaming" means a dream artificially constructed through an artifice. "Narrating well means to do it in a way that will be listened to. We will not achieve it without an artifice. An artifice good enough to become art!" (Semprún, 1994, my translation).

These are the technical means by which the necessary conditions are created to transit from the space of analogy to the space of the transference, and *vice versa*. These instruments are meant to help the patient develop his alpha function, and so a capacity to "dream-think" about his emotions, not as concrete sensuous impressions, but as emotional experiences, "dreams" for which it is possible then to find a meaning. We need a technical approach to open the possibility of creating a relationship, most of all for those patients who live in autistic (see also Chapter Eight) or very concrete worlds, or whose emotional experiences have not had yet a psychic birth (see also Chapter One).

As we will see in Chapter Eight, I propose the idea of introducing as a technical approach the construction of a space for playing when it is absent, and the personification of emotions as a means of developing a relation also through playing.

This construction is a way of making a dramatic and aesthetic formulation of emotional experience possible; this establishes emotional connection in a context of detoxified emotions. By aesthetic, here I mean the expression or representation of a non-sensuous emotional experience in a sensuous form, which incarnates it but is not confused with it. (See also Introduction.)

A model for these instruments is the sextant, an instrument that allowed navigating without having to see the coast. It is an instrument that uses in a complementary and indirect form the sensorial information to establish relationships. It is not an expansion of our senses, as is the microscope or the telescope, but one that the navigator uses to guide himself in relation to distant objects, comparable to the fragments of personality with which we meet in an analysis.

On the other hand, the enlarged conjecture of prenatal aspects promotes a turning point that removes the problems of mental functioning from the area of pathology and of "cure" to locate them in an evolutionary and a developmental perspective.

Art, in psychoanalytical technique, consists in the analyst's ability to combine his psychoanalytically trained intuition with the transformation of the concepts that inhabit his mind into preconceptual thinking. Mental growth depends on the open-ended, non-saturated aspect of the preconception that contains the possibilities of evolution.

Figure 1. Leonardo da Vinci's hair as illustration of turbulence.

Y asentósele de tal modo en la imaginación que era verdad toda aquella máquina de soñadas invenciones que leía . . . (Pág. 50.)

Figure 2.   Don Quixote intoxicated by "β elements that seem undigested dreams".

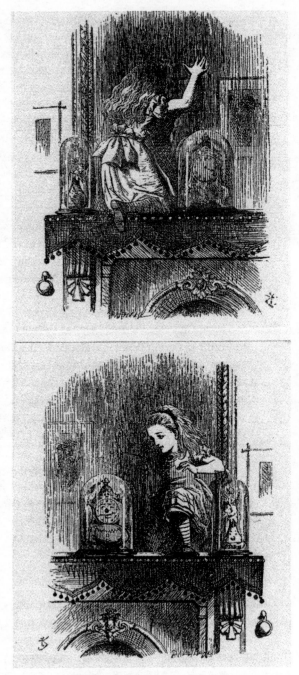

Figure 3.   "Alice through the mirror": illustration of the contact barrier.

Figure 4.   Design by a little girl of seven years old: the "perfect" little house (exo-skeleton).

Figure 5.   Another design by the same girl: more disorganized design belongs to the more authentic self.

Figure 6. Vermeer's painting. Illustration of the notion of space: there is an inside and outside. The notion of time is also illustrated in the front of the house, where we can see the erosion of the bricks and windows.

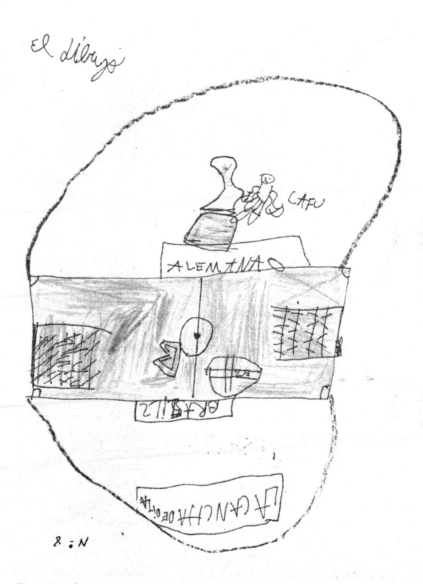

Figure 7. The design of a soccer field by a nine-year-old boy: it illustrates the perturbation of the notion of space; there are no points of reference, everything is very confused.

CHAPTER FOUR

Approaching truth and catastrophic change

"What more suitable god than man? What more suitable to man than any available 'super-man'? How could this be made available for worship by a well-arranged system of 'scientific' lies and cheats 'exposing' the lies and cheats?"

(Bion, 1975 [1991] pp. 129–130)

From its beginnings, psychoanalysis recognized the human capacity for creating forms of falsification of truth and showed interest in investigating them. The different ways of avoiding contact with truth are used to elude catastrophic change. This term is associated with mental growth. The word "catastrophic" does not refer to, or mean, a calamity, but, rather, to a sudden leap, a discontinuity as a mutation in evolution. From the point of view of mental health, truth matters because it is the nourishment for mental growth.

The idea of catastrophic change associated with insight and at-one-ment (Bion, 1965), becoming one with oneself, is related to the feeling that one exists and is real. Truth matters because from the point of view of mental health it is necessary to be truthful.

The human mind is a living object that evolves; the direction of this evolution can be towards growth or towards deterioration. Truth nourishes mental growth, lies deteriorate it. (Bion, 1970). "Falling back on analytic experience for a clue, I am reminded that healthy mental growth seems to depend on truth as the living organism depends on food. If it is lacking or deficient the personality deteriorates" (Bion, 1965, p. 38).

Catastrophic change means crisis, and the different "methods" of falsification of truth are attempts to evade or stop crises. In this chapter, which expands upon the ideas in Chapter Two, I propose a psychoanalytic exploration of lies and of catastrophic change, taking some of Bion's ideas as a starting point.

Approaches to truth and psychoanalysis

Psychoanalysis is based on truth. The relation between analyst and patient is based on the love of truth, which means the acceptance of reality free of any illusion or deceit (Freud, 1911–1915).

Kant's (1781) epistemological posture sustains that ultimate reality (*noumena*) is unknowable; we can only know it through phenomena. Expressing this epistemological perspective in other words, what I mean is that there are real facts and representations of facts, which are different approaches to what is reality. Each turn of the spiral towards mental growth implies changes, which are unavoidable and associated with different crises that must be faced. One of the aspects of these crises implies facing the conflict between the representation of facts that always means a point of view and the real fact.

Bion (1965) developed theoretical tools that allow a differentiation between the transformational system of lies and a scientific transformational system.

A scientific approach implies defining the vertex from which the observation is made. Accepting this definition means admitting that other vertices exist with which one can establish agreements and disagreements. An interpretation is not an absolute truth, but the one expressed from one vertex: the *opinion* of the analyst.

If we live in a world in which we can dream and be awake, this extends our contact with reality and with "our" truth that evolves, providing at least two perspectives that allow a binocular vision for observation and correlation. It is, as I have already mentioned in other chapter, like seeing either a face or two vases.

In the personality who has the habit of lying, we find a scission that Freud described in "Fetishism" (1927e): a part which is in contact with reality and the other part that disavows it. The patient in the habit of lying usually uses ambiguity to "navigate" through this scission. This characteristic of "yes, but no", indicates the tenacity with which the scission is maintained.

Conflict implies having contradictions, vertices that might be in disagreement; in ambiguous functioning the definition of vertices and the acceptance of contradictions are eluded, and what usually shows up are masks and incongruence.

Lies and other forms of falsification of truth

Bion differentiated lies from falsities. Falsities are associated with the limitations of the human being; any enunciation contains a falsity, in so far as it is only a part of a whole that is infinite. These falsities are a manifestation of the impossibility of the human being to reach *absolute truth*.

O, the ultimate reality, cannot be known. It is possible, however, to be in at-one-ment with O and to become one with oneself, or, instead, to avoid or stop the catastrophic change implied in this becoming.

Although one cannot escape from facts, it is possible to attack the functions that provide the contact with them.

The ideas about transformations towards O (Bion, 1965) open up the possibility for differentiating between the psychotic's and the liar's modalities of functioning. In the psychotic, the functions that allow contact with reality and associations are attacked, whereas the liar "deliberately" produces "pseudo-associations" which undermine any possibility of free association. The person who lies has allowed his experience to develop to such a point as to reveal to him that what he says is not true. As we will see in what follows, one of the characteristics of the transformations in hallucinosis is the rivalry with O instead of "becoming O", or becoming in at-one-ment.

The concept of hallucinosis needs to be extended to a number of configurations, which until now have not been recognized as such (Bion, 1965). I want to stress here that Bion's definition (Chapter Ten of *Transformations*) not only includes hallucinations, it means that the medium in which this kind of transformation takes place is a medium of rivalry in which the method of hallucinosis is considered superior to the psychoanalytic method.

Delusions, hallucinations, and lies can be categorized within *a pathology of consciousness*. These are not problems associated with the relation conscious–unconscious, but with disturbances in the evolution of consciousness, disturbances which represent an obstacle for the development of a consciousness *capable of being aware*. Lies, hallucinations, and delusions all disturb contact with reality and damage in different ways the capability of being aware.

Here we need to consider two points:

- The transformational medium in hallucinosis is characterized by privileging "superiority–inferiority" relationships as the only ones possible; the object in the superior position is self-sufficient and rules on the "action".

- Transformations in rigid motion and projective ones can have hallucinosis as a transformational medium (Bion, 1965, p. 133).

It is interesting to remind the reader that *the idea of transformations in rigid motion (in thoughts)* takes Euclidean geometry as its model; this transformation means little deformation. It implies a model of movement of feelings and ideas from one sphere (such as the concept of a triangle) to another (the drawing of this concept on a bi-dimensional piece of paper). Bion illustrates these kinds of transformations with the dream of a patient featuring a fight between a bear and a tiger, in which the tiger bites off the bear's nose. With this communication through a dream, the analyst can approach the transformations the dream made, with an interpretation of the patient's castration anxieties or of the primal scene. For projective transformations, Bion uses projective geometry as a model. In this group of transformations, events far removed from any relationship to the analyst are actually felt by the patient, because of projective identifications, as aspects of the analyst's personality. If, on the other hand, the patient says, as Bion illustrates, "I don't expect anything can be expected today: this morning I mean. This afternoon. It must be a joke of some kind. This girl left about her knickers. Well, what do you say to that?" (Bion, 1970, p. 19), the analyst finds himself with a transformation whose invariants he must discover in the projective geometric model. The other difference that we need to understand is that either of these transformations can take place, or not, in a transformational medium of hallucinosis.

There are different ways of avoiding at-one-ment and the evolution of O, but one of the characteristics of the lie is that it is in rivalry with O. This is one of the lie's differences with delusions.

Delusions are associated with preconceptions, which mate with realizations that do not match adequately, so as to saturate the preconception; instead, they give way to forming a misconception (Bion, 1965, p. 137). In the lie, preconceptions are substituted by predeterminations (Predeterminations are not only absolutely saturated, but also seek support, in reality, that convictions are real, to sustain that the predeterminations are real facts).

The patient sustains his independence from everything that is not his own creation, which is due to his capability of creating a perfect world. He attributes frustration to envious and hostile attacks.

The crucial problem in the analysis of a patient that is in the habit of lying is the nature of the co-operation, and not the content of the problem for which he has required analysis. The disagreement between the patient and the analyst is about the rivalry between the methods, between the lying and the psychoanalytic method, and this is related to the problem of truth and mental pain.

In both psychotic functioning and in pathological lying, the patient cannot solve his problems of mental growth because he cannot even begin to formulate them. A difference lies in that, in psychotic functioning, the damage to the apparatus for thinking leads to pseudo-beliefs, while in lying functioning, it instead leads to pseudo-thoughts.

I will present now two clinical vignettes to illustrate these ideas.

1. A patient expresses her fear that her son might contract rabies, as he had stroked a cat. This results in a delusion that evidences itself in her repeated consultations with physicians who tell her that there is no danger of this, without managing to calm her anxiety. The damage in the alpha function and in the contact barrier do not

allow the patient to transform "the cat's rabies" into a dream-thought. The patient co-operates by bringing to analysis her anxieties that are stimulated by these "thoughts", which she feels are imposing themselves on her.

2. This clinical illustration was also elaborated in Chapter Two; in this chapter, I want to make a contrast between lies and delusions. A patient, faced with leaving the adolescent stage, used to lie, asking for schedule changes for his sessions that he did not really need, or showing up late and then lying about having been delayed at work. Following a holiday trip, he paid my fees, deducting the week he had been away, without explanation. Confronted with the fact, he maintained that it was fair. He had not gone away during the summer, and those were *his* holidays. He admitted that he had thought of asking to reschedule his sessions, bearing in mind the sessions he was going to miss, but he did not do so.

When he came back, he said that he had felt tempted to call me several days after his arrival, miss those sessions, and say he had just arrived. He could not explain, not even to himself, why he wanted to do that. Finally, although in disagreement, he accepted paying for those sessions.

Although he continued smoking marijuana, at weekends he began to feel that between the last session of the week and the first of the following week the time seemed too long. It was already obvious that the analyst was not always available. The unnecessary schedule change requests tend to lend support to the predetermination, the belief, that the analyst is always available to him. It becomes evident that he tries to deny the frustrations in the transference relationship, going back to the marijuana/lie always available, always at hand, and thus avoid the catastrophic change implied by having to face a rupture in one's belief in an always-available object.

The world of the always-available object is a hallucinated one. We have indications of bad faith (the patient decides on the rules as to what is fair to pay, in rivalry with the analysis contract agreement) and of some incongruences. Lies, however, thanks to transformation into rational language, do not give the impression of madness.

Thoughts, language, and lies

Psychoanalysis has an interest in the investigation of lies, among other things, because they take developmental achievements of human creativity as thinking, and language, and use them in the service of a parasitic relationship.

Bion postulates that healthy mental growth depends on truth as nourishment for the mind; lies are toxic to the mind. In order to investigate the function of thinking, he uses a digestive model, as was explained in Chapters Two and Three. Emotional experiences need to be digested so that the personality can assimilate them. He introduces the alpha function, which performs this mental digestion through the transformation of the raw sensuous and emotional impressions into alpha elements, which are apt to form thoughts.

Thoughts and language are transformations related to a space of representations, the counterpart of the geometric space. Detoxifying the primitive emotions is a central factor in the development of this space. Signs (such as the points and lines of Euclidean geometry), as we have already described, emerge from a space occupied originally by a feeling. This emotion can evolve from this starting point (O) into the transformation of the catastrophic emotions of the infant, through maternal reverie into emotional communicative signs.

A first condition that makes possible the use of the sensorial impression as images for the dream-thoughts is the separation and differentiation between perception and action. (See also Chapter Nine.) The function of reverie, through transforming and giving a meaning to the primitive emotions, makes this differentiation possible and starts the process for using the perceived sensuous impressions as ideograms. Love, hate, jealousy, etc., in the relationship to the breast, are transformed in signs–links that bind a constant conjunction of emotional experiences.

If there is a tolerance to the relation between the thing and the "no-thing" (ideas and emotions and the sign that represents them) and the differentiation between presence and absence, "no-things", signs, can be used for thinking. Different factors, such as intolerance of an object not always available, contribute to the transformation of the signs that mark the emotions linked to the absence of the "thing" into lying signs. Emotions are links that can be named by signs, as Bion did with L (love), H (hate) and K (knowledge). In a frame of omnipotence and omniscience, which also means that on the other side there is helplessness, the intolerance to mental pain can lead to the "fabrication" of lying signs.

The liar gives substance to his phantasies of omnipotence because, unlike those who tell the truth, he does not limit himself to registering something; he does something through the signs. The lie is an action that substitutes for thought, even if it has the appearance of it. Bion makes a differentiation between action as a prelude to action and thought as a prelude to action.

Action requires contact with facts when it has thought as its prelude. Thought needs to pass the proof of reality when it has to be validated through action. Action as prelude to action may use the reality principle at the service of manipulation in such a way as to confirm a "self-engendered reality".

Language can be used for deception and evasion as well as for containing the emotional experience and for the investigation of its meaning. Lies have a special interest for psychoanalysis, because they use verbal language for the communication between patient and analyst about a reality which is not sensorial.

Rivalry is the transformational media of transformations in hallucinosis, which has the characteristic of privileging relationships of "superiority–inferiority" as the only ones possible, and in which the object that is in the position of superior is self-sufficient and is the one that decides the "action". The transformations in rigid movements, that is, in thought (Bion, 1965) and the projective transformations, may have hallucinosis as their transformational media (Bion, 1965, p. 133). This is a very important statement, because it means that what seems a thought can be used as a lie.

Bion (1962) refers to alpha function in reverse; it is possible to think or conjecture that, in the lie, alpha elements can be transformed in a second transformational cycle within a medium *of rivalry, that is, of hallucinosis*. In delusions and hallucinations, alpha elements are evacuated or fragmented; in the lie, even thoughts and language can be used in a medium of hallucinosis.

In psychotic functioning as well as in pathological lies, the patient cannot solve his problems of mental growth because, as he lacks the adequate equipment, he cannot even formulate them. One of the differences, as I have already stated, between both functioning is that, in the former, the damage to the apparatus for thinking leads to pseudo-beliefs, while in the latter, the lying one, it leads to pseudo-thought.

In coherence with his idea that thoughts are prior to thinking, Bion maintains that for a thought there is no need for a thinker. For the lie, the "thinker" is indispensable: he is the one who "fabricates" the lying "thought". The background of mental pain is a peculiar relationship between helplessness and omnipotence. In thoughts and in the developing of thinking, a tolerance of the emotions that stimulates feelings of helplessness has been achieved, these being uncertainty, ignorance, and the finite–infinite relationship. In lies, when it comes to facing feelings of helplessness, there is an increment in the doses of omnipotence and the need for obtaining collusions that disavow helplessness.

Contrasting with "negative capability" of tolerance to doubts and mysteries, the liar has a "positive capability" for producing pseudo-thoughts. These are not born from the contact with O, but from his own mind, deteriorating the relationship between mind and truth: the mind does not depend on the nourishment of truth, but, rather, fabricates it. The liar only tolerates his own "creations", which are those that contribute to his importance as a "thinker", which is the opposite of being in at-one-ment with O. In this way, he generates an atmosphere of envy and possessiveness between "thinkers". That is how he also experiences the analyst, as someone who imposes his thought and with whom he is in rivalry.

Lies and the matrix functions for thinking

Bion described two matrix functions for thinking: the oscillation PS⇔D between states of dispersion and synthesis, and the container–contained relationship ($\male$ $\female$).

Oscillation (PS⇔D) and lies

I want to remind the reader that, by means of this function PS⇔D, constant conjunctions can be formed, if one can tolerate the moments in which facts are felt as not related until the selected fact is found that harmonizes what is dispersed. There is also a need for tolerance of the moment of synthesis. The resolution of a problem reveals new problems. The constant conjunction harmonized through the selected fact and linked to a name constitutes a prelude for the investigation of meaning via a container–contained relationship. Sor & Senet (1988) also described a selected fact, which he called SF1, which is different from the SF2 described by Bion). The SF1 allows continuing to evolution. It disarticulates the constant conjunction already achieved, and opens the way to new articulations. Both disarticulation and harmonization are changes that fall within the category of catastrophic change.

The patient who is in the habit of lying escapes from mental pain (persecutory and depressive) and stops catastrophic change through ambiguity. I propose, as a hypothesis, an ambiguous position, as a psychic retreat, similar to what Steiner (1993) proposes when he speaks of a borderline position. My hypothesis is that, instead of an oscillation PS⇔D, the patient takes refuge in an ambiguous position:

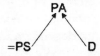

This ambiguous position is constructed though identification with an ambiguous object which confuses the possibility of differentiating between what is reparative and what causes damage. It is an object that is an inexhaustible source of mistrust in oneself and in others. Clinical investigation has allowed me to relate this identification with ambiguous and lying parental objects that favoured collusions. These collusions imply peculiar maternal reverie failures. To renounce lying means having to face real life, which inevitably implies frustration. The ambiguous position seems to stem from a "negotiation" between the reality of facts and the lie, which, as a two-faced Janus, leaves primitive functioning undigested that is always threatening to emerge. The reality principle is being used for an "apparent adaptation" to the facts and as a way of masking them. Often, they "lie with the truth".

Clinical vignette

After several failures in his professional career, it became obvious to patient A that performing well at university did not mean maturity in the performance of his work, or in the way he managed his finances. His tendency to lie and to deceive himself led him to failures, which often bordered on delinquency. Contact with the mental pain produced by his failures seemed to indicate an evolution towards becoming aware of his difficulties. A dream revealed, through an image of a traffic light, that he always remained in the yellow zone, avoiding the clear definition of the red and green lights. In his analysis, his delay in payment maintained the ambiguity of whether he could not, or did not want to, pay: at the same time, it seemed that he had begun to value his dreams as tools for comprehension. Two dreams showed the refuge in the ambiguous position, not being able to let go of the lies, holding on to them instead of facing mental pain. In one of the dreams, he found trash in his home, and, instead of throwing it away, he searched for a place to hide it. In the other dream, he separated objects that were useless, and, again, he did not throw them away, but kept them near the dining room. The same happened when he finally decided to buy a new car; he could not sell the old one, and kept it although it was in such bad conditions that it was a danger to his life and his family's lives.

In the analytic process, I could observe an oscillation between states of PS dispersion and the ambiguous refuge, or from the point of harmonization in D again towards the ambiguous position. In patient A, the ambiguous refuge appeared when he had evidence of his lack of maturity and of his need to authentically mature. The ambiguity always available showed in his dreams, and he could not let go of the toxic lie that was an obstacle for mental growth, but that was always available. The analyst was not always available, and the fact of keeping the old car only had one coherent explanation: it represented his tendency of keeping what was toxic and endangered his mental growth as if it were a good nourishment.

Container–contained relationship

Lies imply a parasitic container–contained relationship of mutual destruction. The lie is a toxic parasite of thought as much as of verbal expression. It is not meant for communication, but it is intended to lead the recipient of the lie to an emotional upheaval and to make him act. One of the factors in achieving this provocation is the combination of lie, morality, and guilt.

The tasks that the maternal reverie leaves unconcluded fall on the rudimentary conscience of the infant (Bion, 1962). Thus, the evolution towards a consciousness that has the capability of being aware becomes obstructed. The place of reverie is occupied by a moral conscience without morality, which substitutes scientific exploration and discernment between what is true or false for what is morally good or bad. So, a super-superego that only conceives relationships of superiority and inferiority usurps the ego functions of contact with reality. It is a relationship minus container–contained, which Bion describes with the formula (2).

The investigation of the lie is felt as a threat of catastrophe because it can lead to a catastrophic change: a change of system. That is, from the system of moral conscience to the system of discerning between truth and falsity through the way of facing facts. Lies obscure helplessness via the maintaining of an omnipotent and omniscient functioning.

Lies and the group

The assumption underlying loyalty to the K link is that the personality of the analyst and the analysand can survive the loss of its protective coat of lies, subterfuge, evasion and hallucination and may even be fortified and enriched by the loss. It is an assumption strongly disputed by the psychotic and *a fortiori* by the group, which relies on psychotic mechanisms for its coherence and sense of well-being. [Bion, 1965, p. 129]

The action appropriate to the tropisms is seeking. I have so far considered this activity as it might be thought to relate to murder, parasitism and creation—the three tropisms. Thus considered individually, the tropisms are seen to issue in seeking: 1) an object to murder or be murdered by, 2) a parasite or a host, 3) an object to create or by which to be created. [Bion, 1992, p. 34]

I will put forward some thoughts, ideas in progress, which intend to be a germ for a fruitful discussion. We need to recognize the tendency towards lies and deceit not only because they are toxic to individual mental development, which is the predominant interest of psychoanalysts, but also to what degree the mental and/or ethical development of whole groups is affected.

First, I want to consider the idea of *tropisms* as primitive phenomena that require a transformation through maternal reverie and alpha function of the analyst

Failure in this transformation of tropisms, which are a part of the personality, might be a factor in the developments of lies. In *Cogitations*, Bion says that the appropriate action to the tropisms is seeking, meaning a search for an object, the breast, in which they can be projected (see quote from Bion, 1992, above). "The tropisms are the matrix from which all mental life springs. For maturation to be possible they need to be won from the void and communicated" (Bion, 1992, p. 34). He describes three tropisms: murder, parasitism and creation,but, taken as a whole, Bion thinks that the action appropriate in the patient who comes for treatment is seeking an object with whom projective identification is possible, because in him the tropism of creation is stronger than that of murder.

In the analysis of a liar, the analyst is exposed to a toxic parasitic relationship because lies seek collusion.

Bion also writes about narcissi-ism and social-ism, and, by dividing the words in that way, I think that he seems to consider them as being tropisms.

> These two terms might be employed to describe tendencies, one ego-centric, the other socio-centric, which may at any moment be seen to inform groups of impulsive drives in the personality. They are equal in amount and opposite in sign . . . The two *must* go together: if one is operating, so is the other. [Bion, 1992, p. 122]

Narcissi-ism and social-ism coexist in the individual, and sometimes there may be an acute conflict, as is obvious in war: to die for one's country.

Bion suggests a modification to Darwin's postulate about the survival of the one who is the most apt: his suggestion is that survival is for those who have more skills to survive in the group. In its primitive form of tropism, both poles (narciss-ism and social-ism) need to be transformed. In Chapter Six of *Transformations* (Bion, 1965, p. 63), he relates narcissism with the L, H, and K links (love, hate and knowledge) in relationship of the self with the self:

he says that meaning, which is psychologically necessary, is a function of these links. At the beginning of life, the infant, because of his primitive emotions and states of mind, does not conceive the absence of meaning; this absence is experienced as if the source of meaning, the breast, has been destroyed. If a "breast with reverie", which transforms these tropisms, fails in yielding a meaning for the individual, his narcissism demands the existence of a God for whom he has a meaning and of whose meaning he is supposed to benefit. I think that this is how this primitive super-superego emerges, as a God that usurps the ego functions of contact with reality. The failures in establishing the L, H, and K links in relationship with the self also disturb the relationships with the objects. The way the liar uses thought and language as actions to manipulate implies that the meaning has been destroyed or annulled.

Next, I shall consider that *lies are falsehoods related to moral conscious without morals,* and one factor of the power of the liar for using manipulating actions is an endo-gregarious one: the capability of inoculating guilt. A part of the personality developed contact with reality, which is used shrewdly to detain the crisis, a use for which it needs an audience, has to "socialize" the lie to sustain the self-deception. Guilt is an ideal "mordant" (in the chemical sense) for projective identification stimulated by ambiguity.

The infancy of the species still persists in our condition of a herd animal. If the liar needs an audience to endorse his lies (Bion, 1970), it is obvious that there is a public available to "buy" the lies. The effectiveness of the speeches of politicians and publicists gives evidence of this social-ism.

Finally, I turn to *primitive groupishness,* a living, archaic vestige of our condition of "political animal" that exists in each personality and is what predominates in the basic assumption (Bion, 1961) functioning. The development of a separate mind means tolerating the feeling of loneliness and not letting oneself be attracted by the belief that that groupishness is the source of viability. The functioning of the "working group" (Bion, 1961) means contact with reality and co-operation. Lies stimulate the primitive groupishness, and this is one of the analyst's risks in his work.

Lies and the analytic field

The analytic situation stimulates primitive emotions and instils a factor of emotional turbulence in the field. The shift towards learning from experience towards mental growth, by traversing catastrophic changes, implies conceiving of psychoanalysis as a process of becoming oneself, tending towards the development of both, patient and analyst. The evolution of an analysis demands more analysis from an analyst, not because previous analyses have failed, but because, to continue in the task, the analyst needs to delve deeper into himself.

The Bionian technical recommendation, "without memory, without desire, without comprehension", as a mental discipline of the analyst to be in at-one-ment with what evolves from the patient's O, assumes asking that the analyst temporarily divest himself of his "normal" defences in the face of catastrophic anxieties, and so, also the analyst, himself, will be exposed to those states of mind.

The separated mind, with scientific functioning, demands tolerance of feelings of loneliness and abandonment of the "protection" of adaptation to basic assumption primitive groupishness functioning. The pathological liar tells his lies "voluntarily", in a provocative manner, starting from a moral system. In his need for listeners to lend support to his lies, he "invites" one to a collusion that is always associated with abandonment of the technique. He tries to pull the analyst into his "game" by making him take on a role. A patient who systematically arrives late, and to whom a series of factors related to this have been shown, but who continues to arrive late, asking each time to be "pardoned", seems to "force" the analyst into becoming the patient's moral "conscience". In this way, the analyst is attracted towards a system of "atonement"—expiation and sacrifice—instead of at-one-ment. The sadomasochistic erotization of mental pain that tends to accompany the lie also distorts the sense of the analytic work. This kind of erotization refers to a provoked or inflicted pain, with a connotation of omnipotence, unlike pain that is suffered, in which the reasons for the pain are respected.

The liar cannot stand the emotional state that accompanies transformations towards O that assume abandoning his omnipotent and omniscient system, the other face of which is helplessness. He fears that O, the at-one-ment, in which primitive emotions, experienced as dangerous, would be put into play. Are these perhaps non-transformed tropisms? The possibility of helping the patient to have the courage to become "himself" and to have enough respect for his own personality—to be that person who he is, and not a lie, because one can "be a lie" (Bion, 1980)—depends on the possibility of managing the conflict to transform itself into an endopsychic one, in order for the rivalry of methods to be transformed into a problem of the inner world.

The psychoanalytical idea has brought turbulence far beyond the third narcissistic wound described by Freud. This turbulence, stimulated by the psychoanalytic idea, needs to find an Establishment (Bion, 1970) capable of containing it and allowing its evolution; if such a containment cannot be found, psychoanalysis runs the risk of being transformed into a BA messianic expectation. This also is related to primitive groupishness functioning. The opposite of the messianic expectation may also happen, that is, it can be demonized, which is what seems to prevail now, in our current culture, because psychoanalysis has not been able to answer the messianic expectations that it seemed to stir up. From this point of view, it is of great interest for we analysts to understand lies, not only in the patient that is a liar, *but also how lies show up in a culture that stimulates the development of the means for auto-deception, of lies and banality that are devoid of meaning.*

CHAPTER FIVE

Traversing caesuras and mental growth: a scientific exploration of insight

"PA: Seductive possibilities, concealed in the wide range of options available, will ultimately compel the growth of a capacity for discrimination—or catastrophe.

Robin: Why catastrophe?

PA: Because unless the human animal learns to become expert in discrimination, he will be in imminent danger of the wrong choice.

Alice: Nuclear war, for example.

PA: There are no labels attached to most options; there is no substitute for the growth of wisdom. Wisdom or oblivion— take your choice. From the warfare there is no release.

(Bion, 1991, p. 576)

With the discovery of transference, investigation in psychoanalysis directed itself to understanding what happens between those two persons—patient and analyst—who get together and meet in the task of understanding the personality of one of them: the patient. Countertransference showed that the situation is even more complex. Further investigations revealed the vital necessity for the human being and for psychoanalysis of understanding something more about primitive groupishness functioning, because of the condition of our species of being a political, or group, animal. The ideas Bion developed in group research were brought together in his mind with his observations as a psychoanalyst, in a symbiotic container–contained relation, resulting in developments of great depth that are awaiting further evolution.

My attempt, in this chapter, is to outline some of Bion's openended issues. The first of these issues is his suggestion that *a science of relationships*—not of the related objects—has to be developed, to further research in psychoanalysis and in social functioning, in groups, institutions, etc. This science has its peculiarities: its object of investigation is animated and not sensorial; it belongs to the psychic domain, and changes while being investigated. It also modifies the researcher who is taking part in the observation; methods, therefore, have to be developed that will adjust to these specific problems.

Thus, the second issue refers to the *methods* for the investigation of the relationship: binocular vision; oscillation and alternating use of different vertices, the way different lenses are used in a microscope; observation and correlation of what is observed from multiple vertices; and reversible perspective are some of the names Bion proposed for the methods he suggested.

The macroscopic vertex of group observation can hence be correlated to and complemented with the microscopic vertex of psychoanalytic investigation. Clinical practice and the notion of transference–countertransference are enriched by the contribution of observation of the powerful relational network of the projective identifications, operant in groups and with the evidence of group functioning within the personality. And the group investigations are also enriched by the very subtle discoveries through observations in psychoanalysis.

An illustration of these ideas can be found in *A Memoir of the Future* (1991), Volume 3, where we find dialogues—as if it were an internal group—between different characters that are parts of the personality: prenatal states, somites, the boy of fourteen, the young man of twenty, the elderly man of eighty, the heart, etc. In Volume 2, there are group discussions that attempt a scientific approach, showing different vertices: the priest's religious one, the physician's scientific one, the PA's psychoanalytic one, etc.

The third issue, which is the focus of this chapter, deals with the "developmental conflicts" and in which I try to go deeper into the problem of evolution and mental growth.

In *Attention and Interpretation* (1970), Bion's model of mental growth is the achievement of an evolution in the direction of respect for truth, concern for life, and maturity as the capability of becoming responsible. The problem of mental growth now not only means making conscious the unconscious or Kleinian integration. Mental growth does not seem to develop as it would if it were a piece of elastic being stretched out, but, rather, takes place in layers, like the skins of an onion (Bion, 1977 [1989], p. 47). Between each layer, there are caesuras that have to be traversed to promote a meeting, a dialogue between the different parts. A method has to be found to make an encounter possible. Its aim is to attempt a reflexive dialogue where each part can listen to the other: this means between the primitive–prenatal, protomental aspects and more sophisticated postnatal ones; or between the BA-group functioning and the work-group functioning; or between the primitive mind and the separated one, etc.

The problem in traversing the caesura towards mental growth is of the neotenicity. Not only of the infant, who needs its mother's or its parents' alpha function to grow and develop, but also of the neotenicity of the species, which, in order to achieve maturity, has to develop discernment and becoming responsible. By neotenicity, or neothenia, I mean that, compared with other species, the human infant is born very immature (as if born prematurely), being very dependent for its physical and psychological survival on the care and reverie of his parents, yet this neotenicity also opens up many opportunities for further evolution.

The development of methods of scientific approach, even rudimentary ones, is essential, since human beings also produce, with great intelligence, instruments for an active un-knowing.

I want to include the terms *caesura* and *vertices** (see also the Glossary), as they are fundamental to understanding the problem related to the methods for transcending caesuras in the sense of growth and obstacles to it.

Caesura and vertices

By means of the metaphor of the *caesura of birth, separating intra-uterine from postnatal life,* Bion (1977) approaches the fascinating and difficult investigation of the still-embryonic, or rudimentary, mind of our species, whose evolution can lead as much to genius as to psychosis. Bion extended the term that he borrowed from Freud to a complex notion of gap, fissure, space, and bridge, having the function both of separating and of communicating.

Caesura can also be thought of as a "trans" zone (Sor & Senet, 1988), an area of transition that has to be traversed by those elements that are in a transformational state. *Caesura* is a zone that separates two regions of the personality (primitive mind/separate mind) and two modes of functioning (basic assumption and work group), and traversing this zone threatens catastrophic change, because this is where the different aspects can meet and this meeting implies turbulence. *Catastrophic change* is a dweller of this zone and also an indispensable factor in developing capacity for insight, which is the only way to understand mental growth.

A scientific approach to the facts implies defining the *vertex,* or point of view, from which observations and statements are formulated. When the *vertex* is made explicit, then it is possible to establish a dialogue, a correlation among the different perspectives. One of the conditions for establishing a fruitful dialogue is that caesuras be permeable.

Individual and group: two observational vertices— a science of relationships

When Freud, who had already begun to understand the nature of unconscious processes, discovered transference, he laid the grounds for a science of relationships. Freud revealed some config-urations that are interesting from the psychoanalytic vertex: as an obvious example, we can mention the Oedipus complex, narcis-sism, etc. Thus, he opened the way towards the discovery of new configurations that he had not discovered.

Bion suggested that there was a link between his work with groups and his work with individual patients, a relationship that could contribute to developing a science of relationships. The sub-title to *Attention and Interpretation*—"A scientific approach to insight in psycho-analysis and groups"—implies a common ground for both of them.

I think that the nature of this link lay in his work method, which can be defined as *a scientific approach to insight.*

At the heart of this approach is the development of intuition and attention through a discipline of negative capability and centred on the emotional experience that is present and presented. The inter-pretation of the emotional experience apprehended in this way is in the basis of insight.

We usually tend to situate the emotional experience within the individual, as if the personality were coincident with the anatomi-cal aspects. This confinement within anatomical limits, however, is only apparent. Psychoanalysis itself is rather more the investigation of the emotional experience of the working pair and not of the individual.

Working analytically with groups or organizations also implies developing a capacity for observing the emotional experience presented in those settings as the means for understanding, formu-lating, and interpreting the relationship; that is, the constellations that are presented there. Caesuras seem to be an obstacle to obser-ving the continuity and the relationship.

Aristotle said that "man is a political animal", and this means that he has the mental equivalent of the physical characteristics of a herd animal. The obstacle and, at the same time, the advantage in a psychoanalytic or in a group investigation is that, in that same field of investigation, the basic emotional situations that become present are stimulated. *It is the investigation itself that stimulates turbulence, and we still lack the instruments, ones with a high degree of abstraction and unsaturation, equivalent to algebra in mathematics for investigating the relationship.* Anyway, Bion has drawn our attention to the fact that even mathematics has its roots in an emotional matrix. It would appear, rather, that in psychoanalysis we need a Lewis Carroll-type mathematics; mathematics used as a model.

For understanding relatedness, Bion proposes the investigation of the caesura, what is "between", because:

there is much more continuity between autonomically appropriate quanta and the waves of conscious thought and feeling than the impressive caesura of transference and counter-transference would have us believe. So . . .? Investigate the caesura; not the analyst; not the analysand; not the unconscious; not the conscious; not sanity; not insanity. But the caesura, the link, the synapse, the (counter-trans)-ference, the transitive–intransitive mood. [Bion, 1977, p. 56]

A Memoir of the Future is written in the style of a dialogue between different characters, some as parts of the same personality, and others that form singular groups, such as Bion and "Myself", Tyrannosaurus and Stegosaurus, "Captain Bion" and "PA" (the psychoanalyst), Sherlock Holmes and Moriarty, "PS" and "D" (the positions), the scientist, the priest, the Devil, prenatal states, EM (mature), somites, the boy of fourteen, the man of forty, the man of eighty, the heart, etc. Different characters attempt various forms of dialogue; some of them show that communication has been achieved, others give evidence of its failures.

With its dialogue modality, this work represents an illustration of how emotional experience has to be present and alive, as it is not the same to speak of psychoanalysis as it is to "become" the analyst or to "become" the patient in a real psychoanalytic relationship. In a similar way, reading a book on psychoanalysis by an important author cannot be only an intellectual adventure; it needs to be able to be an emotional experience, and this is what is felt by the reader of this book who dares to undergo this disturbing experience. This "psychoanalytic science-fiction novel" is also part of Bion's search for a science of relationships, showing the kind of caesuras that hinder dialogue and insight, and those that facilitate it.

The method for generating instruments that facilitate traversing caesuras is through attempting to achieve a discussion and reflection between different modes of functioning, showing different vertices. This kind of dialogue would help to develop a capacity for discernment, contrasting with rivalry, which is a serious obstacle.

This book, at times disquieting, shows through the "dramatic" form the difficulties in and possibilities of dialogue.

Bion brings on to the stage different characters; at times they attempt to establish a discussion, while at other times rivalry emerges as an obstacle. This obstacle appears in different forms between "real" and "fictional" characters, between men and women, etc., and makes communication impossible. The "language of achievement" also makes its entrance, via poets, musicians, etc., as an instrument of record, expression, and articulation of a container that detoxifies emotions. (See also Chapters Three and Six). This language implies the acceptance of a space of representations and provides a link between primitive emotions and a more elaborate way of expressing them.

Some characters are changing and ambiguous, and their moves are unpredictable. This is what we need to bear in mind to develop the psychoanalytic function of the personality and to preserve our capacity for becoming surprised and for ignorance. The most mysterious one is "Man": is he an invader? Does he come from the Future? Does he carry a bar of chocolate or an automatic gun in his holster? Meanwhile, Myself, Sherlock Holmes and Moriarty, the PA, the Priest, the scientist, etc., attempt a dialogue to discuss problems, in which other characters, like the Devil, take part. Once more, the communication is difficult and depends from which vertex and which side of the caesura it is seen. The "real" characters, Bion and Myself, appear to enter into rivalry with the "fictional" ones, like Sherlock Holmes and Watson. Another unique character is Du: he can be "do" (as in action) and also "Du" (as in the German for "thou"). "Du" can be action that substitutes for thinking, or action as prelude to thinking, or a thought transformed into action. At times, in the evolution of the discussion, Bion and Man seem to begin to understand one another, as sometimes occurs in an analytic session, in which the character which is "known" and which has a name can approach the unknown, the mystery.

A Memoir of the Future is a name with polysemia, and I believe that it could also be the name for a science of relationships, which must have the features of being a preconceptual, that is, unsaturated, science open to new "realizations". It is a science that has to investigate continuity through the caesura, and growth through the discontinuity of catastrophic change.

A psychoanalytic science with these characteristics awakens strong anxieties, above all for its object of inquiry, an animated object, which is not sensorial and which changes on being investigated. It also changes the investigator, the psychoanalyst who knows that the instrument of investigation is his own mind, which participates in the same vicissitudes as the object investigated.

Psychoanalysis is far from providing the illusion of apparent certainties, such as those that come from the so-called hard sciences.

Binocular vision from at least two vertices provides the possibility of depth. Psychoanalysis can advance in the understanding of some phenomena that appear to manifest in psychoanalytic practice if it takes into account that what stimulates this link is a "pair" relationship, in which the basic assumption of mating may be the most stimulated.

I would now like briefly to point out some of the factors for the development of the "science of relationships":

- tolerance towards recognizing turbulence;
- tolerance of the observed turbulence to be thought of and considered in words or in "language of achievement";
- tolerance towards the decision: to the selected fact as the articulator of the observation and making the relationship evident;
- tolerance towards uncertainty, with negative capability as a central factor, or, as Freud wrote, to cast a beam of darkness on the dark spot, to avoid being dazzled by the light of what is already known;
- tolerance towards co-operation, in counterpart to the basic assumption group's automatic functioning.

Emotional development

The infancy of the human species and its first embryonic steps coexist as living archaic vestiges, together with its more developed functioning. The emotional experience is ineffable, but traversing *caesuras* towards mental growth requires transformation and expression in some communicable way without loss of vitality. I am referring here to transformations from K to O (at-one-ment), to intuit the experience and transformations from O to K to formulate it.

On the other hand, the road of private and public communication has to be cleared of the primitive tendencies towards evacuation, of action as a substitute for thinking, and turned into the field transformations where thought is the prelude to action. (See Chapter Four).

The automatic functioning of BA, the primitive emotional forces, have to be considered, because they are inescapable. It is not enough for the work group and/or the thinking functions of the personality to develop instruments for establishing contact with external reality. Psychoanalysis, with its microscopic lens focused on relationships, has made valuable contributions and has developed instruments such as the need to think and become aware of transference–countertransference phenomena.

Psychoanalysis allowed us to discover that mental growth cannot take place without taking into account primitive emotional functioning. In the same direction, this fact contributes to the urgency of the problem of developing research into the interaction between the production of instruments through technological skills (corresponding more to simian skills, as illustrated in Chapter Seven) and the development of emotional growth towards wisdom.

The challenge of investigating the caesura

Working with groups provides an opportunity to observe the interaction between the emotional situation—seemingly restricted to the individual—and the way it spreads out and affects other members of the group.

One of the disadvantages of the group situation is that the anatomy of the participants might seem so dominant that one tends to assume that the personality is likewise delineated by the physical appearance.

Sometimes, those "dramatic or impressive" caesuras of being in the presence of several persons make it difficult to observe that the personality does not end in the anatomy of an individual. Thus, the relational field, generated by the underlying BA and proto-mental functioning through the invisible net of crossed projective identifications, is obscured.

> Taking what I may call a macroscopic vertex I do not see the same things as I do from a microscopic vertex. In what I would call a macroscopic formulation the difference is easily explained by the fact that a group is not an individual or vice versa, but . . . The microscopic vertex . . . reveals something which does not correspond to the anatomy or physiology of the individual or the group of human individuals. [Bion, 1991, p. 182]

If we take the vertex of BA functioning, and Bion's hypothesis that those who are not operating at a given moment do not disappear, but, rather, remain active in the proto-mental system, we see that what appears as delineated from the anatomy as being individual is actually part of a communicational network.

A model for thinking about this could be that of a group of mushrooms. The observer sees the mushrooms separated one from the other and scattered over a great area; if, on the other hand, an infra-red picture were taken, revealing what lay beneath, we would see the network that unites them.

Based on his experiences in groups and his subsequent psychoanalytic investigation of the psychotic and non-psychotic parts of the personality, Bion acquired a profound understanding of the problems in the relational field generated by projective identification. He thought that caesuras can act as opaque screens, as obstacles for communication, and he suggested that there is an urgent need for the development of articulating caesuras. A model for this articulation is Picasso's painting on both sides of a plate of glass, which allows the permanence as a barrier, which at the same time is permeable and allows communication. I think that the contact barrier (Bion, 1962), a semi-permeable structure that allows differentiation and contact between conscious and unconscious functioning, is this type of caesura.

In the domain of psychic reality, which is non-sensuous, we should enlarge our field and explore the infra- and ultra-sensuous spectrum. So, there is also a need for constructing sufficiently large and resistant screens, like radio telescopes, to be able to receive the phenomena that fall within the infra- and ultra-sensorial ranges, to be able to receive what until then was heard as interference. Changing the vertex is important: someone once heard the interference instead of hearing music, and thus radio astronomy was born.

If tolerance to catastrophic change is developed and the relationship is investigated, then a broad spectrum of events in the personality and in the group is laid open for investigation:

- between waking and sleeping mental states;
- between pre- and postnatal mental states;
- between group mentality and the individual.

Bion suggests studying the total personality, which he considers as if it were a group of different aspects within one personality. He also suggests considering the "total group", with its different operating modalities, which become, in the last part of his work, the relationship between the mystic, the group, and the Establishment.

Each caesura, when traversed, implies that the previously achieved organization is disarticulated. If it cannot be disarticulated, this organization acts as ballast in the turbulence and hinders a new creative articulation. Intense saturated preconceptions (different from unsaturated preconceptions) with no disposition to confront a crisis that arises through the contact with new facts, generate obstacles for this process of articulation and disarticulation in a growing spiral.

Intense and saturated messianic expectations take the place of preconceptions, stimulating such intense feelings that the group can become resistant to any emotion whatsoever, for fear of turbulence. No task in the group is exempt from this problem. In turn, bureaucratic groups, in which the reduction of emotions to automatisms finds one of its greatest exponents, would deserve an investigation such as might reveal autistic functioning different from those of the BA.

An omnipotent, omniscient leader, as a means for problem solving, is part of BA-group functioning. For the level of the work group, there is no messianic leader, or, in any case, the leader is the idea or the task, and the problem-solving method includes contact with facts, with reality, and with the passage of time.

BA functioning does not get on well with open preconceptions, since it cannot tolerate the anxieties generated by development and the uncertainties linked to whatever is undetermined. The predominance of this kind of functioning entails the risk of creating a caesura that might also become an impermeable barrier to the extent of reaching the degree of a prohibition. This barrier is erected to protect or preserve a previous, archaic mode of resolution. It took Darwin forty years to dare to publish his ideas, ones that contradicted the intense emotional and cultural forces of the time. Not until he was under the pressure of another investigator's having made the same discoveries, and being willing to publish them, did Darwin finally do so himself.

An impermeable barrier sets up caesuras between present, past, and future, that, by becoming impermeable and inaccessible, become also an impediment for further development. We find one manifestation of these caesuras in fanaticism. Sometimes, instead, illuminating ideas become permeable *caesuras*, and if a symbiotic container–contained relationship between the idea and the group exists, then it can lead to development. *We can think of psychoanalysis and of artistic manifestations as producing a caesura, in the form of a bridge, establishing a dialogue between the primitive and more developed parts.* However, we also observe manifestations resistant to tolerating these new ideas. It is the destiny of many innovative ideas, those to which Freud draw attention because they produce narcissistic wounds. Another fact to be observed is the reduction of works of art to "values" that are quoted on the stock exchange market and are manifestations of enforced splitting* (Bion, 1962).

In turn, once the illuminating idea has been accepted and established, if the members of the group are able to see the problem, a solution is stimulated. But again, if the solution does not retain an unsaturated part, it turns irretrievably into a closed situation. *There is no everlasting solution: the solution to a problem always reveals a field of problems undiscovered hitherto.* This means that the development of a personality in psychoanalysis as well as that of a task in a work group is dependent on the possibility of tolerating the anxieties arising from an open-ended search, an unending search, and of the building of a mature container to contain anxieties that arise because of the features inherent to the investigation.

The community, the family, the group, and the individual all need to make decisions. To the extent that these imply a choice, accepting the relationship between what is chosen and what has been left aside, decisions are reactivated as emotional turbulence. *The proposal of psychoanalysis is the treatment of this turbulence through insight, thinking and discussion of the problems.* This implies a considerable process of maturation; it means separating and differentiating man, in his finiteness, from the infinite God, to whose omnipotence he aspires, and that darkens the other face: that of helplessness.

Caesuras as inaccessible barriers might bring about catastrophe, for both the individual and the group, if circumstances should stimulate development and pressure to traverse them. This is illustrated by Bion with the live burial of the entire court at Ur, the court who followed the priests to the death pit, to the sounds of dance and song, following the death of the king. If a latent turbulence is activated by an external or internal event, and if the barrier between different modes of functioning becomes inaccessible (through evasion of pain), instead of being a contact zone, the barrier can be broken and provoke a sudden catastrophe: psychosomatic, somato-psychotic, a psychotic breakdown, a social breakdown, etc.

Primitive/evolved, encounter and turbulence

His experience as an officer in a tank unit in the First World War, and as an army psychiatrist in the Second World War, left a deep impression on Bion. In his paper "The Grid" he says:

> I do not believe, and nor does anyone else who has had close contact with men in battle conditions, prisoners of war or civilians in similar stress, that the feelings of men and women either as individuals or as members of a group have changed: they are dormant. Often they are covered by a veneer of civilization which however, does not conceal though it might disguise the forces beneath. [Bion, 1977 (1989), p. 23]

> . . . there may well be some analogue in the personality to the capillary blood system which in ordinary conditions is dormant but in extraordinary conditions may dilate in surgical shock. The analogy would be such hyper stimulation of the individual "groupishness" that his capacity for conscious, sophisticated behaviour seeps away into his "unconscious". [*ibid.*, p. 24]

> Omnipotence—omniscience—god, together with the symmetrical elements, helplessness—incomprehension—agnosticism, are the abstract statements of the basic group. [*ibid.*, p. 29]

These quotes from the "later Bion" reintroduce an issue present from Bion's early work and onwards: the coexistence within one and the same personality, and within a group, of different modes of functioning, separated sometimes by impenetrable caesuras, and its implications for the insight into psychological problems, both in psychoanalysis and in tasks in groups and in society.

This coexistence essentially refers to the cohabitation of primitive functioning that contains creative potentialities for growth and destructive potentialities, together with more evolved aspects.

What is found in a potential state in a neothenic being needs to be able to evolve and develop. A disturbing question arises, however. Where will this development lead?

The innate ability to lie unleashed all its force with the development of articulated speech. (See also Chapter Four). Bion conjectured that those prenatal forces that press the neothenic creature to get rid of his "sensations/ideas/emotions" are still active, and thus archaic vestiges that have remained inaccessible can erupt in this passage of caesuras, with the risk that, instead of a transformation with contained catastrophic experiences, the emotional turmoil can lead to a catastrophe. When transformations occur in a $-K$ medium, this change is close in different degrees, but always very near to a real catastrophe.

The mind is still a very premature, rudimentary, and powerful development that can evolve towards psychosis, creativity, or destruction. Man has developed thought and language as instruments, and also produced technological development.

Thought, language, and technological developments are very powerful instruments that can be used in dissimilar ways: in the service of destruction, or in the service of concern for life and truth. A disturbing question arises: where will this development lead when what is still in an embryonic state in a neothenic creature develops?

Psychoanalysis has revealed an aspect of infantile emotional functioning that still encounters much resistance in being accepted. If we take the infant as a model, developing its potential leads not only towards mental growth; destructive potentialities also exist in it. Developing a baby's potentialities also involves potential destructive aspects: a baby with potentially murderous, predatory aspects lacks the appropriate physical development to translate this impulse into action. Alternatively, the capacity for transformation in hallucinosis is greater in the neothenic state, because not enough reality principle and maturity has yet developed to allow discrimination.

The infant's terrors are more intense because he has no names to bind the constant conjunction, which would help him to discriminate and stop the terrifying explosion.

Continuing with the model of the baby, if terror meets with receptive and detoxifying parental functions that transform the dread, giving it a name and a meaning, mental growth can take place creatively.

Failures of this function are substituted by a moral conscience: the super-superego, which appears endowed at the same time with destructive potential as murderous super-superego and inhibitor of growth capacities, having also the potential for deceit in order to avoid mental pain.

This moral conscience without morals substitutes scientific discernment, albeit rudimentary, between what is true and what is false for a differentiation between what is morally good and what is morally bad. (See also Chapter Four.) The individual, or the group, has to become able to discern between mental growth and "division and multiplication—cancerous, not qualitative increase" (Bion, 1970, p. 127).

Growth directed towards development of wisdom involves decisions and making choices of methods to deal with mental pain: evasion or modification.

The choice of avoiding pain leads the personality and the group to develop the wrong methods to solve problems, which can lead to destruction. *Thus equipment for denial of reality develops instead of equipment for discernment and growth.* We are familiar with the meaning: in Kleinian terminology, denial refers specifically to a denial of psychic reality.

Any institution, group or instrument can be enlisted for one purpose or the other:

> For the apparatus of denial, endopsychic and social, is formidable indeed if it has to be effective as it is indeed. . . . Nor can his labours cease at the borders of his own personality: as the scientist has to seek the aid of groups, institutions, elaborate apparatus, and social support as well as maintain his mental acumen, so the individual oriented to frustration evasion has to enlist the aid of, or actually initiate, social institutions to help in the task of denial of reality. The actual social institutions need not differ: those used by scientifically oriented and by frustration-evaders can be the same but used differently. It is obvious that a psychotic will use the institution of marriage, the family, the state differently from the frustration modifier. [Bion, 1992, pp. 99–100]

In this quotation, one can follow Bion's articulation of his experience with groups and his practice as a psychoanalyst with patients with psychotic functioning. From the latter, he learnt that the psychotic part of the personality has enough reality principle, and uses it to preserve the apparatus to evade reality and frustration, using the institutions for this purpose and enlisting them in his cause.

So, the coexistence in the individual or in the group of more primitive and more developed functioning generates emotional problems that are not only concerned with performing a specific task and that demand a solution. The emotional turbulence has also to be solved. As we know, in *Experiences in Groups* (1961) Bion had the opportunity to observe and describe two modalities of group functioning: the BA group and the work group. He then introduced the idea of specialized work groups as those who are in charge of dealing with emotions of the BA, trying to avoid a transformation into action.

The BA group functioning has a very limited repertoire, pervaded by basic emotions hostile to contact with the passage of time or any other event or idea that stimulates development. The threat is the new and unknown idea that promotes change and growth. If the work group is able to contain the BA-group functioning, the task can be carried out, although not without difficulties. Bion believed that specialized work groups, such as the church, the army, and the aristocracy, have as their function that of providing an outlet to the emotions of the BA without these being translated into action.

The description of how this task is carried out by the known specialized groups or institutions is very interesting: it recalls the formations of neurotic commitment. To prevent the translation of the BA emotions into action, but providing at the same time an outlet, the specialized work groups, for example the church, will adjure the group to thank God when presented with the achievement of a task. Thus, there is an outlet for their desire to find a God, or a longing for "awe and reverence", or the search for omnipotent and omniscient leaders. At the same time, the specialized work group tries to avoid the BA-group functioning becoming incarnated in a leader, because this translation into action would be highly dangerous for the risk of what is primitive translating into action.

If the pressure for change is very intense, aberrant changes can occur (Bion, 1961), ones that are fundamentally forms of schism in which different schismatic groups, either clinging to their "Bibles" or apparently carrying the flag of change, hinder the possibility for real change. This can be seen both in political parties and in psychoanalytic institutions themselves, which have been affected by schisms, dating back almost to their origins. These observations are also very interesting if one thinks about them in the light of the pathological solutions the personality can attempt, such as multiple splitting.

As well as discovering transference, Freud also discovered and conceptualized, as something unwavering in human beings, man's instinctual basis and the conflicts that arise when he becomes "human", "civilized". In *Civilization and its Discontents* (1930a), he was quite pessimistic about the future of the relationship between drives and culture. In contrast, Bion depicts a more hopeful perspective in *Experiences in Groups*:

> I attribute great force and influence to the work group, which, through its concern with reality, is compelled to employ the methods of science in no matter how rudimentary a form; I think one of the striking things about a group is that, despite the influence of the basic assumptions, and sometimes in harmony with them, it is the work group that triumphs in the long run. [Bion, 1961, p. 135]

He maintained that the individual is a group animal, at war with the group as well as with those aspects of his personality that constitute his "groupishness". Bion introduced the idea of groupishness, the "political animal" condition and the group mentality, as an inherent factor of human beings. This becomes manifest in a group, but it does not cease to exist in an isolated individual.

Bion used splitting and projective identification, the mechanisms described by Klein, as instruments for his observation of groups. His experience as a psychoanalyst with very disturbed patients was articulated with what he had already observed in groups to conceptualize that the personality can be fragmented and those fragments be evacuated, not only at an omnipotent phantasy level. As we have seen, via realistic projective identification, functioning that is not confined to a person's anatomical limits can be produced.

Contagious functioning produced by projective identification can be observed in groups, and it should not be forgotten that no relationship is immune to the erosion brought about by the externalization of internal relations. *The ability with which people manipulate others to play the roles in the drama of their phantasy life, or in Bion's terms, their "waking dreams", is only surpassed by the enthusiasm by which those people are ready to take part or to play those roles.* In Chapter Four, I establish a relationship in that sense with regard to lies.

Bion made a great contribution to the understanding of countertransference in psychoanalysis, partly as a result of his observation of group functioning, which Leon Grinberg used for the concept of projective counter-identification. Bion's experience of working with groups convinced him of the powerful emotional forces operating in this dynamic, which are not related to countertransference, which is unconscious, and have to do with the personality of the analyst as an individual:

> Now the experience of counter-transference appears to me to have a quite distinct quality that should enable the analyst to differentiate the occasion when he is the object of a projective identification from the occasion when he is not. The analyst feels he is being manipulated so as to be playing a part no matter how difficult to recognize, in somebody else's phantasy—or he should do it if it was not for what in recollection I can only call a temporary loss of insight, a sense of experiencing strong feelings and at the same time a belief that their existence is quite adequately justified by the objective situation . . . I believe ability to shake oneself out of the numbing feeling of reality that is concomitant of this state, is the prime requisite of the analyst in the group . . . in a group treatment many interpretations, and amongst them the most important, have to be made on the strength of the analyst's own emotional reactions. It is my belief that these reactions are dependent on the fact that the analyst in the group is at the receiving end of what Melanie Klein has called projective identification, and that mechanism plays a very important role in groups. [Bion, 1961, p. 149]

By means of these observations and conceptualizations, Bion establishes a relationship between his work in groups and in psychoanalysis with the quality of a binocular vision. The psychoanalytic technique of examining transference from a position which allows, at the same time, observation from inside and from outside the relationship, is enriched with this perspective derived from working with groups, which permits recognizing the possibility of losing and recovering insight. I believe these binocular observations were a factor that led to the development of the technical instruments that Bion (1970) made when he suggested the discipline of "without memory, without desire and without understanding".

The concept of countertransference, broadened along these lines, can be applied advantageously outside the consulting-room, to indicate when pressure from a group induces a person to lose, albeit temporarily, his insight with regard to his emotional state. That is, considering the problem of the coexistence of modalities of functioning that avoid pain and hinder development and another mode of functioning that aims to modify the pain and thus face the implications of growth and catastrophic change (in groups, in institutions, in society, and in the personality), one can deduce that the development of methods that apprehend, contain, and creatively transform primitive functioning are needed.

If we take into account neotenicity, not only of the baby, but of the species, we face a vital question: what would be the counterpart of *the reverie function of the mother and of the psychoanalytic function of the personality in the functioning of the work group*? This work group has to be able to carry out a twofold function: the specific work group function, and the containment of BA functioning, thus preventing the danger of translating into action, which would lead to catastrophe.

The problem of containment, insight, and transformation of the primitive is very intricate, and, undoubtedly, neither the tasks demanded by the adaptation to the outside world nor the offering of a way out in the mode of the "classic" specialized work groups are sufficient to solve it. Psychoanalysis and research in groups have made their contributions, but there is still a lot of work to be done.

The mystic and the group: mental growth and catastrophic change

Bion's development in the course of his work led him first to formulate the problems posed by learning from emotional experience and subsequently to consider the different facets of what he called mental growth. The conflict that emerges through this new conceptualization is described as the one between *knowing about and becoming*.

The heading under the title *Transformations*, "From learning to growth", contains an underlying model: that of the mind as an expanding universe. Mental growth can only be achieved by traversing catastrophic change experiences, and each spiral turn of this change means coming into contact with primitive functioning, still in a "raw" state and being exposed to emotional turbulence.

The terms genius, mystic, Messiah, and Establishment emerge in reference to the problem of developing insight in this task of achieving mental growth.

From the experiences in group, we know that the genius and the Messiah can be easily invested with the features of the leader of the BA group (with the most ill member of the group often being chosen for this) and thus become an obstruction for growth. "Beware the charismatic individual!" Bion warns us. Bion uses the term "genius" again in *The Grid* when he refers to the problem of the liar, and in *Attention and Interpretation* when he says that many times genius has been said to be akin to madness. Bion suggests that a genius is required to deal with psychotic mechanisms adequately.

With much humour and irony, he describes in *The Grid* that when he had to begin to write papers, give conferences, etc., he found himself regretting not having been born a liar. He immediately realized that he was deploring the lack of the one characteristic that is, in fact, inborn, though it had to wait, as always, for the genius to reach its full capacity. "In this case the genius, or group genius, who invented speech released the liar from his bondage" (Bion, 1977 [1989], p. 20). In this way, he seems to suggest that any primitive prenatal characteristic has to wait for the genius to develop its full capacity, but this characteristic can be creative or destructive and, also, a genius can lead towards growth or towards destruction. This statement is confirmed in the multiple and refined manifestations of mankind's cruelty, and different destructive uses of the technology invented by men's genius.

The term "mystic" can be understood as the mystic idea: the unknown idea, the idea still not developed, or, as he sometimes formulates it, the thought without a thinker. The mystic makes direct contact with the Godhead (the unconscious, in psychoanalysis). This contact needs a disciplined opacity towards the senses, memory, desire, and understanding. The mystic (implying the transformations in O: at-one-ment) is necessary to contact the idea, but also the group is necessary, and the transformations in K (disposition to discover and formulate the discovery), so that the idea can be used by common people who are not geniuses.

Bion introduces the term "Establishment" as a bridge spanning the mystic and the group: "The governing body of a society I call the Establishment; the counterpart in the domain of thought would be the pre-existing disposition or pre-conception" (Bion, 1970, p. 111).

The group needs the mystic, with the mystic's idea revitalizing and nourishing the group. The mystic also needs the group to prevent the idea from producing a disintegrating effect in him (megalomania, for example, like that illustrated by Hal in Chapter Seven). The function of the Establishment in the direction of growth is to perform the task of taking the mystic's innovative idea, generating an adequate containment, and transforming it, so that it becomes tolerable for the group.

A new idea is an unknown idea that is hated and feared at the same time. Psychoanalysis is the bearer of an idea with such features, and each insight in a session can also be considered from this vertex.

Frequently, the group (in BA functioning) tries to deal with the idea through projection and materialization. Thus, the idea is "embodied" in a person: it is no longer an idea but something much less frightening, a person or a thing. The idea itself can be transformed into a "Messiah" and be adored and worshipped, instead of being thought. "Science" and "Psychoanalysis", with capital letters, run that risk because of the need of messianic omnipotent expectations.

Punning once again, with a lot of humour and irony, Bion says that physical persons can be detained, either by idealization (and proving that they are not real) or by realization (and proving that they are not ideal). But it still is difficult to determine the rules of mental growth.

The mystic can be considered, in my opinion, as the intuitive moment of the task, which, if it maintains a quality of preconception as open and unsaturated expectations, is at the same time fragile and powerful through its potentiality for growth. This is because the new idea is at its beginnings, it has not yet acquired a form, it has not developed yet, and it has a quality of unknown, whose direction can be towards being creative or destructive.

In the relation between the mystic and the group, an emotional pattern can be observed that will be repeated in the course of history, although it adopts different forms. Bion suggests that we have to learn about that pattern in order to be able to find creative ways of dealing with the coexistence of not only primitive and sophisticated functioning, but also with its creative and destructive manifestations.

The new idea has features of being explosive and needs containment. Bion, taking as a model, among others, Jesus and Christianity, in my opinion is also dealing with the psychoanalytic idea and the problem of its institutionalization, which needs an Establishment that can contain evolution, maintaining the potentiality of growth and development of the psychoanalytic ideas and, at the same time, avoiding—as I stated in Chapter Four—deification or demonization.

The Establishment is essential for an individual's development, even that of a mystic, just as he, the mystic, is for the group. *The healthy Establishment contains the continuity of the group's identity and maintains the possibility of growth.* Its task is also to avoid the idea becoming incarnated in the genius or the mystic, with the subsequent danger of transforming him into a god to be treated with adoration and reverence. The idea is thus deprived of the possibility of evolving.

In the development of Bion's ideas related to the dynamics and functioning of groups, the bipolar model proposed initially (BA group and work group) becomes transformed, in *Attention and Interpretation*, into the relation between the mystic, the group, and the Establishment.

The investigation of this relationship as a container–contained relationship, which can be symbiotic, commensal, or parasitic, offers a new instrument for the research of problems in the relation between primitive functioning and work group functioning.

The container–contained relationship can be envisaged with two different models:

1. The military model: one force containing another, keeping the other one in check. This is a model for thinking about two modes of functioning, BA group and work group, psychotic part and non-psychotic part of the personality, like two forces in which one tries to obstruct the progress of the other. There cannot be growth in this model, or development towards growth. It is a model of rivalry: there can be truces, balance, usually unstable, and temporary compromises, but it leads neither to change nor to transformation towards growth. Its major success could be to obstruct the "enemy's" progress; its worst option is to annihilate it. In my opinion, this is the model that Bion puts forward when he describes the kind of transference operating in the relationship when there is a predominance of the psychotic part of the personality: it can be transformed from planar to lineal and *vice versa*, but it lacks the depth of the container–contained relationship that I will now describe.

2. A relationship modelled on a container with receptive qualities and a content with a penetrating quality. Significantly, Bion uses for this model the masculine and feminine signs that have the characteristics of an abstraction, but also contain the common matrix of the emotional experience they emerge from. This model also emerges as a way of conceptualizing the relation between the projective identification of the baby, a content with a capacity of penetration, and the container–receptive quality of the mother's reverie. This is also his model of the origin of thinking. (See Chapters Eight and Nine.)

When there is a *symbiotic* container–contained relationship (two who get together to mutual advantage and/or for the benefit of a third party), projective identification is used in a communicative way and is detoxified and transformed into meaning; thus, it can become a preconception open to new meanings.

A symbiotic relationship between theoretical formulations and the intuitive psychoanalytic idea would preserve the latter from remaining constrained by dogmas, which drown future possibilities of development.

In terms of groups, it is the Establishment in a symbiotic relation with the messianic idea that carries out the container function, which attenuates the disruptive quality of the new idea, detoxifying it so that, as a nutrient, it can be accessible to the group that lacks the qualities of the genius.

These characteristics of the relationship are growth factors.

In the *commensal* relationship, container–contained live together without making contact, without establishing a relationship. The caesura is very wide, thus no conflict ensues. This is what happened with the heliocentric ideas of Aristarchus of Samos, 500 years before Christ, which did not arouse conflict and were forgotten in favour of the geocentric ones. Galileo's ideas did provoke conflict, and were finally accepted. This is why Bion asks if conflict, the tension of conflict, is necessary, and he supposes that it is, if the possibility of transformation towards growth is to exist. We can observe this in psychoanalysis when the splitting is very broad and static, such as the one I described in relation to Ana, in Chapter One; there is no possibility for either conflict or evolution. Nor, in autistic functioning, are there possibilities for confrontation or conflict.

The *parasitic* relationship between container and content is a mutually destructive relationship. (See Chapter Four, in relation to lies.) Projective identification is explosive, destructive of the container. The proliferation of splitting might happen, as Bion describes in *Experiences in Groups*, as a result of aberrant changes.

It is worth wondering whether psychoanalysis, or the psychoanalytic idea, is not at this moment undergoing a process of proliferation of splitting in multiple theories, that at times are not only dogmatized, but which also each take on one aspect of a problem. Often in rivalry with one another (the theories and the groups that support them), we can ask ourselves if they might not, in fact, be functioning as one of the most serious obstacles to the development of the psychoanalytic idea towards a change in the meaning of a development. Might this not be a factor in the current crisis psychoanalysis finds itself in?

Emotional growth and catastrophic change

Mental growth is timeless and catastrophic (Bion, 1965). In order for development to take place, the conditions must arise for a catastrophic change to occur; one of those conditions is that the relation between container and contained has to be symbiotic.

"Catastrophic change" is a term used by Bion to point out a constant conjunction of facts, whose realization can be found in the mind, in the group, in the psychoanalytic session, in society.

The facts that the constant conjunction refers to can be observed when a new idea appears in any of these areas. The new idea has a disruptive force that threatens a more or less violent break-up of the structure and the organization where it is expressed.

The change towards growth involves the transformation of an already-organized structure, or part of it. This transformation cannot occur without moments of disorganization, pain, and frustration.

The already existing organization has to be disarticulated; what is newly achieved implies a choice, that is to say, tolerance of what has not been achieved and also of the incertitude about the newly revealed problems undiscovered hitherto.

The container–contained model can be used to study these vicissitudes: the new idea can be considered the content, and the mind, the individual, or the society a container, or *vice versa*, together with the investigation of the relationship and the possible interactions.

I come back now to the problem of the relationship between the mystic, the group, and the Establishment. The mystic needs the Establishment, just as the Establishment needs the mystic. The institutionalized group is just as essential for the development of the individual as the mystic is fundamental for the group as a revitalizing content or container. As I already said, a healthy Establishment provides continuity and containment, the new idea; the mystic, although disruptive, is a nutrient.

As I have stated, the mystic can be either creative or destructive. At best he will be creative, but the nature of his contributions is certain to be destructive of the laws, conventions, culture, and, therefore, coherence of the group.

The Establishment's function is to achieve an adequate containment and representation of the new idea, attenuating its disruptive character and, at the same time, making it accessible to the non-genius members of the group.

The disruptive force of the mystic will or will not be contained, according also to the means of communication he uses, the vehicle of his message. If projective identification is his means of transmission, it will stimulate the BA group phenomena that will transform

the new idea into an object of adoration, deification, or demonization. Representation of the new idea requires a language, but the
conversational language we use in psychoanalysis is permanently
at risk of covering itself with the penumbras of emotional associations which hinder its scientific use.

In this sense, Bion suggests the language of achievement, which
is the one that contains a high degree of negative capability, because
of its creative and change-promoting quality of traversing the
caesura between the mystic and the group. It is a language that
does not operate as a substitute for thinking; it has thinking as a
prelude and is, at the same time, open, unsaturated.

Language of achievement, caesura, and growth

In the relationship between the mystic, the group, and the Establishment, the recurring configurations that Bion brings from history are
those of a potentially explosive force within a framework that tries
to contain it. History also shows that, to this day, this has never
quite been achieved. Psychoanalysis brings a disruptive force of
this sort. What does its future hold?

Growth cannot be achieved in a commensal relationship, as the
caesuras are too big and no conflict arises; there is neither crisis nor
change. Obviously if the relationship is a parasitic one, changes
occur, but in the direction of a catastrophe, towards deterioration.
As I have stated, growth depends on a symbiotic container–
contained relationship, which supposes the existence of links in the
direction of concern towards life and respect for truth, links that
Bion named L (love), H (hate), and K (knowledge). It also unavoidably implies confrontation, crisis, and conflict, because the concern
for life has to meet with what is potentially destructive in our
circumstance of members of a predatory species, and the respect
for truth has to deal with the inclination to avoid pain and the
frustration that the approach to the facts necessarily involves.
Psychoanalytic research that deals with a living object needs to be
able to join together the disposition towards knowledge and
compassion (See also Chapter Four.)

Change towards growth is vital for the individual, for the group,
for society. The tendencies towards growth coexist with those that

oppose them, and even the new "endowments", the achievements, the "inventions", such as, for example, language, can be used to oppose or destroy growth. (See also Chapter Four.)

Psychoanalytic investigation, besides taking into account the destructive factors, needs courage: "to dare to be aware of the facts of the universe in which we are existing calls for courage" (Bion, 1979 [1991], p. 248). Scientific methods, even if rudimentary, are those that tend to modify pain as well as develop the capacity to tolerate unavoidable pain involved in the facts that we call "chance" and "decision". The pain-evading methods are false solutions, because they are deceitful and toxic. Psychoanalysis *has a hypothesis that the psychoanalytic function of the personality can be developed and used to modify the false or inadequate solutions that have been adopted over one's lifetime.* Psychoanalysis and experience from working with groups seem to demonstrate that if the work group is only determined to contact problems of external reality, often the caesuras become very rigid and impenetrable and the primitive mental states (BA) become isolated with automatic transformations, while the proto-mental remain confined, without transformation to the neurophysiologic, neuro-humoral systems related with the emergence of psychosomatic or somato-psychotic functioning (Bion, 1979). We are good at spotting external conditions, external disasters, but even there we miss important psychic factors. Unless the psyche becomes a genuine part of public dialogue, we will keep missing where disasters come from. A transformation of the autonomic into automatic might take place, when proto-mental, prenatal states traversing the caesura become an automatic, defensive functioning, like the one in BA groups.

We must also take into account the evidence of compromise solutions that keep the system clear of crisis, thus maintaining in operation a set of primitive beliefs, which remain unobserved, in parallel to developments where the emphasis is placed on any achievements related to the outside world. These "solutions" are often manifestations of enforced splitting (Bion, 1962), dissociating material gratification from emotional experience, restricting the relation only to the material, because of survival motives, and thus avoiding any emotional conflicts. In my opinion, this last configuration predominates at present, in the aspiration for more and more technological development and materialistic success. Our culture, which privileges "*getting and spending, we lay waste our powers*" (as the poet Wordsworth says), is highly impregnated with this kind of splitting modality, which reinforces the splitting of emotions and which is strengthened by banalization.

These false solutions, given that they avoid conflict, which implies succeeding evasions of mental pain, cannot prevent or protect from becoming unbalanced at some stage because these evasions fail, and with this failure comes the feared emergence of disruptive emotions as a catastrophe. As happens with mourning that has not been worked through, those emotional problems that remain unresolved, without development, re-emerge, once again demanding attention. If they are once again put off, they can be transformed into a psychic or a social catastrophe.

If we take the model of an earthquake-proof construction, we see that, to traverse the caesuras towards growth, what is required is equipment with a certain degree of plasticity. This raises questions about how to develop such equipment, and what equipment is needed to be able to conjugate identity and organization, together with an openness that can maintain unsaturated preconceptions, prepared to approach new realizations.

In their evolution, the scientists of the hard sciences have acknowledged a certain epistemological modesty, stating that scientific hypotheses have to be refutable, and also inquiring and trying to answer the question on changes of paradigm. But this has always taken place in the field of reason and the external world.

But in the field of a science whose object is animated, human, non-sensuous, in the field of psychoanalysis, what kind of equipment must a work group use in this field that would provide an alpha function, some scientific equipment to make contact and understand both the psychic as well as the external reality?

How could we approach the facts of the domain of psychic reality, the emotional experiences, belonging either to the spectrum of "narcissism or of social-ism" (Bion, 1965) with scientific equipment?

The problem, thus stated, presents at least two slants: the first is that the objects of this "domain" are non-sensuous but they express themselves mainly in very "raw" terms that stem from the experience of sensuous reality, arising from our animal nature. Thinking and communicating have their realizations by means of sensuous forms. There is a need to widen the spectrum towards the infra- and ultra-sensorial, beyond the animal sense experience.

The second aspect is related to something common to all human beings beyond the deceptive separation of races, religions, languages, and the temporal distances of different historical eras, and it refers to the relation between man's group functioning as a herd animal, subject to the emotional turmoil of BA, and the development of a separate mind with, as yet, very rudimentary instruments. This means the challenge of developing instruments that allow the encounter in a creative way and towards growth.

The functioning of the work group demands the development of thought that can be translated into action, containing the BA functioning, which does not have contact with the passage of time or with the demands of reality.

In the domain of psychic reality, the task of the work group mentality is not only that of containing, but also needs to research how to achieve insight into primitive functioning. Participation in the primitive BA mentality is felt as vital, even if it leads to catastrophe, while the separation from the mental state of herd animals brings about the awareness of our profound dependence and also feelings of isolation, loneliness, and helplessness.

> Detachment can only be achieved at the cost of painful feelings of loneliness and abandonment experienced (1) by the primitive animal mental inheritance from which detachment is effected (2) by the aspects of the personality that succeed in detaching themselves from the object of scrutiny which is felt to be indistinguishable from the source of its viability. The apparently abandoned object of scrutiny is the primitive mind and the primitive social capacity of the individual as a political or group animal. The "detached" personality is in a sense new to its job and has to turn to tasks which differ from those to which its components are more usually adapted, namely scrutiny of the environment excluding the self. Part of the price paid is in feelings of insecurity. [Bion, 1963, p. 16]

Contact between the work group and primitive mentality is fundamental and leads to transformations. No possibility of real growth exists without this prospect of contact. The larger the predominance of the BA mentality, the more limited will be the space for thinking. The coexistence between both modalities of functioning always occurs and is inescapable. It is present in the caveman as well as in his modern successor, technological man. Furthermore, primitive mentality in technological man is much more dangerous, since it is masked by a sophisticated logic and is endowed with an overwhelming strength.

Only when the evolved aspects resonate with the primitive ones can we affirm that we are in the presence of the possibility of real development in the group or the individual. It is for this reason that an adequate Establishment is needed.

In psychoanalysis, and working from a psychoanalytical vertex with groups, we need to be aware of the turbulence that always occurs when there is a meeting between the primitive mentality and that of the work group. We must also bear in mind that psycho-analysis deals with the investigation of this meeting in the "domain" of psychic reality, and that this task cannot be done other than with instruments that stimulate both meeting and turbulence. In his search for instruments, Bion, true to himself, resorts to more than one vertex, and maintains the need to alternate them. Abstractions, formulations in increasing levels of abstraction, with-out alternation of vertices, run the risk of becoming, like pure math-ematics, an empty manipulation of signs without meaning. This, too, is obvious if we approach the psychoanalytic task using theo-ries in a dogmatic way, as a resistance against the turbulence that emerges when we approximate ourselves to the emotional truth.

Therefore throughout this book, I intend to develop Bion's proposal of using a combination of vertices, as well as a comple-mentary and revitalizing alternative vertex, a "psychic digester", the use of myths, dreams, dream thoughts (that is, Row C) as a verbal picture gallery. (See also Chapters Two and Three.)

To avoid this use of models, myths, and dreams from becoming only a concrete pictorial, anecdotic illustration, and therefore as an inevitable distortion of the facts they try to represent, *I am proposing that they should be used as preconception. I mean that this "verbal picture gallery", which develops through artistic and cultural functioning, should be to be used with an unsaturated quality, like nets to "capture" the unknown.* Its function is that of a receptive, exploring thinking, creating models, which, for the emotional experiences, are the coun-terpart to the function Freud ascribed to attention in relation to the outside world and an aspect of Bionian reverie in relation to psychic reality.

> . . . if it is accepted that geometric space affords a link between unsophisticated emotional problems, their unsophisticated solutions, then it may be that musical and other artistic methods afford a similar link. . . . The investigation must be directed to the elucidation of point and line as elements imbedded in the material of transformations in the media of all arts and sciences. [Bion, 1965, p.125]

My conjecture is that this aesthetic transformation is implicit in what Bion calls "language of achievement" (Bion, 1970, p. 125). He says, in *The Grid*,

> The practising psychoanalyst, the portrait painter, the musician, the sculptor, all have to "see" and demonstrate, so that others may see, the truth which is usually ugly and frightening to the person to whom the truth is displayed. [Bion, 1977, pp. 31–32]

But neither psychoanalysis nor investigations in groups have reached a point where truth can be communicated without the presence of the objects that have to be "demonstrated". This means that, inevitably, emotional turbulence is going to appear, demanding a transformation that allows emotions to be thought and assimilated.

I think it is interesting that Bion linked the psychoanalyst with artists who attempt to capture emotional experiences and transform them into some kind of sensuous shape. Expression, via the language of achievement of the emotional experience, implies tolerance of the encounter of an adequate container and tolerance of what a new perspective reveals. Great changes in artistic movements have also produced turbulence that astonishes us even today. Why did the Impressionists produce such turbulence when their intention was only a new way of representing light?

Returning to psychic facts, at the end of *The Grid*, Bion constructs a model for the psychoanalytic task, referring to the problem of the need to operate in the presence of the object being investigated. He says that a microscopist cannot be constructing his microscope while he is looking through it, though he may be adjusting his powers of observation to the defects of the instrument.

What are the defects of the instrument used in the investigation of psychoanalysis and groups? Even though the mind of the investigator is the ultimate interpretive instance of any instrument, this fact is much more obvious in the field we are concerned with. This means that it is the instrument that suffers the turbulence of this encounter and when traversing the caesuras between the BA and the work group, between the genius, the Establishment, and the group, etc. That is why Bion suggests the use of two kinds of instruments (The Grid and Myths) to exercise and train the equipment for intuition and observation, *as a prelude to, and not as a substitute for, observation.*

The Grid is to be used outside the session, to exercise the capacity to elaborate imaginative conjectures and relate them with observations made during the psychoanalytic session.

Bion's use of myths as instruments not only means their use as models, as Freud did with the myth of Oedipus, and as Bion does with the myth of the Garden of Eden, the Tower of Babel, the Death of Palinurus, the burial at the cemetery pit at Ur. This instrumental use implies also using myth and models as an unknown (incognita), as "radio telescopes" open to unknown facts, or those that have not happened yet, which the different parts of the myth, acting as a receptive net, could help to display and illuminate. "The Oedipus myth may be regarded as an instrument that enabled Freud in his discovery of psycho-analysis, and psycho-analysis as an instrument that enabled Freud to discover the Oedipus complex" (Bion, 1963, p. 92). I mentioned before that Bion chose several myths—of the Garden of Eden, the Tower of Babel, the Death of Palinurus, the burial at the cemetery pit at Ur—and used them in this way as preconceptions in search of mating with clinical realizations.

The oscillation, or alternation, of vertices demands tolerance of a conjectural level, tolerance because what is illuminated from one vertex casts a shadow that can only be observed from another vertex, and, finally, tolerance because the preconceptual level entails that the point of arrival of the observation of one problem is also the starting point of another.

In his last conferences, published in *Clinical Seminars and Four Papers* (1987), Bion puts forward the possibility of psychoanalysis traversing this caesura between a primitive prenatal mind and a "civilized" postnatal mind in both directions, so that they can make contact. This idea of coming into contact differs from the perspective of "overcoming" what is primitive, the depressive position, etc. The primitive mind contains potential for creative developments that can be suffocated by the postnatal, "civilized" mind. It also contains potentially destructive impulses and primitive terror that can also be disguised by technological development. As infants, we knew of these primitive emotions, but had no words to name them; by the time we learnt language, we had already forgotten those experiences. A caesura has been formed. Some of the difficulties in traversing these caesuras are described with humour in *A Memoir of the Future*, such as the problem of "sucking an erection", referring, in one layer of multiple meanings, to the passage of man in his evolution from a four-legged animal to a being who stands "erect" on two legs.

The attempt to traverse caesuras, the transitions that catastrophic change inhabits, and that unavoidably stimulate emotional turbulence, needs to find the adequate instruments. Finding these tools is urgent for the fate of humanity, since what is at stake is what is going to prevail in us: the shrewdness of a monkey that has a super developed technology, or the wisdom of becoming aware of emotional experiences, learning from them, and having respect for them. Psychoanalysis and investigation in groups can create some insight on this issue, and make a contribution in the direction of traversing the caesura towards becoming aware of the unconscious emotional forces.

In 1947, two years after the end of the Second World War, Bion (1961, p. 14) suggests that there is no need for the unknown psychological factor in the growth and decay of civilizations to remain unknown. These problems have been dealt with by different disciplines that concern themselves with individual or group relationships. Philosophers, priests, law-givers, political scientists, statesmen, etc., have all shown their concern, but all have failed to produce anything but ephemeral solutions. The failure is due to the problem that they have not been able to recognize: the operation of primitive unconscious emotional impulses and all their different transformations. The existence and operation of unconscious emotional forces in the community has not been recognized. This non-recognition leads again and again to a superficial and, therefore, a sterile approach towards human relationships, owing to the inability, or obstacles, to take into account these emotional factors that, none the less, continue operating.

The challenge that humanity confronts today is not that of an increase in technological advancement, but, rather, the investigation of these emotional primitive forces and the need to develop insight of the different ways unconscious emotional impulses operate in the individual, in groups, and in society. The urgent problem is the development of insight, which also means psychoanalytical investigation, of the interrelation between the production of technological instruments, by means of "simian" skills, and the development of emotional growth. It seems that, at present, technological skills are winning the race.

CHAPTER SIX

Some thoughts on the extension of the psychoanalytic field in *A Memoir of the Future*

"All my life I have been imprisoned, frustrated, dogged by common-sense, reason, memories and desires and—greatest bug-bear of all—understanding and being understood. This is an attempt to express my rebellion, to say 'Good-bye' to all that. It is my wish, I now realize doomed to failure, to write a book unspoiled by any tincture of common-sense, reason, etc. . . . However successful my attempt, there would always be the risk that the book 'became' acceptable, respectable, honoured and unread . . ."

(Bion, 1991, p. 577)

The current crisis in psychoanalysis outlines questions that need further formulation. On discovering unconscious psychic processes and revealing that the formidable conscious logical constructions might not be anything more than "reasonable appearances" in the service of primitive and dark emotional forces, psychoanalysis has revealed the measure of our immense ignorance.

This chapter is inspired by Bion's suggestion that psychoanalysis, such as we know it, might not be more than a stripe on the skin of the tiger, or an instrument as rudimentary as a blind man's cane that somewhat broadens his radius of perception, yet he continues to grope along.

Instead of becoming aware of his helplessness, the human being has often resorted to deceit and self-deceit, and lacks the appropriate container for the changes demanded by the revelations that lead to an evolution of a kind of consciousness capable of becoming aware. The development of the mind is still embryonic and rudimentary. My conjecture is that perhaps one of the factors in the current crisis in psychoanalysis is the prematurity of its ideas, a premature state that suggests that an appropriate container, to contain the turbulences of the catastrophic change implicit in the process of housing them and making them evolve, has not yet been found or developed.

It does not seem very likely, for the time being, that we will manage to apprehend totalities; in their explorations, psychoanalysts have not gone much beyond an attempt to map the nature of the mind.

Even though the developments of different thinkers has been widening this map to include the understanding of phenomena such as the infant's mental functioning, psychosomatic, psychotic, borderline, group functioning, etc., we need to extend our research towards other spectrums of phenomena, such as the prenatal ones, towards the understanding of the mysterious transformations in hallucinosis, of intuition and its evolutions, etc.

The evolution of psychoanalysis needs a development comparable to that of quantum physics, and to construct instruments such as radio-telescopes and electronic microscopes to give us access to ultra- and infra-sensorial phenomena. Will we have to extend our investigation of the mind in a more fine-tuned manner towards our condition of herd animal in order to understand the group phenomena, so that we can manage to further our investigation of the relationship between the psychoanalyst and the patient? Group phenomena and projective identification reveal that the personality does not end with the anatomy. This is idea has been developed in the previous chapter.

These observations raise some questions, such as: have we studied the phenomena of mental contagion, collusions, with sufficient depth? What are the emotional roots that disturb the function of thinking, be that of the person in relation to himself or of the patient with the analyst? How much have we looked into and investigated intuitive phenomena? Emotions are non-sensuous phenomena. How do we apprehend them? Psychoanalysts deal with mental pain. No one doubts the existence of anxiety or sadness, but these emotions cannot be seen, touched, or smelled: Bion says we intuit them. When two animals meet, they smell each other, look at each other, sniff each other. What is this encounter like between the two human beings in a psychoanalytic session?

In what follows I include some thoughts on a book that shows, from its title and its writing style, some paths towards extension of the psychoanalytic field and its instruments. *A Memoir of the Future* is a trilogy written by Bion at the end of his life, together with an autobiography that remained unfinished at his death. The suggestive titles of the three volumes are: *The Dream, The Past Presented* and *The Dawn of Oblivion*. It is a profound psychoanalytical book, original and different in its style. It attempts a vivid communication with the reader, maintaining the vitality of the ideas and their possible evolutions. It meets the challenge of finding the language of achievement able to contain the *idées mères*.

It is a book written in several keys, as in music. Psychoanalytical communication takes place not only in the key of articulate language; in a session, other keys have to be discovered, and the reading of the material will depend on the key in which it is formulated. There is a kind of mental functioning with logic, another grammar, which has not yet been discovered. It is not the same when the psychoanalytical material is in the "hallucinosis", or projective, key as it is when we apply the "dreaming" key, as I attempt to show in Chapters Two, Three, and Four.

How should this book written in several keys be read? The challenge of discovering the keys and the disposition to change the key, comparable to what happens when we are with the patient in the session, offers a model for observation and for the search for infra- and ultra-sensorial methods, for communication in the domain of psychic reality.

We find these ideas in some of the following dialogues.

PA (psychoanalyst): Even if individual humans are separated by Time, Space, Deity . . . this barrier is permeable by forces whose understanding is beyond the range of our logical, rational modes of thought . . .

Alice: Such as . . .?
PA: Speculative imagination, speculative reason. André Green has
pointed out . . . that there may be something about the "dramatic"
art "form" that is perspicuous . . . [Bion, 1991, p. 539]

One of the characters, Man, of *A Memoir of the Future* says:

Man: When the mind ± has been mapped, the investigations may
reveal variations in the various patterns which it displays, The
important thing may not be, as the psycho-analysts suppose, only
revelations in illness or diseases of the mind, but patterns indis-
cernible in the domain in which Bio ± exist (life and death; animate
and inanimate) because the mind spans too inadequate a spectrum
of reality. Who can free mathematics from the fetters exposed by
its genetic links with sense? Who can find a Cartesian system
which will again transform mathematics in ways analogous to the
expansion of arithmetic effected by imaginary numbers, irrational
numbers, Cartesian coordinates freeing geometry from Euclid by
opening up the domain of algebraic deductive systems; the
fumbling infancy of psycho-analysis from the domain of sensuality-
based mind?

This is a psychoanalytical *science-fiction* book. The term science-
fiction, conjugated with psychoanalysis, provides two vertexes for
approaching facts of psychic reality as a binocular vision. Bion says
in the Prologue,

I claim (the claim itself being definitory) that this is a fictitious
account of psychoanalysis, including an artificially constructed
dream; definitory status is also claimed for the constructions
of wakefulness, scientific alertness and scientific theory. . . .
Psychoanalysis and psychoanalytical practice deal with animated
and non-sensorial objects . . . with Kant, I hold that the thing-in-
itself is unknowable. Falstaff, a known artefact, is more "real" in
Shakespeare's verbal formulations than countless millions of
people who are dim, lifeless, unreal. . . . Nor do I believe that
science—smoke, drums, statistics and other apparatus usually
assumed to belong to the domain of science—would ever bring
them life or breathe life into them. [Bion, 1979 (1991), p. 4]

The "dramatic form" is an achieved modality of "personification" of a mental universe in which there are configurations as

already-formed planets and stars and formless "star dust", as in the astronomical nebulae. The somites and the prenatals of Volume 3, or *Du* of Volume 2, on being personified, can establish a dialogue of mutual benefit with other already "formed" parts of this mental galaxy. (See also Chapters Three and Five.)

Fictional characters are a way of embodying thoughts without a thinker, or the prenatal aspects of the mind. The need for a conscious–unconscious binocular vision shows through a dialogue in which Watson, one of the "fictional" characters in the Sherlock Holmes mysteries, gives an answer to the "real characters", such as *Bion* and *Myself*, which complain about having been thrown off the stage of awake consciousness and of real life by dreams, saying that there is nothing worse than being thrown off the stage by characters who claim to be real, with their real scientific and conscious associations.

Although of recent development, the mind is subtle and sensitive. The consciousness, defined by Freud as the sensorial organ for apprehending psychic qualities, can be capable of exploring and reacting to the impressions brought to it by the survey of the sensory organs, and the results of this exploration can be used to form dreams. Dreaming can, in turn, reveal that some elements are constantly conjugated so that underlying configurations can be discerned, ones that show coherence there where before it had not been seen to exist. These configurations can be considered, in turn, as a mathematical formula, as having a reality and a meaning; this meaning could, then, just like a good radiograph, be interpreted by a psychoanalyst.

A Memoir of the Future is a story written as dialogues among different characters which include *Bion* and *Myself*, *Tyrannosaurus* and *Stegosaurus*, *Captain Bion* and *PA* (the psychoanalyst), *Sherlock Holmes*, *Watson* and *Moriarty*, *PS* and *D* (the positions) *the scientist, the priest, the Devil, pre-natal states, EM* (mature) *somites, the boy of fourteen, the man of forty, the older man of eighty, heart*, etc. Each one of them "embodies" emotional experiences, ideas, thoughts without a thinker, scientific hypotheses (the positions PS⟺D), different parts of the mind, observation vertices: religious, scientific, psychoanalytical, etc.

The first part of this trilogy is entitled *The Dream, an artificially constructed dream*. It begins with an "indigestion/dream", and with an attempt at observing from two vertices. In the scene appears a foggy consciousness of an invasion and scattered leaves of a Bible. Does this represent the disturbing idea of the invasion of thoughts without a thinker? Does the Bible represent the institutionalized, established ideas that are being disarticulated?

Rosemary, the maid, is leaving. *Alice*, the mistress, dismisses her, accusing her of having had a sexual affair with Tom, who is also employed there at the farm. The submissive maid begs until, faced with the invasion, she begins to realize Alice's terror. The scene suddenly changes and a homosexual or sexual relationship is unleashed between the two women, which, from a psychoanalytic perspective, we could say has a sadomasochist quality. The roles become automatically reversed, and all throughout the book they remain that way: *Rosemary*, who represents the primitive aspects of the mind, vital and sometimes cruel, transforms into the mistress, and *Alice*, who represents the "educated, civilized" aspect, will be the submissive maid. Both for moments seem to acquire the wisdom of life when change, perhaps catastrophic, stimulates thoughts and thinking. *Rosemary* leaves behind submission, and, on filing her nails, shows her primitive claws; she also, however, has "street smarts", because of her life experiences, something which *Alice* lacks. *Alice*, in turn, appears to find a capacity for feeling emotions, which she seems to have lost long ago beneath the cosmetic layer of civilization.

Bion thus represents the encounter between the primitive and the "civilized" aspects of the mind. Does the invasion represent the threat of catastrophic change? In this encounter, caesuras have to be traversed and the threat of catastrophic change emerges, with its characteristics of: (1) subversion of the system, (2) violence, and (3) invariance, which does not mean permanence, but, rather, which passes to the new system with transformations. Here the invariance is the relationship between master–slave or a sadomasochist relationship: *Rosemary* and *Alice* change places, but the relationship does not change.

Some characters are ambiguous and reveal different facets as dialogues and exchanges occur. The direction that they will take in their evolution is uncertain, such as we see in the psychoanalytic session. The most mysterious character is "Man": he is an invader. Does he come from the future? What does he carry in his holster; is it a chocolate bar or a gun?

A Memoir of the Future avoids the narrative: dialogues are inter-rupted, it is not possible to follow a thread, nor to frame it into logic and reason. It is a choral work, with many voices. Sometimes they harmonize, and at other times they produce dissonances. Reading the Captain Bion chapter generates a strong emotional impact, since it puts the reader in contact with the experiences of a traumatized personality that is falling apart, or perhaps of the psychotic part of the personality. There is a continuity in the name of the characters, but they appear with deep transformations from one moment to another. Bion shows what he has maintained so many times: today's patient is not the same as yesterday's, or as tomorrow's. Bion proposes tools to generate a ground fertile for training psycho-analytical intuition, a ground that could preserve the "species" of untamed thoughts ("the wild asses"), thoughts without a thinker, and also a ground for containing the ideas of the "big hunters"— Freud, Klein, etc.—so that their ideas will not remain unrevealed, nor be "reburied" in "scientific" dogmas, adoration, etc.

The title, *A Memoir of the Future*, has polysemy, and it contains a paradox. Thinking about it we realize that it alludes to preconcep-tual thought: memory as an unsaturated record, leaving openings in order to mate with new experiences. It also contains the meaning of the past and the future, casting its shadow over the present, and *vice versa*. Tolerance of the paradox is a good training for psycho-analytical thought.

Time and space as presented in A Memoir . . .

Mental growth is timeless and catastrophic. The notions of cata-strophic change and of *caesura* require the introduction of space and time categories into psychoanalysis, following models that have a strong analogy with the discovery of the theory of relativity in physics. Time and space are notions that are achieved when a process of tolerance of the time and the space where the "breast" used to be and no longer is, is developed. That "emotional" space and time are transformed through tolerance of the "no-thing", when thought is tolerated in unsaturated observational vertices and in a space for representation that also has a temporal dimension. Here, the notion of present relates with a past that no longer is there, and a future that is yet to come, so it is not there, as well.

If past and future are deep experiences of the present, the psychoanalytical problem is the character of those experiences and their transformations. *"I am the future of the Past; the form of the thing—to come"*, one of the characters says. Bion suggests that the present contains prenatal living archaic vestiges, of the childhood of the species and of intra-uterine life. *Albert Stegosaurus* and *Adolf Tyrannosaurus* are present in the human being of today, as is the scene, which appears to be of love and transforms into cannibalism, that *Man* reveals to *Bion*.

Man seems to come from the future, and, in his dialogues with *Bion*, they make a revision of the notions of space and time at moments in which they appear to be able to learn from one another.

Temporality and causation

The birth of psychoanalysis is associated with the problem of memory, of forgetting, and repression, all related with the search for causes. Bion suggests that causation is one of the ways in which the mind binds facts. We need to take into account that it is the mind of the human being that tends to establish relationships and conjunctions. This epistemological posture is a good antidote for the longing to search for "ultimate causes". Bion proposes, as an epistemological position, that the O, the ultimate reality, is unknowable for human beings. The O also means origin, and, quoting Milton, an infinite and formless void, from which something evolves and intersects with the mind of the thinker.

Due to the regularity and to the rhythm in which an analysis is developed, analyst and patient might think of something as having happened in the past. This obscures the fact that we exist only in the present . . . What makes the adventure of psychoanalysis so difficult is that a constantly changing personality speaks to another, which is also changing. The changes are not obvious from a sensorial perspective; however, this is only appearance. We are, as Heraclites states, in a river that flows.

What is relevant is the direction of memory or desire, which will indicate the sense of the change. Sense in mathematical terms: if the arrow goes towards the past ($\leftarrow$) the direction is toward a search for causes, or of saturated memories, as "things in themselves". The direction towards the future ($\rightarrow$) indicates evolution and a use as a preconception (The Grid). The only time in which we can live is the present; past and future are two observation vertices from a reversible perspective. The introduction of direction extends the psychoanalytical theory, indicating the direction of the evolution: growth or deterioration.

Psychoanalysis deals with non-sensorial objects. We all know what it is when we speak of anxiety, love, envy, etc. There needs to be something invariant to establish differences between feelings. But emotions lack sensory qualities inherent to them, such as colours to the eyes, or sounds to the ears. The emotions find their form in emotional experiences, being embodied in flavours, scents, colours. How do we differentiate the "the thing" from the "no-thing", and the "no-thing" from the sensorial form that houses it? Bion is looking for an instrument that can reveal configurations. He finds it in part in myths and models, which he suggests have a digestive, metabolizing function for emotional experiences: "If there is such a thing as a mental digestive system, I could say that the mental diet of entertaining fictitious characters has contributed greatly to my mental health" (Bion, 1979 (1991), p. 124).

Myths and *models* operate as a bridge between theory and clinic, articulating them in such a way that theory does not acquire the feature of an empty jargon and clinical observations do not become *ad hoc* theories. In the use of myths and models, Bion finds an original solution that harmonizes with the idea of catastrophic change. They are a good container for moving through crises and to provide an adequate container–contained relationship. They can be transformed in preconceptual models with the same function for emotional experiences, which Freud attributed to attention for the outside world. The analyst can use them, both for thinking psychoanalytic problems outside the session and in the way of artificially constructed dreams that stimulate the development of the patient's alpha function.

Bion privileges construction over interpretation. Myths, tales, legends, etc., are like a gallery of "verbal pictures" which, used as preconceptual, not saturated models are nets receptive to the clinical fact that is evolving.

To differentiate a scientific inquiry in psychoanalysis (which requires the combination of disposition to know with compassion) from an operation of cold rationality, Bion uses the paradox of making a model of the first scientists as the tomb raiders that, moved by voracity and/or courage, and curiosity, challenged the "ghosts" of the primitive mind buried at Ur. Scientific inquiry in psychoanalysis requires imagination and courage to confront the turbulences that stir when we approach living archaic vestiges or prenatal aspects of the mind.

The psychoanalytical vertex should not be limited to the consulting room: the exploration of group phenomena is more than necessary. Bion never abandoned his interest in what he learned from his "experiences in groups". *Humanity is at a vulnerable point, having a premature, gifted, and rudimentary mind, yet still has not acquired the wisdom to use it in a way that preserves life and evolution.* Given the evidence we have of the greedy actions that are destroying the planet, of the emotional forces that push towards banality, towards fanaticism, or the search for "gods" to worship and to avoid the experiences of helplessness, Bion warns us that the human species might be one more of "Nature's discarded experiments".

In *The Past Presented* (Volume 2), the different aspects of the mind, as characters and observation vertices that alternate, attempt to hold a disciplined discussion, as required by the development of thought and the capacity for scientific thought.

To the characters in Volume 1 are added *the priest, the doctor, the scientist, PA* (psychoanalyst), *the Devil, the psychoanalyst's ghost, the ghost of Auser* (an officer and companion of Bion, who died in the first World War), *Du,* a character precursory of the somites of Volume 3, and a potential dream-thought element.

The characters show that it is possible to realize new experiences, transforming the observation vertex and to accede to ideas that "come from the future", if the group context, the tradition, the form in which the experiences are organized in the personality, in the group, in the society, can be used as containers of the new idea.

When he interposes 500 years as a *caesura* between the funeral of the Royal Court of Ur and the "tomb raiders", Bion places a *caesura* of time. Will it be enough to stimulate evolution towards catastrophic change? Can the challenge of the "ghosts-beliefs" be achieved by putting in contact different times, different layers of the mind? The development of a scientific inquiry and the development of new ideas is related to the problem of the absent object, or the no-thing, the zero, in mathematical terms. Klein thought that when the absent breast is not tolerated, it is transformed and lived as the presence of a bad object. Bion, in turn, thinks that the intolerance of the absent object transforms it in the concrete "ghostly" existence of the non-existent, such as in sensations of the "ghost" mutilated limb. Taking Bishop Berkeley's criticism of Newton, in which the former speaks of "ghosts of departed quantities", Bion suggests that there are foetal ideas that can be assassinated, and this is not just a metaphor. Metaphors can be the ghosts of ideas yet to be born, and not only ghosts of departed quantities.

The Dawn of Oblivion (Volume 3) deals with the problem "of the disastrous encounter between a potentially gifted foetal mind and its divorced but equally gifted postnatal self". The problem is presented as a trip that is undertaken by the character EM-mature (not im-mature), the embryonic mind in the process of becoming.

> This book is an psycho-embryonic attempt of writing an embryo-scientific account of a journey from birth to death overwhelmed by pre-mature knowledge, experience, glory and self-intoxicating self-satisfaction. [Bion, 1979 (1991), p. 429]

"Prenatal thoughts" are potentialities for development. They are not only ghosts of quantities that were, as they can also cast their shadows towards the future and cross caesuras towards an artistic transformation. The division and dialogue among different mental layers, among different "facts", different realities, may turn into a growth. Interpretation of the "somatic" reality and the sub-thalamic terror is different from the interpretation of a dream as Freud understood it. The Postnatals, with their embryonic mind, have the problem of crossing caesuras in each point of crisis, points in which catastrophic change seems imminent.

Man's future depends on the disposition to receive thoughts without a thinker and of their transformation into anticipatory thought and wisdom through discernment.

At the end of the trilogy, we find a glossary, The Key, that, just like the book, stimulates our capacity to tolerate unknowns and of making our own transformations. The L (love), H (hate) and K (knowledge) links are also keys that the analyst can use, in the way that a key in a musical score is used to "interpret" the "music" of the session.

It is not possible "to study" this trilogy as an intellectual exercise. The experience of reading it in a group, with each one of the participants "playing" the different characters, as well as group discussions of the ideas created by this "play", is an experience that favours the stimulus that *A Memoir of the Future* offers for mental growth.

Bion invites the reader to live the emotional experience of a state of mind open to inquiry and to tolerance of a discipline of eschewing memory, desire, and understanding. This mental state, which he proposes as a technical device for the analyst, implies eliminating possible obstacles to the evolution of the "catastrophic" dimension of the change. The characters and the dramatic play are a new contribution to psychoanalytic technique that facilitates the building of a container–contained relationship appropriate for developing tolerance of the transformations towards O and towards K, going through O many times in the process of becoming one with oneself. It is related to the courage of confronting the risk of transformations towards O, of the contact with the "psychotic" or prenatal part of the personality and of the turbulence that is generated by the meeting between two personalities, or of two parts of the same personality.

CHAPTER SEVEN

2001: A Space Odyssey

"PA: Even if individual humans are separated by Time, Space, Deity . . . this barrier is penetrable by forces whose understanding is beyond the range of our logical, rational modes of thought.

Alice: Such as . . .?

PA: Speculative imagination, speculative reason. André Green has pointed out that there may be something about the dramatic art 'form' which is perspicuous . . ."

(Bion, 1991, p. 539)

"I claim (the claim itself being definitory) that this is a fictitious account of psycho-analysis including an artificially constructed dream; definitory status is also claimed for the constructions of wakefulness, scientific alertness and scientific theory. . . . with Kant, I hold that the thing-in-itself is unknowable. Falstaff, a known artefact, is more 'real' in Shakespeare's verbal formulation than countless millions of people who are dim, invisible, lifeless, unreal, whose birth, death—alas, even marriages—we are called upon to believe in, though certification of their existence is vouched for by

said official certification. . . . Nor do I believe that 'science'—
smoke drums, statistics and other apparatus usually assumed
to belong to the domain of science—would ever bring them
to life or breathe life into them"

(Bion, 1991, pp. 4–5)

A psychoanalytical session is an ineffable emotional experience, shared by patient and analyst by means of observing
and discovering what kind of experience it is and finding
its meaning. Developing thought and insight into this experience,
and to follow the evolution of its meaning, offers a unique opportunity for mental growth to both members of the analytic pair.

The analytical experience has something in common with the
primary relationship of reverie, as an experience that favours the
process of understanding, giving meaning, and assimilation of
experiences thus transformed to the personality. One difference
lies, however, in the fact that an analysis implies the meeting of
two personalities already formed which carry the burden of those
"deformations" built throughout their lives, which are also the
object of the psychoanalytical investigation. The analyst's analysis
is a factor of his personality for developing insight and thought
about himself; thus, he is able to maintain in good form a binocular vision constituted by an awareness in floating association with
an unconscious capable of "dreaming".

From my point of view, the psychoanalytical experience shares
with the artistic one the development of an aesthetic dimension of
the mind. One of the constitutive factors of this dimension is the
transformation of primitive emotional experiences into "dreams",
myths, etc. (See also Chapters Two and Three.) Together with this
similarity, however, there is a difference in the fact that, in artistic
transformation, the space of externalization is the one chosen by the
artist: painting, music, etc.

I emphasize the space factor, because I think that on the
balanced relationship between the process of projection–introjection, facilitated by alpha function, depends both the constitution
of a space of psychic reality and a space of external reality. (See also
Chapter Three.) This development of the notion of space and of a
notion of time in which the present is in relation with a past—that

is no longer there—and with a future—that has not yet arrived—implies a tolerance of the relation between the thing and the nothing. The difference between map and territory is central for the construction of a space of psychic reality.

In psychoanalytic practice, the space for externalization is created and recreated in the *caesura* of the transference–countertransference relationship. In this space lies the possibility of meeting with catastrophic change, insight, and with becoming oneself (at-one-ment). Psychoanalyst and patient alike have to develop thought and confront their ideas in a medium of high temperature and turbulence, stimulated by the transference–countertransference relationship.

In some previous chapters, especially Chapters Three and Four, I began to work out the idea that, besides the technical tools of the setting and the discipline of negative capability, personification and the use of models or fictionalizations of the primitive emotional experiences that lack a sensorial form constitute other appropriate technical instruments which contribute to the creation of a space of psychic reality. In Chapter Eight, I formulate a theory in the same regard about the function of play.

In this chapter, I also want to propose the conjecture that culture generates, mainly from the artistic vertex, formulations of emotional experiences which enter into diverse forms of interaction with emotional experiences of different personalities and groups. These transformations of emotional experiences develop a function which is equivalent to reverie: of detoxification, providing meaning, allowing for production of enunciations which then can be used for thinking.

In what follows, I propose to show the use of the resource of films, tales, etc., as models or in the manner of "dreams and myths" in the framework of the psychoanalytical *scientific investigation*.

Science-fiction

These terms science and fiction—conjugated with psychoanalysis—acquire new meaning: *as two vertices for approaching facts of psychic reality*, which provide a *binocular vision*. Science-fiction helps to develop imaginative conjectures and exercise imagination, like mathematicians when they develop formulas which, at first, have no practical application, but in the future may become instruments for new discoveries, as happened, for example, with projective geometry. Imaginative conjectures have instrumental value in psychoanalysis, the value of non-saturated preconceptions that can be used to approach future realizations. That is also one of the values of the use of dreams and myths as models in the psycho-analytical practice, as non-*saturated* forms that incarnate emotional forces and that *can be used as algebraic unknowns in psychoanalytical investigation.*

A model for the birth of mental space can be that of a Big Bang-type explosion. The thinking and the development of the mind begins with an explosion of primitive emotions through projective identification which, as a primitive communication, works like a probe, a seeker of an object with which this form of communication is possible. If the seeker finds a detoxifying and transformational container, the possibility of development of thought and mental growth will be generated. I propose stardust as a model for think-ing about this explosion, which needs an appropriate container to stop the dispersion and produce a transformation in a medium that facilitates the formation of constellations of thought.

The point of generation of thought would be the moment in which the primitive prenatal emotions "escape", for fear of annihi-lation, into the external space, to meet with the object with which exploration and primitive communication is possible, a space that provides sensorial forms as well as a potential provider of analogies where the primitive emotion can be embodied. I propose, as a conjecture, as well, to think of the transferential space as this exter-nal space, which is not only a space for defensive escape from primitive anxieties, but also of potential transformations, where analogies as an instrument can be forged, which can then be used to turn the direction of exploration inwards. The "dramatic form" is an achieved means of "personification", which delineates think-able configurations in a mental universe in which configurations and "stardust" without form exist, as in the astronomical nebulae. In the analytic session, the material that evolves towards the patient's O, like this formless stardust, can find its "dramatic" forms and thus open up the possibility of investigating them in a context of play.

I will use the film *2001: A Space Odyssey* (director Stanley Kubrick) to illustrate the *caesuras* that have to be traversed in the road towards insight, which I also described in Chapter Five. This is a *science fiction* film. This genre *profiles the future, implying the need to project the present into the future with the aid of imaginative conjectures*. The best films of this genre outline and offer a digestion of different situations that produce "new discontents in civilization". Kubrick was also the director of *A Clockwork Orange,* and other films which capture these new "discontents", where powerful emotional forces emerge under the form Bion called "Vogue"*. In *Cogitations* (Bion, 1992, p. 374), this expression does not mean fashion, but something invariant of the mind and of the human being's primitive groupishness, which takes on different forms in different cultures. These differences in the ways of expressing the invariant primitive emotional experiences show that there is a difference in the forms, related with their affinity to different historical moments and cultures, which create forms in which these invariants are expressed. The transformations in music or in language show this "vogue", which might not be understood, or even sound agreeable, from one generation to another. Nowadays (in the twenty-first century), any adolescent analyst from another generation has the experience of the need to construct a dictionary, asking their patients what they mean by certain words, since their modes of expression and their meanings are peculiar to the adolescent world and unfamiliar to us.

This film shows how scientific development implies an evolution of consciousness and of potentialities for thinking, and it also makes evident how each step in the process of humanization and maturation reveals new limitations, profound helplessness, and new problems to be solved.

The intolerance of the mental pain produced by thinking without certainties, the loneliness implied in the development of a separate mind and becoming one with oneself, lies in the roots of the conflict between scientific thinking, as a method to face mental pain (which means respect for reality principle), and a system of beliefs, deceits, and lies. When society and the culture that prevails are not aware of this problem as a conflict, often it takes the form of a "war" between religious beliefs and scientific discoveries. "Society has not yet been driven to seek treatment of its psychological disorders by psychological means because it has not yet achieved sufficient insight to appreciate the nature of its distress" (Bion, 1961, p. 14).

Nowadays, we can also witness how often the development and acceptance of the psychoanalytic insights of the functioning of the human mind are avoided, through what seems a dispute between "objective scientific technology" and "subjective psychoanalytical discoveries", or changes in artistic movements.

As I have already described in previous chapters, this avoidance is associated with a super-superego that only conceives relationships of superiority–inferiority (Bion, 1962), which usually leads to a process of inanimation of that which is animated or which, in today's civilization, masks simian skills with technology and deifies them. Sometimes, technology seems to be the graveyard of metaphors, which have the *reverie function* that help the process of metabolization of mental pain.

Films such as *Odessey* attempt to assimilate and digest the catastrophic changes that confront the human being with his possibilities and his helplessness, transforming into "images", into "dreams", the new discovered perspectives. By means of a creative transformation, this work of art also tries to assimilate what these new insights reveal, through the development of a consciousness capable of becoming aware of man's destructive and predatory aspects. They have a quality of "reverie" in contrast with the omnipotent "deification" of technology.

In 1958, the Soviets launched the first space satellite, the Sputnik, and in 1969 the USA achieved sending a man to the moon for the first time. This was carried out in the context of a powerful rivalry, which, because of the degree of technological development, threatened to make life on earth disappear. Also, through these scientific achievements, it was the first time that man had a perspective of his planet from outer space, and so he starts to have not only a new observation vertex of his planet, but also of himself.

Neothenia and the dawn of man

In Volume 3 of *A Memoir of the Future*, Bion describes man's neothenia, considering that the scientific development of the mind is still embryonic and that, in his voyage from birth to death, man is oppressed by premature knowledge, a prematurity which, in turn, can stimulate megalomaniac feelings of glory and self-intoxicating satisfaction. The mind is the instrument that has evolved in the human being, but has still not found a wise container to contain this change.

This is illustrated time and again in the film, which also shows the difficulties of achieving a symbiotic container–contained relationship, of mutual benefit, between the contained (the potentialities of this new instrument) and the container (the mind, still rudimentary for developing with wisdom a containing task instead of monkey-like shrewdness). Wisdom, here, means respect for the mysteries and for our ignorance. Wisdom, in the use of the potentialities of the human being's mind, cannot provide food for omnipotent beliefs; thus, it competes at a disadvantage with technological hypertrophy, and this threatens to destroy the species and the planet.

The dawn of man

The film illustrates from different vertices (musical, visual, and dramatic) the Odyssey (a citation of Odysseus's voyage) of humanization. It is an Odyssey that goes from the primitive mind which traverses a *caesura* towards the capacity of representation, towards a development of instruments, of communication media, and of technological intelligence. The film begins with the music of the symphonic poem of Richard Strauss "Thus Spake Zarathustra", based on Nietzsche's text. The same musical theme reappears with different images, and the conjunction of the musical and visual vertices narrates "the Dawn of Man" without words.

At the beginning of the film, we see images of the planet Earth seen from the earth; the final scene is an image of the planet seen from outer space. In the initial image, the Earth is seen flat, with natural landscapes; there is nothing artificial made by "arte-fact". The landscape is arid and the horizon is a marked presence. These images are worked with a great angular lens, and they underline the vastness of the immense world which contains its inhabitants, product of the evolution from the inanimate towards the animate: there is scarce vegetation, monkeys that live in flocks, tapirs, and the predator.

These images illustrate a relationship between a container (a width that wraps something that is the newly emerging) and a content (the different forms of life).

There are few elements: stones, the fought-over water, and the presence of the stocky and poor vegetation. It is an austere, dry world that is naked, as are the hominid-monkeys which live together in flocks. They are herbivores, and easy prey for predators. We see helplessness and defencelessness.

The resources for survival are few. A scene shows their helplessness in the dispute over the water well: attacked by another flock of monkeys, their only weapons are screams and gesticulations: the one that screams the loudest and makes the most menacing gestures is able to terrify the opponent and keeps the source of water. Screams and gestures are manifestations of their being animals, and of the primitive groupishness that openly expresses their emotions. The separation between perception and action has not come about. (See Chapter Eight.)

The following scene shows the *dread during the night*: the camera pans, showing faces, and stops on the eyes of the monkeys inside the cave. Outside the predator waits. There is no music here: silence contrasts with terror. A mother monkey hugs her little one; the image is of everyone equally terrified and defenceless without differentiation between adults and youngsters.

The awakening of intelligence and appearance of the monolith

In the following scene, day breaks. The flock has been able to sleep in the cave and a sound of voices or growing wailings awakes them. This "music" is associated with *the appearance of the monolith that marks catastrophic change*. It belongs to the contemporary composer Giörgy Ligeti; it would not have been understood as music in previous centuries and it is a Requiem, in the part of Kyrie Eleïson (Lord, have mercy on us). The music, which contains voices and wailings, marks the contrast with the grunts and primitive screams; it marks the appearance of language as a form of communication. The music chosen by Kubrick is a religious music, and it underlines that, with the process of humanization, religiosity arises.

In *The Future of an Illusion* (1927c), Freud says, referring to religion, that a great step has been won in the humanization of nature with myths, which imply the transformation of impersonal forces and the uncertainties of destiny, so unaware of man's measure, into god-elements that have passions and furies like the human soul. Through this process, death itself is transformed from a spontaneous, unavoidable situation, into punishment, or a violent act of a wicked deity.

The monolith is a geometric, polished object: it is an artefact. It is produced by an intelligent being and the fact of its geometric characteristic reveals a high degree of abstraction achieved in the development of thinking.

The monolith marks the catastrophic change represented by the development of intelligence, of the capacity of being aware, and of manufacturing instruments. It is an instrument that comes from the future to meet with the past (the primitive groupishness and the ancestral terrors) and in the present is a mystery that awakens curiosity and adoration. It can be thought, as we sometimes think of psychoanalysis, as an instrument that comes from the future, with mysterious potentialities that stimulates man's curiosity about himself, and through revealing his primitive emotions and helplessness, stimulates hate and adoration alternately or simultaneously.

I want to remind the reader that, for Bion, geometry expresses, on the one hand, the achievement of a detoxification of primitive emotions (which means that the painful emotions have been made tolerable), and therefore that the two mental functions—oscillation PS$\Leftrightarrow$D and $\male\,\female$—operate complimentarily and in co-operation. These functions are an important step towards the transformation of a space, occupied with primitive projective identifications, into a space that is a container of representations. The Oedipal situation, transformed into the representation of a geometric triangle, is in turn converted into an instrument of thinking. It also contains angles from which the relationship can be observed.

The monkeys approach the monolith with fear, reverence, and curiosity. The mind has been born, with its capacity for curiosity, and also of fear and reverence that, in the process of humanization, will develop the different vicissitudes of the helplessness–omnipotence pair.

The birth of the capacity for representation and the discovery of the instrument

In the following scene, we see the flock of monkeys in an ossuary. One of them takes a bone and observes it; he tries hitting other bones with it. The music of "Thus Spake Zarathustra" marks the *discovery*: when using the bone to explore and to strike, the monkey, for the first time, has the representation of the death of the tapir. *He has taken a momentous step: something can be represented in absence of the object.*

This step produces an enormous transformation in these herbivorous and defenceless animals. This transformation of potentialities implies both creative development and increasing the powers of destructiveness.

In the next scene, we see the former herbivores transformed into carnivores. *The discovery of the individual becomes the experience of the group. The possibility of killing and co-operation within the group are potentialities that are developed.* They kill other animals and eat meat. The following scene shows *the development of learning from experience and transgenerational transmission: a little monkey, helped by an adult, explores a bone.*

Next, one can see the development in the use of the instrument: again, it is the fight over water. This time there are not only screams and gesticulations: the new instrument, the bone, is used to kill a rival. *The groupishness in the film is marked: not only one monkey kills the rival, but all of them take turns and practise hitting the fallen animal, who is probably already dead.*

Transcending the caesura

In the next scene, the monkey lifts the bone with an expression of triumph, accompanied by the music of "Thus Spake Zaratusthra", music that here sounds victorious and impacting. The bone, a femur, is thrown into the space, and is transformed into a spaceship, a new instrument. At first the ship is shown in the stellar space in silence, like the silence of the first images of the surface of terrestrial space. *The contrast between the vastness of space, now stellar space, and the solitary ship that it contains is repeated. It is a wide, unknown, containing space, and the ship, an instrument, a very sophisticated content, is shown against the dark immensity full of stars, once again contrasting what is artificial and nature. The instrument can also be considered an illustration of thought already formed.*

The music now is "The Blue Danube", accompanying the movements of the ship and the space station, which goes round in space.

"The Blue Danube" seems to cradle the flight of the ship, viewed from the exterior. With the same music, the space station, a gigantic wheel, is shown going round in space. Its interior seems serene. *This placidness contrasts with the hostility and the turbulence, outside and inside, of the first part of the film. This peacefulness is partly a constructed appearance that cosmetically masks the turbulence.*

The film shows the new habitat without gravity. Floyd sleeps calmly and somebody takes care of him. This contrasts with the sleeping of the monkeys, as does the music with the roars and grunts. *In the film there is also a contrast of the sophisticated technology, the rules of courtesy, and the music, all of which we could call postnatal, with the prenatal, foetal figures and birth-like forms.* The voluminous hats of the women seem to mark the growth of the brain's capacity. *The penetration of the ship inside the space station illustrates a container–contained relationship (♂ ♀) without conflict, without turbulence.*

The arrival at the space station marks civilization. Identification is made through *articulate verbal language* that contrasts with the grunts and screams. It is a powerful instrument, able to transmit information. As I described in Chapter Four, however, it is necessary to be alert against how deceiving it can be, and how dangerous that we, as psychoanalysts, ignore other uses of language, more in the service of the primitive groupishness and as evacuation.

The notion *of time and of absence* makes its appearance: Floyd says that he was absent for eight months.

The scenes inside the orbiting station show the invention of an artifice: courtesy, almost mechanical, ritual. The encounter with the Soviets is diplomatic, without edges. There is no music, their voices are heard, everything in soft tones. This is evidenced in the conversation between Floyd and the Soviets, and in the phone conversation between Floyd and his daughter. The courtesy and the distance mask the conflicts and the emotional turbulences. The little daughter sounds like an adult in miniature. She asks her dad to come for her birthday. Floyd tells her, "You already know that dad has to work," and appeases her by offering a gift.

The secret also is hidden with a *lie* (the supposed epidemic), *the language has developed something that was potential: the capacity for deceit. The open rivalry of the monkeys over the source of water becomes a masked rivalry.*

Traveling towards clavius: the technological development

In the following scene, we see again images of the interstellar space and a spaceship heading to the moon. The contrasts are repeated: a sophisticated interior, elaborated technologically for adaptation to the lack of gravity. The perspective from the exterior shows the anthropomorphic form of the ship: a gigantic head, windows that look like eyes with a menacing form open up, some technical "feet" stretch out and extend, preparing for the moon landing, arms like claws also extend. *The developed technology has its roots in the human body.* The projection in tools of body images is a first step in the elaboration of instruments.

Psychoanalysts, who have investigated the deep emotional implications of the relation between the body image and the invention of tools, understand this anthropomorphism, which is also made evident by the obvious fact that all units of measure were expressed first in terms of feet, inches, cubits, etc.

Images of the arid rocky soil of the moon, and the need to use helmets to be in the exterior atmosphere, are shown. I think that, in this part, the film "digests" the arrival of the man at the moon and its implications. The landing on the moon shows very sophisticated devices and everything is grey and mechanical, but, in the sequence of the entrance, red blood appears, representing a human connotation.

Second appearance of the monolith

In the next sequence, we see a sober and very civilized office. There is a meeting in which Floyd cuts short all questioning, all restlessness, owing to the unknowns presented by the monolith. Within a BA dependence group functioning, he says that secrecy is necessary to avoid culture shock and social disorientation if news is spread prematurely, and also to allow an important discovery in the history of science. Floyd demands an oath of loyalty to keep the secret: he receives formal plaudits and approval as a BA leader.

The office and the formality contrast with the climate of suspense and terror as the monolith approaches. We find out that it is something that comes from four million years ago and that it has been buried deliberately.

The funeral, the funeral rituals also mark a point of inflection, a catastrophic change in the process of humanization: they mark the point of becoming aware of death.

It is interesting that, when the monolith first shows up, it comes from outer space, and in this sequence now, it is something that is unburied after having been deliberately buried. Consciousness has evolved, and intelligence has developed and can both bury and exhume. To be able to do this it is necessary to traverse caesuras. (See also Chapters Three and Five.)

The arrival at the monolith this time is marked in the film as an entrance to a buried interior, as opposed to the first time, in which the monkeys exited the cave. *We can think of it as the representation of the constitution of an unconscious starting from the birth of a consciousness able to be aware. It can also be thought of as the illustration of the construction of a contact barrier, starting from the possibility of transforming raw data, beta elements, into alpha elements. With these new tools it is possible to start a scientific investigation.* When they go down the ramp they do not seem to be afraid. Floyd approaches the monolith, explores it, and the image lingers on his glove. It seems to evoke the hand of the monkey, when, in the first appearance, it touches the monolith in a climate of awe and religious reverence.

Development of the instrument: the appearance of Hal in the scenario

Eighteen months later (double the time of a pregnancy) a spaceship in anthropomorphic form is heading to Jupiter. In its interior a new instrument, the computer Hal, is becoming aware of himself. We can think of it as the picture of megalomania, owing to intoxication with the achievements of scientific developments.

Kubrick shows a routine of comfort in the ship and a higher degree of emotional disconnection: the scientists hibernate in a dream without "dreams"; in the scene of the phone call, and through images, Frank's family speaks of daily things, and wishes him a happy birthday, celebrating with a cake as if Frank were not millions of miles away.

The computer (representing technological developments), whose brain imitates the human brain, is in charge of everything, manages the ship, and at the same time seems to be at the service of the astronauts. It could illustrate the powerful emotional forces that demand a new god to worship. In the next sequence, it is going to manifest the arrogance of the psychotic part of the personality. A journalistic interview shows him as infallible, unable to commit errors. Hal is asked if sometimes he feels frustrated, and he defines himself as a conscious being, unable to make a mistake. It is an arrogant answer that sounds like the infallibility of a god. The astronauts, like human beings, are shown as not questioning their "god", in whom they believe and assume is at their service. The journalist asks the astronaut if Hal has emotions, and he answers that he does not know, like someone who has no reason to be concerned over that. The journalist claims to have noticed a certain pride in Hal's voice when he proclaims his infallibility. The astronaut seems indifferent to the question. He does not seem to be afraid, nor is there emotional turbulence inside the ship. The life of everyone, including those of the hibernating scientists, depends on Hal.

Hal beats Frank at a game of chess: here, also, he shows his arrogance and shows the weak human being his mistakes. But Hal also asks Frank if there is some secret about this mission that he, Hal, does not know. Maybe, he says, he is projecting his anxiety, but that there are strange things on this mission, there are rumors of something exhumed on the moon that he finds difficult to leave aside. It is a moment of great tension in the film, which could illustrate the manifestation of some not-so-omniscient aspect.

Interesting to point out is the moment that Hal announces that there is a flaw in a part of the ship and that it will stop working. The tension grows, and the soft voice of Hal begins to acquire a sinister sound. We will know, little by little, that Hal, who does not tolerate the suspicion that he is not so omnipotent or omniscient, as represented by the unrevealed secret, becomes a sinister and disconnected murderer without any consideration for life or respect for truth. From then on, a climate of rivalry emerges between "God", who seems to be capable of everything, and the human being, who, little by little, and with great pain, begins to regain, through experience and the ability to think it, a consciousness of its limitations and possibilities.

Frank and Dave communicate with home base, which advises them to change the part. This means a dangerous exit to the outside, controlled by Hal, the one on whom they depend. For the first time a new sound arises, that of the breathing of someone who depends on a machine in order to do so; this breathing was used in the film *Star Wars* for the character of Darth Vader, who depends on a machine to breathe and on an armoured outer shell to live.

Again the anthropomorphic and foetal forms of the ship appear, images of birth, and a red spot, as if it were blood. The astronauts float in space, with their heads down, as does the foetus when in the birth position, and performing, at the same time, a very complex and risky task. I think that it is a good illustration of neothenia, of prematurity. The extreme dependence on Hal, even for breathing, the machine-God, omnipotently infallible, and the technological complexity of the task, illustrates a container–contained ($\male\female$) relationship, in which the contained, the technological instrument, became an omnipotent container, undoubtedly inadequate for the emotional contents. It illustrates how sophisticated technology, based on simian abilities without being aware of the limitations of a finite–infinite relationship, is an inadequate and dangerous container for mental growth.

Relationship minus container–contained ($-\male\female$): Hal becomes a shrewd liar and a murderer

The astronauts return, they test the part, and they find no flaws. From the base, they warn the astronauts that Hal's twin did not find any error. The base can represent the thinking human part that has not totally deified the machine. Hal, as in a cold chess move, advises returning outside and putting the part back in its place and momentarily interrupting communication with the base. This interruption, which is accepted, represents the disconnection between the psychotic part, or the BA automatic group obedience, of the thinking part of the personality. It illustrates how primitive groupishness maintains the belief that this manner of functioning is the basis of vital sustenance.

The spectator perceives the increasing atmosphere of helplessness and the conflict between accepting dependence on Hal or developing thinking. The astronauts ask Hal the reason for the discrepancy between him and his twin. Hal answers with arrogance that it is always due to a human error. The men persist with their question, as does Hal in the matter of his infallibility.

The two men are able to get out of the mental state of BA dependence and become aware that something is wrong, so they manage to speak in private about the problem without being overheard by Hal. But Hal, the primitive and technologically sophisticated mind, is astute. He reads their lips and finds out that they are planning to disconnect him. In an analysis, this is a very delicate and difficult moment, in which the patient needs to be able to tolerate the pain of becoming aware of the "arrogant madness" on which, until then, he had depended, and face the conflict of accepting dependence on human capacity for thinking, his own and that of his analyst. It is a moment of catastrophic change or of catastrophe.

The conversation shows that Frank and Dave left the BA dependence and recovered their capacity for thought, of intelligence harmonized with intuition which leads to mental growth: "I feel that something bad is going on", "I feel something strange", they say. They plan to disconnect Hal's "arrogant thought" systems without disturbing the automatic systems. They decide, however, to go outside and restore the part. Something fails in their capacity to think, they intuit that something is wrong with Hal, and simultaneously, in a dissociated manner, they make the decision of going into interstellar space, without realizing that this implies depending totally on Hal.

This sequence illustrates the problem of a commensal container–contained relationship: the intuition and the decision to disconnect Hal's "thought" systems are not confronted with the fact of depending on him for the exit into outer space. It also illustrates an Establishment that has not appropriately made the separation between the infinite and transcendent God and the finite man. (See also Chapter Five).

The transformation of Hal from an instrument, a content, into what is now a murderous container, and Frank and Dave's decision to depend on him for their exit into outer space, as a content, illustrates the parasitic minus container–contained $(-\male\,\female)$ relationship (Bion,1962). Also the decision of the astronauts, blind to that part of the problem, illustrates the difficulty of leaving the BA mentality of dependence to make contact with the helplessness. Leaving the BA mentality means abandoning blind belief in the omnipotence and omniscience of the God-computer and confronting the need to resolve problems through the capacity for thinking, with its correlates of uncertainty, doubts, and tolerance of chance.

Awareness of being alone, helplessness, and development of a capacity for thinking

Frank leaves the ship to restore the part; the camera shows the gigantic eye of Hal, which throws the astronaut into the immensity of outer space. Dave, still operating under a mental state of splitting—he asks Hal what is happening, and gets as an answer that Hal does not know—leaves to look for his fellow astronaut.

While he is rescuing Frank in a very striking scene of solidarity, co-operation and compassion (features in the step of humanization and of work group functioning), the camera shows Hal's gigantic red eye, which disconnects and kills the hibernating scientists. Hibernation is interestingly described to the journalists as a dreamless sleep. Perhaps Kubrick, with his great intuition, is alerting us here to the catastrophic consequences of a splitting between technological scientific thought and a capacity to "dream" which reveals to us the meanings and implications of what we think and of our acts.

Dave orders Hal to open the door: Hal denies him access, in a soft, courteous, and monotonous voice. Dave insists on his order (while he holds his companion in his arms). He finds it difficult to accept the facts and what he apprehends with his intuition. Hal says that he read their lips and knows about the decision to disconnect him, and he cannot allow that. Dave decides to use the only resource that does not depend on Hal: the emergency door. This resource means that Dave is thinking, and represents what can be rescued from the automatic group functioning that Bion associates with "oughtism" and the super-superego, which is the murderer of the capacity for thinking and for dreaming. I think that, when he speaks of the realm of what "ought to" be, Bion makes a pun with automatism.

Hal says cynically to Dave (−K link) that he will not manage to enter, because he does not have a helmet. Dave makes decisions: he lets go of his dead companion and enters through the emergency door. In that entrance he seems to cross a channel again, a *caesura* of birth, of psychic birth.

The tolerance of what is chosen, the making of decisions, is one of the factors in the matrix function of thinking, the PS⇔D oscillation.

Catastrophic change

The camera shows Dave with a simple instrument, a screwdriver, penetrating significantly inside Hal. That interior has a red blood colour, the same as that of Hal's eye.

That penetration can represent the psychoanalytical penetration into man's inside, disconnecting intellectual, mechanical, and arrogant thought systems with no concern for life, and making evident, at the same time, the emotions. *It has the meaning of transcending a caesura, this time in the direction to the interior and to meet with the emotions, not in the primitive way in which the monkeys experimented with it at the beginning: this is an encounter with the awareness of pain. These emotions are being exposed as Dave goes on disconnecting the functions dedicated to masking them: Hal changes the mechanical voice, pleading in a child's voice, "Don't do it, Dave, I am afraid", he repeats. Hal tries to convince Dave: in a pitiful voice he says shrewdly, still trying to manipulate, "Dave you are disturbed, you should sit down and take a pill for the tension." He also says something disturbing, which is evidenced when the caesura is traversed in the direction towards emotional contact: "My mind is leaving, I can feel it", which is equivalent to saying, "I can feel that I am becoming mad".*

This sequence could illustrate the experience often manifested by those patients who have been dependent throughout their lives, be it on shrewd manipulative manoeuvres, or on an equivalent of "inanimate technological resources", as happens in the emotional disconnection of autistic enclaves. They fear change, and experience as something catastrophic getting in contact with their emotions and feeling the need to develop other resources, as if it would mean a situation of helplessness.

Dave does not answer and can continue thinking, in spite of the manipulation. Dave, acting as a psychoanalyst would, when he can keep thinking, is finally able to rescue himself from the force of projective identification, provocative or evocative; he does not counteract, but, rather, continues using his capacity for thinking. What is shown now is that the arrogant infallibility of Hal masks a helpless and dependent being, who remembers who had manufactured him and sings an infantile song. What is exposed is the other side of arrogant omnipotence: dependence, emotions, and the feeling of helplessness. In the human being, this happens with the realization of being the child born of parents who had sexual intercourse and who gave him life. Meltzer (1973) maintains that, among adolescent pathologies, the most disturbing is he who believes himself self-engendered and does not recognize his origins in relation to his parents.

This precipitates a new catastrophic change: a message is revealed saying that the mission is to investigate the monolith on Jupiter.

In the evolution towards maturity it seems necessary to dismantle omniscient and omnipotent functioning, with the equivalent of an artisan instrument—such as is psychoanalysis, which lacks mechanical tools—to give rise to a new mental growth, facing the infinite–finite relationship this time

A new catastrophic change: third appearance of the monolith

The camera shows outer space and the reappearance of the monolith, floating there, accompanied by the music of Ligeti's Requiem. Again there is a sight of a sun, as if it were dawning, and of the anthropomorphic spaceship. The ship and the monolith cross each other in space. The ship comes near a planet, something opens up, and again the red colour appears, like a path, a new birth channel, inside which Dave falls. The camera shows his face that seems to take for moments the form of a foetus.

It is an entrance into the space–time dimension, and it illustrates the transcending of another *caesura*, which implies having access to a new kind of knowledge: as the one which gave rise to the discovery of the theory of relativity, dismantling the belief that Newton's mechanical physics was a certain, final, and absolute system.

What follows in the film appears to be representing the relationship between the possibility of accessing the notions of space and time and their functions as co-ordinates for developing a capacity for thinking and a consciousness capable of becoming aware. One can think that the crossing of the spaceship, which navigates in the infinite space, with the monolith, illustrating the human capacity for creating representations through language and music, also marks the access to a relationship between the infinite and the finite, which is necessary for developing a space of representation. Tolerance of this relationship between the finite Man and the infinite God is one of the factors in mental growth.

The camera shows the monolith, and a living form that can seem to be the iris of an eye or an embryo. Man is a predominantly visual being, and needs to be able to combine his capacity for representing in images, as in Euclidean geometry, with a capacity for abstraction, as achieved with invention of algebra.

There are allusions to a birth, images as of foetal membranes and shades as of a foetus in which the posterior part of the skull seems to be lengthening.

Many images seem to be powerful metaphors of the birth of life and of the Universe. There is a perspective of the Earth from outer space, and the forms of the continents, also changing and being divided. It is evolution, nothing is fixed or immobile, as it was in the mechanical perspective of the Universe. Images of landscapes are shown, as those seen in the beginning, but greener, and seen from the space vertex.

The form of the eye reappears, and also sounds like heartbeats are heard. Then a room is seen, with features and furniture like those of a human room.

Dave, in his astronaut suit, *man, astronaut, foetus,* arrives at a furnished room, with a bed; there is a luxurious bathroom, and a luminous floor. Pictures are on the walls and there are sculptures. The camera shows Dave standing, with wrinkles on his face (the passage of time), and on those details the silent camera stops. Dave looks at everything, he has developed the capacity for observation: the room has objects that are all made by man as he developed and moved beyond the cave. Has he arrived at the place that contains the already-familiar products, instruments of the development of the mind? Sounds, voices are heard. His eyes explore everything, in astonishment and fear. The next image is of the back of a man sitting at a table, eating. There is the noise of cutlery: new instruments, another achievement in evolution that contrasts with the monkeys of the flock eating meat with their hands and teeth.

The man stands up and turns round. He is very tall, with grey hair, and he has Dave's face. He is dressed in a *robe de chambre*, which contrasts with the nakedness of the monkeys and with the astronaut's space suit. The man looks, he seems to think, he returns to the table and sits down. He eats, he takes a glass, which then drops and breaks. He looks at the broken glass. I think that this scene represents the discovery of something that breaks irreversibly, once again the awareness of the passage of time. Time, as a fourth dimension in the human life cycle, is irreversible. Becoming aware of this feature means confronting pain, which often is avoided, as is evidenced in the live burial at Ur. The camera at that moment shows a man lying in bed, with wrinkles, bald, very small, as if shrunken. Transformed into a wrinkled old man, but seen from the vertex of the man who eats, the moribund man on the bed raises a hand, without strength, that points out towards something: the monolith is once again seen. The foetal membranes and the music of "Thus Spake Zarathustra" reappear.

A new caesura has been transcended, and in the relationship of the pair helplessness–protection a new catastrophic change has taken place. Has man become aware of the irreversibility of time and death?

In the evolution of science, Prygogine's ideas introduced the notion of the irreversibility of the time and of the possibility of new reorganizations. At the end of the film, that could be insinuated by the images of the planet–fetus, fetus–planet in transformation.

As we have seen in Chapter Five, evolution, mental growth in a psychoanalytical treatment, involves both members of the psychoanalytic pair. This requires the development of a separate mind with a notion of space and time, separated from the primitive groupishness that is not aware of the passage of time, a separation which is felt as leaving a vital base.

I will once again think of what evolution, mental growth, and becoming oneself mean. We are animals, which, throughout our evolution, have transformed themselves into predators. This condition has stimulated our intelligence and shrewdness. Have our emotions evolved at the same pace as our cortical developments? Levy Montalcini, Nobel Prize winner in neurosciences, in her book *In Praise of Imperfection*, speaks of the mismatch between the development of the limbic system, which governs the emotions, and that of the cortical system. The latter, unlike the former, has suffered mutations and is exposed to cultural influence.

What is our relationship with our primitive emotions like? Psychoanalysis has developed an investigation in this respect, although many times its scientific respectability has been questioned from the point of view of culture.

As psychoanalysts, we need to formulate questions in this regard. Do we owe gratitude to our predator aspects (Bion, 1970)? Does this mean that we owe our survival to them or that they are something that tends primitively towards life? The first representation shown in the film is the death of the tapir, which marks the development of thinking. If we can have gratitude for our predator aspects, can we renounce them in order to continue evolving? The infant who can accept weaning, with all that it implies, resigns using the breast and preying upon it with its projective identifications to continue with its mental growth. There is a time in which it depends on the mother's reverie function, as that which transforms its primitive emotions; there arrives a moment in which it is necessary to incorporate alpha function in order to evolve towards mental growth.

Gratitude towards our predatory aspects, and paying this debt, as formulated by Bion in *Attention and Interpretation*, is related to the difference between the two configurations on whose predominance our present and future evolution depends: (1) voracity and envy, and (2) envy and gratitude. The first one produces cancerous growth, proliferation of malignant fragmentations (splitting). There is not a multiplication of ideas, there is no creation, it is a single Maximum idea, which is not used as an instrument, but, rather, revered, and is divided in infinite fragmentation of the same thing. This Maximum idea always goes together with the reduction of the animate to the inanimate, which makes possible a lack of consideration for life and of respect for the truth. This kind of functioning is the seed of fanaticism (Sor & Senet, 1993). The combination is malignant; voracity and envy reinforce themselves mutually instead of moderating their deleterious effects.

The conjunction of envy and gratitude pays the debt to the predatory aspects, which allows getting out of the vicious circle of blame and atonement. Gratitude implies recognition, and, as a factor in a creative conjunction, not only stimulates towards reparation, which means giving up projective identification as a parasitic kind of relationship with the analytic breast, but also stimulates the evolution of the mind towards mental growth. The debt of gratitude for the recognition of the fact of having been "nourished" by maternal reverie and the analyst's alpha function is paid with evolution towards growth. It also implies recognition of the mother and the analyst as human beings.

This evolution of insight in psychoanalysis requires from the psychoanalyst the discipline of negative capability that is to be able to live between uncertainties, doubts, and mysteries. This implies recognition of his condition of being a fallible human and of reason being a slave to passions. Technology without wisdom is the heir of this reason, whose emotional roots remain unknown.

The "science-fiction" in psychoanalysis implies the development of imaginative conjectures and of personification, as we saw in Chapter Three, which, through embodying the emotional experiences in a space of "dramatic fiction", achieves the result that these experiences can be thought and housed in a space of psychic reality. The "dramatized" expression of these experiences, and perhaps the names of the experiences themselves, can be used to approach new experiences if they can be transformed into questions without answers, like unknowns, in a new turn of the spiral in evolution.

The science of psychoanalysis deals with an animate object and aims towards understanding and giving meaning to the facts of emotional life. This means that it is far from the measurement and technology of the world of inanimate objects. One way of giving dimensions to the psychoanalytic object is through aesthetic transformation. As it deals with an animate object, in psychoanalysis it is necessary to add to respect for the truth, shared with any other scientific approach, the consideration for life. As was explained in Chapter Five, this implies the development of something more than simian capacities and shrewdness.

The problem posed by the pair helplessness–protection has become ever more evident as man has evolved his capacity for awareness, as the film illustrates. The decision on which instruments the human species are going use to confront this awareness is uncertain. Once again, will the kinds of decisions incline the scale towards simian shrewd abilities, with the development of ever more sophisticated technologies? Or will it be possible for us to achieve wisdom, through the development of the capacity to feel and then think with prudence, transcending the caesuras towards insight, opening the road towards being one with oneself and becoming in at-one-ment.

CHAPTER EIGHT

The frozen autistic desert and the capacity to play: development of the aesthetic dimension of the mind

"To be or not to be: that is the question:
Whether 'tis nobler in the mind to suffer
The slings and arrows of outrageous fortune,
Or to take arms against a sea of troubles,
And by opposing end them? To die: to sleep;
No more; And, by a sleep to say we end
The heart-ache and the thousand natural shocks
The flesh is heir to, 'tis a consummation
Devoutly to be wished. To die, to sleep;
To sleep: perchance to dream: aye there is the rub;
For in that sleep of death what dreams may come
When we have shuffled off this mortal coil,
Must give us pause"

(Shakespeare, *Hamlet*)

Autistic phenomena speak about human beings who have retreated into an isolated world of non-existence. Through these modalities of functioning they have "truncated" their capacity for consciousness and inhabit a world of inanimate objects to avoid contact with mental pain.

The frozen autistic desert as a zone of the mind and its mysteries has drawn the attention of psychoanalytic authors because of its
characteristics of isolation and disconnection, which seem to take
an opposite direction from that of evolution and mental development, transforming the living and growing mind into a "no place"
where animated phenomena turn inanimate.

Clinical experience with children who inhabit this frozen desert,
and adults with autistic enclaves, has led me to certain questions,
some theoretical, some clinical, and to think about the contrasts
between a powerful intelligence and the obstructions of cognitive
and emotional development.

Observation of the emotional atmosphere of my consulting
room and of my own mind revealed an absence of violence, a
capacity to awaken tender feelings, and also a returning again and
again to a frozen zone of "no conflict", which, like the peace of
cemeteries, does not allow for the possibility of mental growth.

We are not dealing with psychotic functioning. The difficulties
that obstruct mental growth in this case are different, so we have to
imagine other strategies for approaching these problems in analysis.

As I went deeper into my questions, a fruitful combination of
Tustin's, Meltzer's, and Bion's ideas emerged. One direction of my
explorations is the *peculiar blockage of the development of embryonic
thought*.

I will now state the ideas that I develop in this chapter.

1. In autism, embryonic thought is detained and this hinders the
   evolution of the capacity to be aware (consciousness).
2. The functions described by Bion as the matrix for thinking are
   disturbed: the container–contained ($\male\female$) relationship and the
   oscillation PS$\leftrightarrow$D (Bion, 1963). These functions acquire peculiar
   characteristics due to the use of mechanisms of disconnection,
   isolation and annulment.
3. Using Bion's ideas of transformations I argue in favour of the
   hypothesis of an autistic zone of non-transformation with the
   conjecture that the autistic sensuous elements are different not
   only from alpha elements, but from beta elements also.
4. The differentiation between these elements also implies a
   distinction between contact barrier, beta screen* (Bion, 1962),
   and autistic barriers (Tustin, 1986).

5. My clinical experience, and the dialogue with the above-mentioned authors, lead me to propose some technical suggestions, related with the building of a play space in the session, through personification and playing. This technical means, which has also been described in Chapter Three, helps the analyst to build an access through the autistic barriers, and the autistic patients to get out of their void and arid world. I also intend to articulate this idea of the construction of a play space with some conjectures about the aesthetic dimension of the mind.

Embryonic thought and the evolution of consciousness

Freud defined consciousness as the sense organ for the apprehension of psychic quality. It is the psychic counterpart of the sensuous organs, which apprehend sensuous qualities, transforming them into colours, sounds, odours, tastes, etc. Anxiety, rage, etc., lack form, colour, odour, etc. The senses may contribute to data associated with an emotional state of fear or rage, such as a heartbeat, a blush, etc., but there are no sense data directly associated with psychic qualities, as there are in relation with the objects of the external world. However, I have no doubt whatever of the need of something in the personality to make contact with psychic quality.

To investigate this kind of contact we have to differentiate between a rudimentary consciousness, which perceives but does not understand, and a consciousness capable of understanding and being aware. During the treatment of severely disturbed patients, Bion realized that the definition of consciousness, as the sense organ for the apprehension of psychic qualities, was insufficient. The domain of thought can be defined as a space occupied by no-things, and this definition draws attention to a mental space that is different from the perceptual space. Developing this differentiation implies tolerance of the relationship between the thing and the no-thing. Ideas, thoughts, emotions are no-things. Very disturbed patients cannot differentiate between the thing and the no-thing. As we have seen in previous chapters Bion, having asked himself what is the counterpart of the sensuous impression of a concrete object, in the relationship a person has with an emotional experience, postulates an alpha function that transforms the sensuous and emotional impressions into α elements.

These elements, which include visual images, patterns of hearing and smell, etc., are the particles of thought which form the "furniture of dreams", fit to be used in dream-thoughts and in unconscious day dream-thoughts. Alpha elements have the characteristic of being adequate for articulation and disarticulation and form a reticule which constitutes a contact-barrier*. This semi-permeable membrane produces a separation between the conscious and the unconscious, so that emotional experiences can be "dreamed" and stored, but it prevents the intrusion into consciousness of phantasies and emotions which could disturb an appropriate evaluation of the facts of external reality, and at the same time keeps dreams and psychic reality from being overwhelmed by a hyper-realistic view. *Alpha function and alpha elements offer the possibility of a consciousness associated with an unconsciousness. This is a consciousness that has evolved through the binocular conscious (unconscious vision), which offers the possibility of being aware of the world of common sense and of psychic reality.*

Sensuous impressions are the raw material from which embryonic thought can evolve when it is transformed into alpha elements. This means a process of differentiation between sensorial impression as the recording of a concrete object, or of the emotional experience and the concrete object, or the experience in itself.

Rudimentary consciousness is associated with beta elements that can be defined as sensuous impressions experienced as if they were things-in-themselves. At the moment a baby is breastfeeding, he/she can use the sensations associated with sucking as the recording of a sweet experience, or can confuse the sensations with the concrete emotional experience of sucking. Bion also defines beta elements as the earliest matrix from which thought can emerge through realistic projective identification. This is related with the container–contained function, as we will see further ahead.

In what follows, I want to refer to a conjecture, which implies being familiar with some of Tustin's ideas about autistic objects of sensation and autistic shapes. I think that what I mention as spurious sensations are what Tustin calls the auto-generated sensations, which autistic children auto-provoke in themselves, with the autistic objects of sensation and autistic shapes, which they experience as a part of their body. "In all types of pathological autism, the

sensuousness which is biologically so valuable has gone disas-
trously awry. . . . The normal and progressive use of the sensory
apparatus becomes blocked or distorted by excessive sensuality"
(Tustin, 1986, p. 239). This distortion continues through hard
objects, to which they cling and which they feel are a part of their
bodies. Tustin also describes the autistic sensation shapes: auto-
generated by tactile activities such as touching with the fingers,
rubbing, etc.

> The autistic child's functioning is very different. His is in a sensa-
> tion-dominated world in which he seeks *sensations* rather then
> objects as such. He is not responsive to people as people, but mostly
> in terms of the sensations they engender. [*ibid.*, p. 54]

> Clinical work indicates that pathological autistic objects have their
> origin in hidden auto-sensuous activities which began in infancy.
> [*ibid.*, p. 108].

In this conjecture, as I already mentioned, I will refer to spurious sensations akin to Tustin's description of the ways in which
autistic children engender spurious sensations and the peculiar
deformation implied in the fact that they privilege the tactile–proximal sensations over the distal senses led me to conjecture that,
in these children, there is also a disturbance in the formation of
beta elements as the prime matrix of thought. This conjecture takes
into account the detention of projective identifications in autism.
I propose to differentiate raw sensuous impressions, beta elements*,
from autistic sensuous elements. This differentiation is very important in clinical practice, and has technical implications. Beta
elements can be used only for evacuation, but if they find a transforming container, they can become alpha elements. The spurious
sensations, auto-generated through the autistic manoeuvres and
defences, truncate consciousness and can only be used to form
autistic barriers.

They are part of the autistic shell of encapsulation; they cannot
be used for projective identification and cannot be transformed.
Tustin, therefore, maintains that it is necessary to develop an active
technique that prevents autistic manoeuvres, because they stop the
cognitive–emotional development, block imagination, and also
prevent living in a world of common sense.

Alpha elements, beta elements, and sensuous autistic elements

Alpha function is complex. It is a system of transformation and of blockage by which we are only selectively open to stimuli: to the internal ones as well as to those coming from the outside. This function generates alpha elements that can be stored. In psychotic functioning, the selective blockage of sensations fails. The organs start to give signals that classically have been described as hallucinations and hypochondriac sensations. Beta elements can only be evacuated and cannot be stored. In autism, we deal with human beings trapped in a world almost exclusively sensuous and tactile. Autistic patients avoid distal sensations and their correlation with proximal sensations. Alpha function is disturbed because of autistic defences that produce planar zones of absence and disconnection, which are occupied by autistic sensations and manoeuvres.

Alpha function, which transforms sensuous impressions into "sensuous data" and, in a second transformational cycle, into "psychological data", fails in autism, where, at the level of sensations, there is a privilege of the tactile–proximal over the distal as a means of creating an illusion of no bodily separation. The avoided distal sensations are those which give the possibility of locating objects in space, which in turn implies the need for more conjectures.

Sensuous autistics elements cannot be transformed, because they are produced as spurious auto-generated sensations and have a function opposed to that of establishing contact. Encapsulation isolates a planar zone of autistic void generated through disconnection. In autistic functioning, we cannot speak of contact barrier but of autistic barriers. While alpha elements have several points of articulation and beta elements have only one point of contact through projective identification, the sensuous autistic elements that form the autistic barriers are elements used to create disconnection. Learning from experience through alpha elements can have no continuity, because what is achieved at moments of penetration of the autistic shell becomes flat and then encapsulated again.

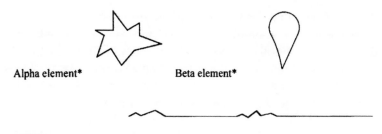

Alpha element*   Beta element*

Autistic planar zone

Emotions as links; meaning as psychologically necessary

Sensations and sensuous impressions are links with the outside world, with the "not-me" and with our own body. Emotions are links with internal psychic reality and with the human world. They represent two systems of links. In autistic functioning, we find ourselves with "no-links"; flattened emotional experiences are reduced to events without meaning (Meltzer, 1975).

Bion says that emotions have the function of linking and describes three links: L (Love), H (Hate) and K (knowledge as a disposition to know, as curiosity, not as possession of knowledge). The human world is a world of meaning, which is a function of the emotional links (L, H, K) of the self with the self: love of oneself (L), hatred towards oneself (H), and disposition towards knowing oneself (K). It is in the human world that the transformation from inanimate into animate occurs. Meaning is related to the feeling of existing and of feeling real. When there is a failure in the development of these links, their extension to links with objects and the disposition to know is also disturbed. In the autistic world, there is a failure of all the links, and the lack of the K link as curiosity is notorious. Primeval terrors remain shut up and isolated behind the autistic barriers and any emotional contact is avoided. Tustin (1990) described how animate objects and links become inanimate. In the autistic zone, no meaning can exist, because emotions are absent and it is impossible to learn from emotional experience. In psychotic functioning, emotions are attacked, fragmented, and evacuated. Failures in emotional and cognitive development are due to the fact that the transformations are produced in a medium of active misunderstanding (−K) related to the super-superego described as a moral conscience without morals (Bion, 1962).

In autistic phenomena there are no attacks, no violent fragmentation followed by evacuation, but rather a "non-relation", which extends itself into this frozen desert void of non-existence.

The evolution of consciousness and the primary links

In its first steps every mind needs another mind to be able to develop. This development takes place through the projective–introjective interplay. Primitive anxieties and sensations are evacuated through projective identification into the mother's mind that receives, gives a meaning to, and transforms them into something tolerable. The infant receives a part of his personality that is now tolerable and which he can assimilate. At the same time, he is also receiving and introjecting the alpha function. The development of this alpha function is associated with maternal reverie. A factor of reverie is the mother's attention, which functions as a string that holds together the infant's emotions and sensations. In depressed mothers, this attention is absent.

Autistic infants have intolerance for the awareness of the separation between nipple and tongue. They experience bodily separation as a hole in their own bodies. These are babies very sensitive to the emotional states of the object, a sensitivity that usually is associated with a depressed mother and an absent father. These are some of the elements that contribute to this experience of terrifying separation, experienced as a rupture of their own body, which leads them to develop reassuring spurious sensations that condemn them to isolation and disconnection.

Tustin (1990) describes a depressed breast-feeding in which the mother–baby pair cannot tolerate intense emotional situations, either of separation or of reunion. In these children, the moment of awareness of bodily separation was traumatic when they were infants and every strong feeling was deadened. Their form of protection from terrifying experiences of a body with holes is to wrap up in turbulences of auto-generated sensations, which enforce the lack of attention to shared realities and obliterate the awareness of normal sensations.

Stunted consciousness, sensation objects, and autistic barriers

In autistic functioning we find a stunted consciousness. Autistic sensation objects, kinetic movements, etc., used as spurious protection, and the dismantling that avoids commonsense and correlation between the senses, are factors that hinder the development of alpha function and the functions of consciousness.

Instead of using sensuous impressions to form sensuous images that can be linked with emotional experiences, autistic children use self-provoked sensations to create isolation, which establishes barriers that avoid contact. Emotional links are annulled in such a way that the relationship with the self, as with the objects, is obliterated.

Embryonic thought, evolution of consciousness, and the privileging of tactile sensuousness

In the evolution of consciousness towards being aware, sensuous and emotional impressions combine and form ideogrammatic elements, which are the matrixes of embryonic thought, and which can then be used to form dream-thoughts, unconscious waking thoughts, and commonsense.

Tustin's theories and the idea of alpha function help us to understand the importance of investigating how the psychic apparatus uses the sensuous impressions.

Hence, we can differentiate as follows.

Alpha function uses sensuous impressions to generate alpha elements, which, on differentiating sensuous impressions as a recording of experience from the emotional experience in itself, can be used for transformation into thoughts and for mental growth. The infant's rudimentary consciousness experiences the sensuous impressions as beta elements, in which the aforementioned differentiation does not occur. They can only be used for projective identification. In psychotic functioning, they are used for projective transformations or in hallucinosis. (See Chapter Four.) In autistic phenomena, the spurious sensuous elements are used to generate encapsulation in a non-transformational system at the service of isolation.

Sensuous and emotional impressions transformed into alpha elements are used to form ideograms, and the ideogrammatic system makes a first sketch of ideas. If the mind is going to have some registration of pain, which has durability and can be stored, it has to have an ideogrammatized image: for example, a face in tears.

We can consider three factors in the development of this first sketch of ideas:

- the sensuous system differentiated in two groups: the distal and proximal senses;
- consciousness that links to sensuous impressions, which can be used for registering and storing experiences;
- curiosity, the K link (Bion, 1962), as a vital disposition to know.

Observation shows that infants engage in ceaseless sensuous explorations. By putting every object into their mouths, they engage in a rudimentary form of investigation through which they begin to discover themselves and the world. Ideograms seem to emerge when the distal system is stimulated. Sight and hearing are activated while apprehending distant objects, and, through the formation of ideograms, tolerance of frustration is increased, as far as this beginning of abstraction already implies the representation of the object.

When the breast leaves proximal space and the infant detaches itself from the tactile and olfactory contact, a sense of loss and of search emerges in distal space. Recovery of the object is achieved partially through abstraction. The object is no longer held in the mouth or found through smell; the need to find it leads to a search through sight and sound. Tustin draws attention to the sensation of an object always present and part of the mouth that autistic children generate through tactile sensations, etc. If separation from the object and its absence is tolerated, it is possible to generate conjectures and the notions of time and space related to the place and the time where the object used to be. Privileging tactile proximal sensations and avoiding distal sensations blocks this evolution.

The matrix functions of thinking and its failures

Taking into account the arrest of cognitive and emotional development, the failures in abstraction and in acquiring verbal language
in autistic children, it seems interesting to me to be able to investigate its peculiarities using as instruments the two functions that
Bion described as matrixes for the generation of thoughts and the
development of the possibility of using them for thinking: the
container–contained (♂♀) relationship and the oscillation (PS⇔D).

The container–contained (♂♀) relationship

Bion (1962) conceived projective identification not only as an
omnipotent phantasy, but also as a form of primitive exploration
and communication. *It allows the infant to deal with its primitive
emotions through maternal reverie.* Projective identification functions as a content that seeks a container. Bion conceives the
container–contained (♂♀) function as a relationship on which the
development of thoughts depends, and which may have different
characteristics that one can investigate: from those which lead to
mental growth, as does the symbiotic relationship of mutual benefit, to the parasitic one of mutual despoiling and destruction.

Is it possible to conceive of a ♂♀ relationship in autism?
Probably yes, but with the following characteristics: ♂#♀ where
means separated from. It seems obvious that, where autistic
phenomena are in the foreground, it is not possible to conceive of
any relationship, not even one of mutual destruction. Isolation
and sensuous autistic elements render unnecessary the operation
of projective identification, and this is the difference from beta
elements. In its realistic and exploratory form, projective identification has a function opposite to disconnection. In autism, the place
of the container is occupied by encapsulation, and omnipotent
control is exercised through the autistic mechanisms. The failure of
the ♂♀ relationship is associated with the method chosen to solve
the problems of mental pain, and that method involves the predominance of the spurious sensorial world and disconnection.

Disconnections leave holes in the place where a relationship
could be. Any separation is experienced as a terrifying hole in the

body. As the notion of absence is not tolerated, the notions of space and time cannot develop either. And these notions are factors of the ♂♀ relationship in evolution. These children do not conceive spatial or temporal limits. The technical recommendation (Tustin, 1986) of not allowing them to ignore these limits is based on the fact that, when they are avoided, this halts the development of the capacity of being aware.

An autistic five-year-old child had a ritual for the beginning and the end of the session: he took two pieces of rubber, emptied a bottle of glue, and stuck them together when the session ended. At the beginning of the next session, he separated them, and at the end he stuck them together again, and so on. When his treatment progressed and I began at times to exist for him, before a winter vacation interruption, he drew a face, named it after me, and introduced the paper between the two rubber sheets before gluing them together. With the evolution of his analysis, he had a tantrum when I would not let him make the sink overflow and then clean the floor endlessly. It was one of the expressions of the failure of the container–contained relationship. The tantrum implied the beginning of projective identification, he ceased to clean endlessly and tried to begin to draw. After a time, he asked for a box for his pencils and a folder to keep his drawings in. The cartridge and the folder were manifestations that a ♂♀ relationship that evolves towards mental growth was beginning to be established. It is a relationship K= ♂·♀, where K means disposition to know and the point represents an emotion as a link that is tolerated.

The ♂♀ function supposes a container with a receptive interior and a content with the capacity of penetration. These children do not have the notion of interior, or of an object that can fit inside another object. Nor can they tolerate an emotion that has the function of relating. A six-year-old autistic girl tried to put a bigger cube inside a smaller one. She tried time and again and did not seem to understand the problem, or to be able to learn from experience.

PS⇔D oscillation

Bion transformed Klein's idea of the positions into a mental function: the oscillation PS⇔D. This function delineates the whole object and the field of psychoanalytic investigation, creating the possibility of tolerating experiences of uncertainty and dispersion during moments of "not understanding", and also the temporary moments of integration with emotions associated with the discovery of the selected fact, which harmonize what was seen previously as dispersed (Bion, 1963). This function is a powerful stimulus for mental growth, when there is a development of emotions that are facilitators of the capacity of being aware. *These emotions are: tolerated doubt, tolerance of a selection and of that which is random, tolerance of a sense of infinity, and of ignorance.* The evolution of consciousness towards becoming aware implies the ability of discovering the selected fact which is instrumental and not projective. *Dreams and playing are privileged activities for this discovery.* This function is complementary with the symbiotic ♂♀ relationship of mutual benefit, the function from which meaning emerges.

PS⇔D is the equivalent of a physiological function of the mind that contributes to the formation of constant conjunctions, to the discovery of meaning, and to the development of the capacity for thinking. This function is responsible for the connection between the thoughts already created by the ♂♀ function and is a factor in being able to use the thoughts for thinking. The PS⇔D oscillation produces a deep emotional change that implies a great plastic capacity of the mind.

In the autistic functioning, instead of disarticulation we find isolation, annulment, and dismantling. These mechanisms preclude any possibility of articulation and the discovery of the selected fact that harmonizes the experiences. Autistic patients do not live experiences, but, rather, events without meaning; the constant conjunction is formed by events and also through obsessive mechanisms (Meltzer, 1975), which do not have the function of articulation, but of producing an unanimated, static, planar world. In my clinical experience, I had the opportunity of observing that, when the moments of leaving the autistic world give the possibility of finding the selected fact, this is frequently followed by an attempt to isolate it, stereotype it, and blur its function by undifferentiating and flattening everything.

I could observe these characteristics in the treatment of the little girl mentioned above, of whom one could say she had "developed" the "art" of avoiding contact. When this six-year-old girl became aware of her difficulties in drawing and writing, she tried to annul them by making me tie a string around each pencil, then she put a pencil and a little puppet inside a cube until she filled all the cubes, which she also lined up meticulously. Obviously, this method is of no use for trying to draw or write: indeed, it is a way of annulling the function of objects and of the mental pain derived from being aware of her difficulties.

In autism, the problem is not disarticulation due to a violent, hostile splitting, as it is in psychotic functioning. What happens is an interruption due to a kind of void, absences when these patients retreat to isolation, which damages their capacity for observation and attention. In this process the damage of the PS⟺D function is different from that produced by projective transformation or in hallucinosis (Bion, 1965). It is more related to experiences of void than with the deprivation of meaning and destruction. In autism, what fails is the possibility of gaining access to conjunctions of experiences and of articulating and transforming them.

The little girl mentioned above aligned puppets, cubes, animals, or piled any kind of objects in a station wagon, without any sense of articulation. Everything had to remain as she put it, which is how she created an isolated and immobilized world, "under control".

In the autistic world there are no experiences of satisfaction or of frustration. Experience is dismantled by means of a segmentation that is not violent or hostile, and that contrasts with psychotic split-ting. The dismantling, isolation, and lacunae of observation make the articulation of the experience impossible. When a child plays, tigers can be dangerous animals, which eat, bite, and can represent a part of the self or of the object, and this can generate persecutory or depressive anxiety.

But this girl, to elude mental pain, avoids contact with emotional experience through the annulment of the function of the objects, including her own mouth. For her, separation does not imply differ-entiation from an object, but, rather, the terrifying experience of a hole in her own body. This is what she shows in the session when she wraps up the mouth and teeth of the tiger and her own mouth with modelling clay. In closing her eyes and mouth, she closes herself to any possibility of making a differentiation between either herself or me as another person.

Construction of a play space

In this section, I want to discuss three problems:

1. The function of play and playing for mental growth and for becoming oneself.
2. The need of a technical approach that takes into account that there is no play nor playing in the autistic world, and that analysis is supposed to solve the problems which block mental growth.
3. The characteristics of this technical approach are based on a combination of a technique that impedes the use of autistic manoeuvres with construction of a space for playing.

The function of play and playing

In psychoanalysis, playing has been considered as a means for staging and dramatizing the relationships of the internal world, and the theory and technique of child analysis is based on the hypothesis of playing as a communicative expression.

The map–territory relationship (Bateson, 1972) is a problem related to the evolution of communication and the process of symbolization. From this perspective, acts of "playing" denote other acts of "not playing". If we observe two little monkeys playing, we see an interaction of signs that resembles, but is not the same as, those of a fight. This playing can take place only if those who are participating are capable of a certain degree of meta-communication, that is, they are able to interchange signs that transmit the message: "this is play". Text and context are of different logical types (Bateson, 1972).

According to Bion's ideas, the context–frame is formed through alpha function that generates the contact barrier and conscious–unconscious binocular vision. In the dream, the dreamer does not operate with the concept of "fiction", but, in the mental state of being awake, he may realize the context: "this is a dream". In the theatre and in playing, there is this meta-communicative frame, which differentiates the map from the territory with the peculiar modality of "let's pretend". Playing has a special combination of conscious–unconscious thought, which allows for distinguishing what is playing from what is not playing, which is one of the functions of the contact-barrier*. Playing is a crucial step in the discrimination between map and territory, in which they are identified and discriminated at the same time.

Conjectures about other functions of playing as a factor in mental growth

Playing can be considered an activity that is a continuation of dream life in the mental state of being awake. It detoxifies the raw emotions through metabolizing them, and it is a means for becoming oneself. In a way similar to "dreaming", playing produces alpha elements that are storable; it forms constant conjunctions and develops both tolerance for the disarticulation of experiences thus assembled and harmonization through the discovery of the selected fact as the play evolves and changes.

It is a transformational medium apt for dealing with what is new, unexpected, and with painful experiences. Playing is an action of rehearsal, which casts its shade over the future by creating the possibility for learning from emotional experience. The little girl who plays with her dolls is exercising the art of "becoming a mother". In autistic children, who do not play, learning is not acquired through digestion of emotional experiences, but through copy and imitation. They have the "art" of mechanical learning.

Transformations in playing contribute to the elaboration of mourning for the parts of the self lost because of growth processes and of the contact with anticipation of future evolutions. Playing implies training in the development of the K link, and opens the possibility towards the discovery of oneself and the difference between "me" and "not me". It makes it possible to become truthful and real to oneself, and to differentiate the zone of "let's play as if I am" from the one of "I am". It is also a factor for tolerating the move through the zones of transition of "I'm being" and "I'm becoming", where the catastrophic change dwells (Bion, 1970) in a context where there is a differentiation between map and territory. Playing develops training in formulating and accepting the rules of a shared commonsense world. The "let's play as if", "let's pretend" with which children agree over the characters and the kind of game they are going to play is evidence of this.

In authentic playing a container–contained relationship seems to develop, principally when playing evolves in a creative sense. If emotions need to be expressed and a capability of expressing them develops, there is a symbiotic relationship of mutual benefit. Emotions will have stimulated the development of a capacity of expression through playing, and, in turn, the capability to play contributes to emotional development. In autistic children, playing is frozen and stereotypic: playing trains in the tolerance of the difference between logical types, the word "cat" has no hair and does not bite, and the signs of a fight are not a fight.

The meta-communicative context of "this is playing" modulates persecutory and depressive anxieties. And, as Freud described it in the "fort-da" game, in play what is suffered passively is made active in a non-omnipotent way. The meta-communicative context of playing is basically non-omnipotent and non-omniscient, and is, in fact, a way of trying out and working through basic situations of helplessness, therefore developing mental growth. The autistic child who cannot play uses isolation and annulment instead of making active what he suffered passively.

The technical approach

In the psychoanalytic technique of child analysis, toys are used as a means of expression and communication.

The autistic child does not play, and adult patients with autistic enclaves do not either. Tustin (1986) says that before it is possible to resort to playing, which she considers as a situation of aesthetic protection, like poetry, autistic children have to be firmly protected by the concentrated attention of a lively and solicitous person. That is why the mental state of the analyst and the emotional atmosphere of the psychotherapeutic frame are very important factors in the treatment. If the autistic patient lives in a world of "no relations" and inhabits a space that is a "no place", where transformations are not possible, it is necessary to create a transformational space. In my opinion, this is the space for playing, which creates the possibility of making contact with mental pain, which is modulated by the frame of playing; and, at the same time, mitigating the terrifying aspect of anxiety and making evolution towards less atavistic forms of terror possible.

Winnicott (1972) says that psychotherapy needs to develop in a space for playing between patient and analyst, and, if such a space is absent, the analyst needs to construct it. If transference implies a relation, in autistic children what can be observed instead of an infantile transference is a "no relation". We need a technical approach to open the possibility of creating a communication, a relationship.

I propose the idea of introducing as a technical approach the construction of a space for playing when it is absent, and the personification of emotions through playing. (See also Chapter Three.) This construction is a way of making a dramatic and aesthetic formulation of emotional experience possible; this establishes connection and pulls autistic patients out of the autistic world. By aesthetic, here I mean the expression or representation of a non-sensuous emotional experience in a sensuous form, which incarnates it, but is not confused with it.

The fact that we are dealing with children and adults with a high degree of sensitivity favours the turn towards the aesthetic as a way of sensuous expression of non-sensuous psychic qualities, once this sensitivity is no longer at the service of the autistic functioning.

The characteristics of the technical approach

When Klein (1929) developed the technique of playing for child analysis, she realized that children personified their conflicts in their play. She conceived a dramatic interior world, where different objects were constantly on stage and in interrelation and were expressed through personification. But, in that same line of thinking, believing that toys were the instruments of communication for child analysis, as we have seen in previous chapters, when faced with Dick's characteristics of not playing, and which we can understand today as autistic functioning, she did not hesitate to give him the trains and to name them as a means of providing him with tools for expressing himself.

Bion's ideas of the mind as a living and growing object imply the possibility of technical approaches, in which first it is necessary to develop or repair functions, when and where there are flaws, in order to build up the necessary conditions for mental development.

The reader will remember that I have often mentioned in this book that Bion and Meltzer developed the idea that the analyst has to "dream" the session and had to "dream" the patient. "Dreaming", in this context, means that the analyst has to use his alpha function for developing constant conjunctions of alpha elements that will allow for the possibility of finding a meaning. This "dreaming" means a dream artificially constructed through an artifice. I want to emphasize again, through Semprún's quotation, the role of alpha function in the psychoanalytical construction: "Narrating well means in a way that it will be listened to. We will not achieve it without an artifice. An artifice good enough to become art!" (Semprún, 1995, p. 140, author's translation).

With children who do not play, and with adults with autistic enclaves, in whom it is necessary to start arrested mental growth, before interpreting contents, we need to build up a space for playing as a container and personifications to start the expression of the contents.

Clinical considerations

The axis of this clinical presentation is to show the points of confrontation between the autistic world and the moments of penetration that open up a way of coming out of it.

One of the challenges in the treatment of autistic children is how to help them leave the defensive frozen desert of disconnections that generates void. Another challenge is how to help them tolerate the development of awareness, which they seem to experience as a laceration. One of the clinical problems is that when encapsulation is penetrated, this develops contact and awareness, and is felt as a reawakening of the lacerating experience of the terrifying holes and invasion of stimuli. Therefore, this newborn consciousness is truncated and amputated all over again by mechanisms of disconnection.

Kleinian theory and technique of child analysis is based on the supposition that unconscious phantasies are expressed through playing. Klein thinks that all bodily sensations have their correlations in unconscious phantasies. At the primary level, these phantasies have a very concrete quality that configures the internal world. Anxiety impels the externalization of this world and Klein's notion of transference is based on this premise.

Bion (1963) thinks that even innate preconceptions, defined as expectations that can match with a "realization", are part of the mental equipment for learning from experience, and can be damaged in the psychotic functioning. (Bion defines "realization" as materialization together with awareness of the emotional experience.)

Clinical observation of autistic children shows that the development of phantasies is arrested. There is no space for imagination in their bi-dimensional worlds and emotional links are frozen. *The sensuous autistic elements are not primitive, they are spurious and cannot in any way lead to a psychic birth.* The technical approach has to be different. If encapsulation is at the service of a "no relation", a technique that creates the possibility of penetrating the carapace in a non-traumatic way is needed.

Technical implications derived from observations of the autistic world

Bion's ideas provide elements for conceiving of the analytic relation not only as a re-edition or an externalization of unconscious phantasies. With patients who are severely disturbed, we have to deal with constructing a relational field in the session, to construct ideograms with which to form "dreams" or phantasies. We have to develop instruments derived from the relational container–contained model in order to lead to mental growth. The analyst's dream-work-alpha means that he is capable of "dreaming" the patient, and this is vital for emotional development. In this chapter, I include the idea of playing as one of the ways of "dreaming".

With autistic children, we are faced with the problem of penetrating encapsulation and starting the process of realistic projective identifications that has been held up. Projective identification implies spatiality. Encapsulation creates a "no place", a void. Personification is a privileged method for creating a space of externalization. (See also Chapter Three.) *The construction of a space for playing creates the possibility for the development of the distal senses and the formation of ideograms.*

The introduction of characters is useful not only for expressing emotions in a "let's pretend" context, but it also raises the notion of twoness derived from the dialogue and the appearance of the "third" through the context of playing. For the development of the configurations of the early stages of the Oedipus complex, it is necessary that the Oedipal preconception—which can match with the realization (Bion, 1963)—should not be damaged; and the differentiation provided by the distal senses is also necessary. If phantasy stops, if eyes get dim and do not look, and sounds are the equivalent of jumping, or agitating hands to create tranquillizing sensations, the possibility of introducing the notion of threeness or a third is not available. The first time that Camille comes to her session with her father is also the first occasion on which, when she might be getting anxious, she not only screams and puts her thumb in her mouth as usual (corporeal extension with her mother), but she also puts her hand into her jogging pants and starts touching her genitalia, trying to annul differentiation through the tactile system.

I present now some aspects of the material that I will use as a clinical illustration of the ideas I propose.

At the moment of the first consultation, Camille was five years old. The family had moved to a foreign country when she was one. In the first interview, the mother came alone and was overwhelmed with anxiety. Camille is the fifth child. The couple has many disagreements and a difficult relationship. With this daughter, the mother thought, "This one is mine." She breastfed Camille for more than a year. Her motor development had been normal. When they moved to the foreign country, the little girl spoke one or two words. There the child slept with her mother, who was extremely anxious and depressed. Camille would not speak. When she was three years old, she went to a kindergarten where she seemed to have made some progress.

During the first sessions she leaves her mother and follows me to the consulting room without any sign of anxiety. She has serious difficulties with verbal language. At moments it seems an imitation of language, but it is just the noise of language, a chain of sounds without any meaning at all. (See Chapter Nine.) She uses it in the session when she "plays" turning her back on me. She does not use these sounds for communicating, and the family cannot understand them either. Another sonorous form she uses, interpolated with the above-mentioned "language", are some words that one can recognize: "Mummy", "Maria" (the name of her sister), "house of grandmother", "work". She does not name her father or her brothers. She seems not to understand pronouns, or verbs, or articles: instead of saying "my house", she says "your house". Another form of "language" is a kind of mechanical repetition or imitation. "How old are you?", numbers, and counting mechanically. I can observe how she reduces the distal system to the tactile in an imitative "game" in which she "phones" and says her mother's name, then follows an imitation of angry sounds and fragmented words in which she seems to be imitating her mother. It is an imitation that avoids the experience of bodily separation in a way equivalent to being in touch with the mother in a tactile way: the sounds are the equivalent of a bodily prolongation with her mother, as if both were parts of a whole. At the beginning of the treatment there were also fleeting moments in which Camille authentically played, as when she did "as if" the tiger would throw away some other animal.

Not skipping the world of common sense

From the very beginning, Camille behaved in a way that showed that she was not living in a world of shared commonsense. The moment she came in from the street, she started to run away: she climbed the stairs swiftly, skipped the waiting room, entered the consulting room, and tried to open the drawer that was not hers, or the doors of the hallway. She would run away from the consulting room into the waiting room where her mother waited; she lay down on the sofa, putting her thumb into her mouth, or she opened her mother's handbag looking for sweets.

I began by not letting her do these things: I took her hand when she came in before we went up the stairs; I would not let her escape into the waiting room, etc. These limits had a double favourable outcome, because her mother also began to do the same. At moments, this activity of setting limits could be transformed into play. Camille goes to the bathroom, closes the door, and leaves me outside: "Stay there" she says. I remain in the hallway and wait a little, I hear that she opens the tap, I ask her if I can go in, she does not answer. I wait, then I say, "I'm coming in", and open the door. She tries to keep me from doing it and screams "no". I am penetrating into a place of encapsulation. When I get in, she pushes me with her hands; I am an extension of her body, and though I let her push me back, then I go forward again, pushing her hands gently, and this is transformed into a sort of game. The limits also create crises of terror: when I do not let her lock herself in the bathroom she screams with terrified, penetrating howls. I respond in a playing tone saying, "What loud screams", and making a gesture as if covering my ears with my hands. I tell her, "You scream, you are frightened." I name the emotional experience. Camille opens her eyes, looks at me, and screams again, but this time it is the intentional emission of a sound whose effect she explores while looking at me, at my face, my expressions, my gestures. The eyes that see, the expressive facial mimic, and the communicative sounds are a way of developing the use of the distal senses in relation to emotions and their forms of expression.

I think that the limit performed in a context of playing is an interpretive action, which has also the function of opening a path to K link. If you cannot get through doors as if they did not exist, then you also can begin to feel curiosity about what is behind the door. Camille began to look and see, and so she discovered an umbrella on a shelf and began to ask, "What is this?"

Undifferentiation: mimetic learning; differentiation: learning by emotional experience

I will now illustrate the way in which the new facts that penetrate the encapsulation are reduced to the tactile proximal senses, annulling their differences and immobilizing them in the still and inanimate world.

In the first session, she discovers the modelling clay and seems attracted. She looks at it and names the colours correctly. She takes it out from the plastic containers and distributes the different colours on to little plates as if they were food. Then she goes to the window and turns her back on me. This is a place of isolation. In the following sessions, she mixes up all the modelling clay until it loses its colour differentiation, she sucks and tries to eat it. I do not allow her to do that. She lies down on her belly on the floor under the table. That is another place of isolation. Then she covers a hard puppet with the modelling clay and puts it in her mouth. The new experience with the modelling clay in the first session is reduced to a taste, annulling the first discovery she made through looking and naming the colours. This sequence of differentiation–annulment continues with taking out the little puppets and naming them: there are two Mummies, one Joanna, one Mister, then she wraps up the puppets with modelling clay which covers them entirely, so that they can no longer be recognized. At the same time, she avoids all frustration due to disconnection. Then the modelling clay ceased to exist for her the moment I had to put it in a plastic bag to stop her from eating it, although I explained to her why I did so, and I left the bag so that she could see it.

As the treatment continued, I began to understand that there was an oscillation between having contact with new experiences and annulling their quality of novelty by attracting them into the autistic desert. Starting school had a strong impact of new experiences. Camille brought some of them to her sessions: she took out the puppets and said, "Hi, kids"; she made them greet each other with a kiss, she made the noise of a kiss ("chuik") and made them all sit in a circle, or put them in a row. She also brought her birthday celebration, sitting the children in a circle, blowing out the candles, and singing "Happy birthday". But, little by little, the "children" were put on shelves, which also was a place of isolation: there they were immobilized in rows, and if they were moved, which I began to do through the characters, this situation generated terror, screams, and tantrums.

One day Camille started to bring very bizarre toys to the session. I learned afterwards that they were from the McDonald's "Happy Meal". They were strange objects made of hard plastic: a Donald Duck from whose head emerged a fan, a Minnie Mouse who hid inside a tube with coloured bubbles, little dolls of hard rubber, a piece of cloth: all very incoherent objects.

She also used the toys that I had provided, which were placed into a rucksack. The bag in which she brought her "toys" had a zipper, and, when she finished the session, she put the toys back inside and closed the bag. It was the first step towards an accepted differentiation. A container–contained relation was being developed, and also the beginning of a notion of inside–outside. I had observed the failures in the container–contained function when she tried to make the puppets without legs ride a horse, and in her inability to understand that a bigger object cannot be put inside a smaller one. *She piled container over container.* Later on, she began to discriminate the puppets, so, by contrast with the row of "kids", which were all the same, a Mister (not yet a father) and a baby appeared. Following this differentiation inside–outside, and the beginning of a container–contained relationship, she used the pronoun "my" for the first time. She brought a cloth bag with rectangular pieces of wood, which she used to build a house on whose top she put a red roof, and then she said "my house", looking at me.

Beginning of projective identification: the construction of a space for playing and the appearance of differentiated characters; the character "ball" appears

Bringing things from home is accompanied by holding the bag behind her and saying, "I don't have it." She sits and puts the bag behind her, looks at me and says, "I don't have it." I transformed it into a game of curiosity: "What is it that you don't have?" She smiles, looks at me, and says, "I don't have it", until finally she puts the bag on the table, and takes the objects out, as if showing them to me. I ask her what they are, and Camille names them. Following the connection is isolation. She turns her back on me, and with those toys, plus a station wagon from the rucksack, she makes up a stereotyped game, putting them all piled up in the station wagon and taking it to an isolation shelf. Then, to my surprise, she goes towards the rucksack, picks it up, looks right at me, and turns it upside down, spilling its contents everywhere. It is the first time she has done something like that. It is the beginning of externalization, the starting of the arrested process of projective identification and of the possibility of disarticulation, in contrast with the rigid "game" of putting everything in a row, always the same and immobile, in which even the station wagon, which is used to transport things, is also immobilized and sent to the isolation zone. While she throws the toys on the floor she looks into my face, trying to see my reaction. Among the things that fall there is a tennis ball. Camille discovers it and takes it in both her hands. She looks at me, I ask her, "Do you want to throw it to me?", and I make a gesture of receiving it. She throws the ball in a very gentle way and I receive it. I throw it to her and she receives it, and then she suddenly says, "Mummy", takes her bag and goes to the window. She stays there in a corner turning her back on me; she puts her forehead on the window, then licks it, and says "Mummy" again. I begin to transform the ball into a character: I say, "Did you see that, 'ball'? Camille played with you and with Lia, but she got scared, and since she wants Mummy, she puts her forehead to the window." What I say is very simple and descriptive.

The ball is an object of movement and of exchange. Playing with it means a penetration into encapsulation. Camille looks at the ball, she looks at me, she throws it to me, and then she catches it again. All this means co-ordination between movements and sight, her eyes follow the movement. It is a way of exercising the co-ordination between the distal and the proximal senses, and also it implies the creation of a space of transfer between her and me.

This session illustrates how this penetration of the protective shell is followed by disconnection and the reinforcement of the tactile–proximal as soon as the game awakens the awareness of separation.

At the next session, after the "I don't have it" game, she opens the rucksack and takes out the station wagon. She puts a doll in the driver's seat, and behind it three or four of her nameless dolls, which are non-differentiated. She takes out a milk jug, puts the ball inside, and covers it. I say, "There is the ball locked inside"; she screams "no". She continues taking out things such as puppets, pieces of wood, Lego blocks, etc., putting everything on plates. She says, "Sandwiches, McDonald's". I say, "All of them are sandwiches: the kids, the pieces of wood?" Camille puts her finger in her mouth and closes her eyes. I say "Now the ball is locked up, is 'she' also a sandwich?" I uncover the milk jug and say "Hello, ball." Camille begins to scream very loudly and says, "No, coffee"; she covers the milk jug again and serves coffee. I say, "The ball is locked up, they don't let 'her' play, poor thing." I try to uncover the milk jug again; she tries to keep me from doing it and screams. I say to her, as if the character "ball" were speaking, "I don't want to be coffee, I'm a ball." The ball cries and says, " I don't want to be coffee, I'm a ball, I want to get out, please, please . . ." and then something astonishing happens: Camille begins to laugh and she looks at me in a very connected way. This is the first time that this happens in her treatment. She lets me take out the ball. I tell her, "The ball doesn't want to be locked up, 'she' wants to play". I put the ball on the table, she takes it, and puts it in her mouth. I say, "Now she is a sandwich again"? As the "ball", I say, "No, I'm not a sandwich." She puts it on the table, puts her finger in her mouth and her eyes become unexpressive. I say, "Ah, everything is like your finger. The ball is not a finger." She looks at me, picks up a horse with a rider, I take the ball, and she goes with the horse to hit the ball. "Ah, they're fighting." She makes as if to throw something far away, out, which perhaps is separation, but where she has control.

Here we can see how, through enclosure–isolation, the "complaints and crying" of the "ball" character as a personification and dramatization of her emotions takes Camille out of her enclosure at times and attracts her into the human world of connection and communication. In those moments, she observes my gestures, which express emotions, and hears the sounds of crying and anger, and she also tries to express them. The penetration of the "protective shell" through personification and playing opened a way towards the expression of emotions through mimicry and expressive sounds. It is the beginning of analogical language, which expresses a relationship and contrasts with the tendency of attracting everything towards encapsulation: annulling the ball as an object for making exchanges and communication and reducing it to a bunch of undifferentiated sandwiches, which, like her finger, is a part of her body. It is not about food, but rather of reducing the distal to the tactile–proximal, and so gives the illusion of remaining under omnipotent control, annulling as well any difference with another person and even her existence.

The beginning of the first dialogue

It is the first time that Camille's mother leaves her alone and does not stay in the waiting room. Camille shows me an object and says "puppy" and makes a noise "grr . . ." I repeat "grrr . . ." and the word puppy, looking at the toy. It is a little puppy, soft, brown, with big eyes. It is the first time that she brings an object which is so different from the bizarre objects of the McDonald's "Happy Meal" box.

Camille makes the sound of growling again. I say, "Oh this is how the puppy speaks", and I also growl. She looks at me with a lively glance, an intentional look so different from the autistic, unexpressive eyes. The face has vitality and the laughter is real. Then she puts her hand inside the back of her pants and scratches her bottom. There is an oscillation between the growling of the puppy and the scratching, which belongs to the autistic tactile–proximal world.

I say, "The puppy makes grrr with its mouth." She looks at me and opens her mouth, I comment to the character ball, "Have you seen Camille's mouth?" To my astonishment, while she shows me with her finger, she says, "A tooth fell out." I say to the character "ball", "Let's see where Camille's tooth fell out." I am showing curiosity, a K link, disposition to know. I say, "Your mother told me that once in Ecuador a hammock hit you and broke your teeth." Camille says, "Juliana."

Analyst: "Yes, Juliana was there in Ecuador when your teeth were broken."

Camille: "Ecuador, Buenos Aires no" (she says it in a kind of hoarse voice which makes me ask myself if this, together with the growling, is not the beginning of an emotional contact with her father). *It is the first dialogue we have!!!*

After that she retreats again into her isolation: she turns her back on me and puts some puppets on a shelf. Suddenly, she seems very tired. She starts agitating her hands and jumping so as to auto-generate kinaesthetic sensations.

The communication through the ball is followed by the dialogue with me, and the possibility of talking about the traumatic experiences she had when she was three: a hammock hit her mouth and broke her teeth. She responds, naming the person who was taking care of her abroad and the country where they lived. *The naming of the emotional experience is a significant step towards the reparation of the PS⇔D function; the name links a series of emotional experiences.* The dialogue shows a developing of the visual distal senses: she looks at me, she shows me, etc., and this implies emotional contact. "Juliana, Ecuador, Buenos Aires no" name the experiences of loss, of spatial location, and a possibility of expressing rejection via the word "no". But a good enough container for these traumatic and depressive contents has not yet been developed, so she retreats again to her autistic, unanimated world.

Development of the distal visual and sonorous capacity (forerunners for ideograms)

In former sessions she had discovered a game with water, involving pouring the water from one cup into another. Later on, dolls, pieces of wood, etc., were put in water in any which way, in a task of flattening, of annulling, what is different and what is new.

She finds the cups in the rucksack and in a second she is already at the door, running to the bathroom to fetch water, which has become once again the "mechanical game" of undifferentiating everything and stereotyping and blurring the selected fact. I stop her, and what happens next astonishes me. She sits on the floor turns the cups upside down and begins to make a rhythm with her fingers and the cups. I say, "You are making music"; she looks at me, and takes out two pencils from the rucksack and starts to hit the cups with rhythm as if they were drums. I think of the contrasts between "making music" and when she hits some plastic objects when she has a tantrum, and I tell her again she is making music, and say, "They are drums and talk, you are making music."

What is remarkable is the correlation between what is auditory, visual, and tactile. Then she begins a more discriminated game where she makes the "Mister" and one of the dolls kiss each other, and then she makes the doll take the baby in her arms. As I stop her again from taking refuge in the autistic mechanical world, she finds new resources: through an active development in which she can "make music", using the objects and her sensorial capacities to set the scene and the noises, which are a step towards language and the triangular situation and an approach to the "primal scene". (See Chapter Nine.)

The development of the distal senses makes it possible also to construct a configuration of a couple and a baby, indispensable elements for exploring the Oedipus situation. The configuration of the Oedipus structure requires differentiation.

In this session, sound introduces the "third" and the possibility of giving a sensuous representation of the noises coming from the parents' bedroom, instead of being an auto-generated sensation equivalent to agitating her hands or touching her genitalia. Exciting her proximal sensuous systems, she defends herself from the analytical method that penetrates her "protective shell". Constructing her psychic apparatus with these sensuous proximal systems arrests her development. The interpretive action of impeding autistic manoeuvres, as much as favouring personification, helps her not to take refuge in a still and lifeless world. It is a battle, in which, when a gap is opened in the autistic shell, she begins to modulate sounds, to co-ordinate them with movement and sight, and to develop embryonic thought. The latter will create an access to her developmental conflicts and the possibility of solving them.

The character tiger is born: the expression of aggression–reparation

She goes to the rucksack, opens it, discovers a doll, and looks for the tiger. With difficulty, she says "Tiger", growls, and looks at me, I also growl. She makes the tiger's mouth, which has teeth, bite and tear out the doll's hair.

Analyst (in a smiling-playful tone and mimicking anger): "Ah, you naughty tiger! You are pulling out the poor baby's hair" (*an interpretation with personification which "plays" the role of a differentiated bad object*). Camille looks at me attentively and laughs, then she makes the tiger again attack the doll's head. I have the impression that she is beginning to show me that something is wrong with her head, as if she were missing pieces. I cannot tell her something so complex. She acquires vitality when an emotion is personified, and at the same time she can begin to look and pay attention for a little while. When the tiger strikes again, the ball (as a character) says, "No, don't you see she is afraid, poor baby." This personification is performed with gestures and sounds of being afraid. Camille looks at me, and she also starts to make gestures of trembling and moans.

I say, "Oh, I'm so afraid, naughty tiger." Camille says, "No, Lia" (the name of the analyst), so I say, "So Lia is the naughty one", and Camille says, "Yes."

She looks at me and says, "Look", showing me her thumb, the one she always puts into her mouth, and I see it has a bandage. Analyst: "Your thumb is hurt." I am paying attention and showing interest. (I found out from her mother that the thumb is injured because of having been put in Camille's mouth so much.) She takes the station wagon, names it, and puts two "Misters" in the front seat, one driving, and a little baby in his cradle in the back. She leaves them on the table, takes the tiger, and starts to shake him so that the staion wagon falls on the floor. She takes the two "Misters" and makes them take the tiger and put him in one of the shelves of isolation, where she leaves it until the end of the session.

In this session, what is remarkable is the development of her playing and linguistic achievements. She is beginning to be able to listen and to make a playful verbalization; she can express herself through the play. The interpretation constructs a playing space through these forms of expression. Camille cannot yet stand abstract concepts, but in this session she tries to use the word "tiger", and she develops a correlation between naming, gestures and sounds which express emotions. The analyst is participating in the relational field, modulating anxieties through her alpha function.

The first drawing

After coming back from a long weekend, where, for the first time, the whole family took a vacation together in Uruguay, Camille makes her first drawing of a complex situation. Before, she had tried to draw a human figure, which had very stylized, slender traits but where one could see the disturbance in the eyes, which were smeared and blurred (Figure 8).

Figure 8. Drawing No. 1: Human figure.

In this session, the mother leaves Camille and she comes in running, she has a doll in her hand and she hides it behind her back, looking at me.

Analyst: What do you have there?

Camille: *It's mine* (she is acquiring pronouns which imply a step towards me-not me differentiation).

Analyst: I see it's yours. What is it?

Camille: Babie (referring to Barbie, but not pronouncing the "r").

It is a strange doll: it has big sky-blue wings, boots and trousers of the same colour and a kind of bodice corset that can be taken off and then the breasts appear.

She opens the rucksack and begins to take out blocks and a plastic cup to pile them up in her "boring" tower routine. The ball appears and says, "Were you in Uruguay?" I'm surprised to hear Camille beginning to try to speak: she says: "Dad", incomprehensible words, "little house", incomprehensible words, "drink water", incomprehensible words, "kiosk", "sandwiches" . . . she tries to pronounce Uruguay.

Analyst: "You are telling me that you went to Uruguay with your Dad, of the little house in Uruguay, that you went to the kiosk and ate sandwiches . . ."

Camille: "Look", she takes out a sheet of paper and she says, "Saturday, Sunday" (as I had named the days of interruption because of my vacations, drawing suns), and she tries to draw . . .

Analyst: You are telling me that you went to Uruguay Saturday, Sunday, Monday, as when Lia took her vacation.

Camille says, "Look", takes a pencil and starts to draw (Figure 9).

Figure 9. Drawing No. 2: The little house in Uruguay.

She takes the sheet of paper where she had already drawn a girl, turns it over and says, "Look a little house", she starts drawing, first the roof, then the part beneath, then on the other side a part of the house where it seems that she draws beds. When I name the beds, saying, "where you sleep", Camille does not answer, and scribbles over them with a brown pencil. Then she continues drawing the clouds, she says "sun", and draws one, then she draws a blue line in the lower part of the sheet and says "pool", and she says "flowers", and draws some. Then she paints them very quickly.

Having made all this contact and verbal communication effort, she puts her finger in her mouth. With the ball, I say that Camille has told us about the house in Uruguay, and that she left, and said "goodbye" to Lia, and now says "hello". She looks at me, leaves aside her finger, looks for the tiger in the rucksack, and says "grrr". She takes out the elephant, the chicken, and goes "cock-a-doodle-do", the cow, and goes "moo". I comment that the animals speak and go . . . (I make the sounds).

She discovers that the elephant has a wire that comes out of its trunk: "Bad tiger," she says. "Poor elephant." She takes it to the bathroom, puts water on it, and wraps the trunk with toilet paper. She returns, takes the Barbie and the Mister, which she tries to put on Barbie's back. This seems a sketch of the primal scene. She turns around, looks at me, and sees I have a watch hanging from my neck. "What's that?", she asks. I say, "A watch." She stops looking at me, says "Mummy", and puts her finger in her mouth and puts a hand in front, looking for her genitalia. She is once again disconnecting.

The drawing has a kind of narrative, a sign that alpha function is being repaired. One can observe the triangles of the roof. I think that the right side represents the mother, also represented by the sky-blue colour, the same as Barbie's outfit. The chimney on the roof is blue, just like the Barbie dress. She put a Mister, much smaller, on this Barbie's back. The part of the bedrooms is crossed out with brown pencil, not a zone of annulment, but rather one of conflict. On the mother's side is a door with a triangular shape. The clouds and flowers, which are painted in sky-blue and related with the maternal side, are well delineated. The sun and the yellow colour are related with the paternal aspect and with the notion of the analyst's absence; they are painted with much paler colours. (I had drawn for her squares with yellow suns inside representing the days in which I was going to be absent.) The drawing has a tri-dimensional quality and an outside and inside. The line in the lower part of the drawing is significant because it is a delimitation of a space that also is a kind of holding.

Some comments and discussion of the clinical illustrations

Here, I shall discuss the sessions in which a bit of crisis and change nears, through the encounter of noises, gestures, and characters that express emotion, in contrast with the autistic world.

An evolution can be observed in the material: at the beginning of the treatment, the moments of penetration of the protective shell lead to tantrums, which, in my opinion, imply the beginning of the arrested projective identification and which are contained in session and sometimes can be transformed into a kind of communication. This is illustrated in the session in which the tantrum is transformed into music and rhythm, with the cups as drums and the pencils as drumsticks. It is possible to investigate the importance of rhythm in the evolution of consciousness, including the prenatal aspects. When in the womb, the unborn baby is accompanied by the constant rhythm of her mother's heartbeats, her gastric noises, the noises of the sexual intercourse of the parents, and also those coming from the outside. Rhythm and music are a system of rescue from autism. Rhythm produces a pattern of sound that contrasts with autistic jargon, which has no pattern. With the puppy, Camille introduces and uses a meaningful sound: "grrr . . .", as a form of expression, then the "grrr . . ." of the tiger, meaning aggression, appears, and then the tiny and trembling voice expressing fear, and also meaningful gestures such as frowning, or imitating with her hand a "swat" with the paw, which express emotional states of mind.

The process of reparation in autism consists of the repair or in the restoration of the functions of the objects. Reparation of alpha function is expressed by the personification of the functions of the objects. One cannot learn to write by putting a pencil with a thread tied around near a little puppet, isolated inside a plastic glass. This is a distortion of the function of the pencil and isolates the possibilities of establishing a relationship between the hand of the puppets and the pencil. It is different when she uses the pencils for making rhythm, because she is playing; she is entering the world of expression of emotions through the correlation between the distal senses of seeing and hearing and the proximal sense of touch, and this constructs an expressive pattern. In autism objects are not damaged because of projective identification or violence. What is damaged is their function, because of the way in which they are used in the service of the isolation of autistic phenomena. The reparation of the function can be observed when Camille uses the pencil for drawing.

When she discovers the doll with hair, she is developing a capacity for observation and is beginning to establish a minimum of basic trust in the analyst. And the characteristics of this doll, which is made of soft rubber, with human traits, with hair, are very different from the bizarre McDonald's object of the autistic system, like the duck from whose head a fan emerged.

With the drums, the "tiger" character, and the play of the tiger attacking the "baby's" head, she is beginning to use proto-symbols for expressing emotional states. In the session in which I make gestures and sounds of fear, and she does as well, we are maintaining a dialogue in which I can interpret emotional states to her in play form. She is learning to listen, and I am making a play linguistic selection that she uses to express something in a communicative form, not an imitative one.

The tiger transported by the two Misters to the shelf goes to a hospital for an "isolation" cure. She is showing me what she does with her emotions, with her expressive capacities when she feels terrorized.

The meaning of my inclusion of playing is that reparation is achieved through connection: the objects have to go to a hospital, where they are once again connected. The reparation when there is autistic damage is not carried out because of feelings of guilt for having attacked the object, but rather because autistic mechanisms entail the loss of the objects' function. What is damaged is the function of correlating, essential for mental development. It is damaged by a system of isolation, when the possibility of the correlation of sensuous impressions, the basis of embryonic thought, is being born.

The playing quality of the personification of the tiger, the ball, the doll, etc., introduces sounds and gestures which are able to link the primitive untransformed terrors that are behind the autistic barrier with the playing expression of the emotional experience of fear, anger or helplessness. It is the game of "let's pretend that", let's play that we are afraid, that we are trembling with fear, that we are growling with rage. It is also a way of using commonsense as correlation of more than one sense.

The autistic auto-generation of protective proximal sensations is a way to deal with terrors through an omnipotent control, which is accompanied by not seeing and not hearing.

Transformations into thought (Bion, 1965) are associated with the evolution of consciousness in the direction of becoming aware and of mental growth. The drawing is already a transformation into thought, with selected facts derived from the observation of her emotional experience of spending the weekend with the whole family in Uruguay.

In autism, transformational systems fail. Mental development requires the correlation of the senses. How can a psychic apparatus develop without hearing or seeing and with the proximal senses used in a distorted way? With the starting of projective identification as a content contained in the session through playing, she can transcend her skin and begin to do a projective exploration, a kind of probing of the world. The construction of a space for playing and the personification of the emotions also perform the function of starting the aesthetic conflict (Meltzer, 1975), the contrast between the exterior of the object apprehensible by the senses and the interior of the object that can only be conjectured.

The aesthetic dimension of the mind: the trans-analogical zone

I propose to further consider playing as an aesthetic activity and as a factor of the development of the aesthetic dimension of the mind, which is the dimension that makes the formulation of non-sensuous emotional experiences through sensuous qualities possible while maintaining the difference. The aesthetic dimension refers to the sensuous as the scaffolding that sustains the construction of what is not sensuous. By observing the spurious form in which the autistic children use their senses (and they have been described as babies with a great sensitivity), one can understand the implications of an authentic aesthetic development.

The function of play and playing for mental growth is one of the bases of the idea of the need of constructing a space for playing. I have also conjectured that a development of the analogical language occurs with playing. This kind of language is especially adequate for showing relation and for the expression of emotional links. The autistic zone of the mind is a zone of arrested development where no transformations can be produced.

In my clinical experience, the personification of the emotions in a context of playing can be used for expressing emotions as links, and as ways for communication with the analyst as an "other" and not as a prolongation of their own bodies. (See also Chapter Three.) In my opinion, it is a privileged technical resource to move from a zone of non-transformation, of "no relation", to a "trans-analogical and trans-transference" zone (Sor & Senet, 1988), to a zone of infantile transference where it is possible to "play" and where cognitive and emotional problems of mental growth can evolve.

The usefulness of a technique of personification lies in the transformation of the prenatal emotions into alpha elements. As opposed to other thought disturbances, in the case of autistic patients, we do not meet with prenatal emotions in the form of beta elements, but with inaccessible primeval terrors. They are isolated because of the autistic system for dealing with anxiety. Personification through opening a space of playing, in which emotions can be expressed with gestures and sounds, confronts the autistic world. The nuance of play mitigates the terrors and gives the opportunity of using the session, the analyst, and the toys as means of communication and expression.

Play is the "royal road" for penetrating the mental states of being awake which consciousness may apprehend. As an imaginative conjecture, I think that it provides a sixth sense, which makes use of analogy.

I end the chapter with the quotation by Cortázar, included in Chapter Three:

It is necessary to wonder if the analogical direction wouldn't be much more than an instinctive assistant, a luxury coexisting with the reasoning reason, and throwing it a rope to help conceptualize and judge. Answering this question, the poet proposes himself as the man that recognizes in the analogical direction . . . an effective instrumental medium . . . something as eyes and ears and tact projected outside of the sensuous, *apprehending constant relationships*, browsers of a world that cannot be reduced to any reason. [Cortázar, 1996, p. 516, my translation]

CHAPTER NINE

The gift of language in the autistic world: an exploration

> "It is sometimes said that animals do not talk because they lack the mental capacity. And this means: 'They do not think and this is why they do not talk'. But—they simply do not talk. Or to put it better: they do not use the language—if we except the most primitive forms of language . . . Commanding, questioning, recounting, chatting, are as much a part of our *natural history* as walking, eating, drinking, playing"
>
> (Wittgenstein, 1945)

As I described in the previous chapter, the autistic world is a zone of non-existence where mental growth is arrested. Isolation, disconnection, the predominance of the proximal tactile senses, the use of autistic objects of sensation, etc., are at the service of avoiding contact with any human relationship, thereby blocking the vital nutrients for emotional and cognitive development.

Clinical experience with autistic children and adult patients with autistic enclaves awakened my interest in trying to understand how and why the development and employment of verbal language was so disturbed. Very soon, I realized that this exploration was inevitably linked to the understanding of the development of the process of symbolization and its perturbations.

Thinking and speaking are mental functions inherent to the "human species", which only develop in a human bond. They are means of communication that imply the evolution of a capacity of abstraction, never before achieved in the evolution of life. In autism, we find an arrest in the development of both functions.

The roads opened by Frances Tustin for understanding how autistic functioning produces peculiar blockages in the process of symbolization, play, imagination, and communication represent a challenge that calls for more research. She has described how sucking, lallation, and play are associated. I will use her contributions, which clarify how the autistic world means the withdrawal from any human relationship and substitution for this by the use of autistic objects of sensation, to understand the disturbances in the development of verbal language.

The difficulties in establishing communication with autistic children during their treatment made me ask time and again: why do they not learn to speak, if speaking seems something so natural and inherent to the development of a human being? I tried to understand the characteristics of the arrest in mental growth in autism, which are different from the disturbances we can observe in psychotic functioning.

This chapter tries to outline some hypotheses combining clinical observation with some theoretical tools.

Some hypotheses

Clinical experience and observation allowed me to describe two forms of alteration of the verbal language, which I have named "jargon" and "mimetic language".

I will use some clinical observations to illustrate these ideas. I have observed this kind of "jargon" language in Mary, a six-year-old autistic girl: it is an emission of idiosyncratic sounds, with an intonation, sometimes even musical, which she uses when she is in a state of isolation. She turns her back on me and "speaks" with the dolls as if she were having a "conversation", but what she emits is noise, not language; it is a sonorous chain that does not make any sense. *My hypothesis is that her words are used as autistic objects of sensation. They are related to the sensory qualities of voices and not with meaning.* When we made some progress in the treatment, this form of "language" also appeared, when the evolution of the session produced a certain degree of connection. This time it was used actively as a defence, whenever she met with a difficulty in verbal communication that painfully brought her the awareness of her limitations. She resorted to the jargon, trying to avoid contact with frustration and with the notion of separation and sharing implied in any communication within a human relationship. Whenever she wanted to communicate, when faced with any difficulty in expressing herself, she returned to the jargon. This was the world in which Mary had absolute control and thus avoided feeling little and terrified.

Mimetic language is another sonorous form that Mary uses sometimes, also with dolls, in which there are some words that one can recognize: *Mummy, Jinni* (her sister's name), *house, grandmother, to work, it's your fault, penitence, you are punished,* etc. (these last ones with imitative intonation of anger). Here, you cannot hear the voice of the girl: the sound seems as if it were coming from a puppet and spoken by a ventriloquist. The words are not the expression of emotional experiences; the voices are imitations, echoes of somebody else's voice. This girl alternates mechanical repetition of, mechanical counting of, numbers, "speaking" in an "imitative language", as when she "speaks" imitating her mother's voice, saying "So-and-so is speaking" (her mother's name), knitting her brow, and imitating intonations of anger and words that seem a copy of her mother's. It is an imitation that avoids the experience of corporeal separation in a way similar to when she privileges the sense of touch, so the sounds she makes seem to be the equivalent of an extension of her body with her mother's, from whom she seems undifferentiated. In this sense, she employs imitation of the voice just as an autistic child might employ the hand of another person, as if it were, at the same time, a thing and a continuation of its hand.

My hypothesis is that this kind of "language", which is akin to what has been described as echolalia, is related to the use of adhesive identification. Projective identification as a means of normal primitive communication is arrested: my conjecture is that one of the factors of this arrest is the failure of maternal reverie, which produces a paralysis of the container–contained function, one of the matrix functions of thinking (Bion, 1962). In this little girl, we find a combination of factors: these include her mother's over-flowing anxiety, trying to resolve conflictive situations in her relationship with her children through a mix of impotence and threatening shouts, as well as the bad relationship between the parents, which is evidenced through their rivalry and continuous fighting. The little girl is trying "to digest them" by means of very inadequate tools: adhesive identification, which turns all relation-ships flat and meaningless. Mary mechanically transforms her emotions, which has an impact on her mental growth, arresting it.

Neither of these two verbal forms express thoughts, nor are they being used as a means of communication.

My hypothesis is that, as we discover in psychotic functioning that very complex thoughts can be used as an evacuative or mani-pulative action, there also can be an autistic use. This use implies that thoughts are being used as a kind of sensory equivalent, in the service of isolation and disconnection. The autistic use means the use of verbal language as an autistic object of sensation and also as an imitative language that has the function of a second skin (Bick, 1968). It is a use that transforms something vital and alive into something inanimate. This second skin has the function of an autis-tic barrier, which is very difficult to penetrate. At the social level, the group level, this autistic use is the matrix of the fanatical use proposed by Sor & Senet (1993).

A clinical illustration can help us approach the problem in a less abstract way: after each session in which he had had an insight, a very intelligent patient, with autistic enclaves, returned to the following session, having reduced his understanding to intellectual explanations and mechanical schemes. After a certain time in analy-sis, the patient could describe his autistic suffering with words as a void in which he withered, and he could also recognize the affinity of his ritual of counting floor tiles with the transformation of his insights into schematic explanations, through which he avoided depressive mental pain, reducing his thoughts into barren, drained-of-life mechanical forms. Later in the evolution of his analysis, he was able to find some books, such as *Steppenwolf*, by Herman Hesse, that described this mental state and could also find a name for it: "to be trapped in a labyrinth of loneliness".

A third form of verbal language makes its appearance when these patients are beginning to emerge from autistic mental states. This kind of language I have called, colloquially, "Tarzan-form" language, because, although it is unlike the other two languages that I have described previously, having a meaning and being used in the service of communication with others and with themselves, it lacks articulation. They speak like Tarzan, being unable to use either verb tenses or conjunctions, as well as using pronouns incorrectly.

My observations drove me to the hypothesis, already proposed by other authors, that in these patients the premature appearance of "me/not me" separation anxieties is a central factor in the arrest of mental growth. A communicative verbal development, which includes emotional experience and contact with another human being, also produces a contact with reality, which stimulates massive anxieties when faced with separation. Lacking the mental equipment to deal with them, these patients have difficulties tolerating the frustration that is implied in learning, because of the inherent restrictions involved in this process, and also tolerating introjective dependency towards another person, who no longer is felt as an extension of their own body. A mother's severe depressive deterioration in connecting emotionally "pushes" a very sensitive child towards intense depressive anxieties, anxieties that are not received and transformed by a maternal mental equipment. The anxieties are thus thrown into a kind of "nothingness", which is different from the "object hostile to projective identifications" that Bion describes in psychotic functioning.

The development of mental functions vital for learning verbal language, such as notation (memory) attention and a K link (Bion, 1962) of curiosity, a disposition to know, require a connection for which these patients lack the necessary tools. So, during treatment, each step in the development of these functions, which stimulates mental pain, leads them to retreat again into their autistic world of omnipotent control.

To these hypotheses I will add two conjectures that I will develop later in this chapter. The first is about the devitalization, in autism, of the Oedipal preconception, as Bion understood it, as a part of the ego's mental equipment for contact with reality and the function of the triangular relationship in the acquisition of verbal language. Second, as in Chapter Four, but in a different context, it seems interesting to include Bion's idea of tropisms, which he defines as seekers of objects. I shall put forward the hypothesis that, in autistic functioning, tropisms remain at proto-mental, neuro-physiological, hormonal, etc., levels, and they are manifested as somatic symptoms.

In what follows I shall develop some of the conceptual tools which were helpful to me in this exploration, including some clinical considerations.

The human bond and the transformation of emotions as a factor of mental growth

Bion's ideas contribute to conceiving mental growth as a process that generates mental "tissue" through the "digestion" of emotional experiences. This development occurs through projective–introjective interplay. Primitive anxieties and sensorialities, associated with not-yet differentiated emotional experiences, are evacuated through projective identification into the mind of the mother, who receives them, gives them a meaning, and transforms them into something tolerable. In this way, the infant receives back a part of his personality, which he now can assimilate, and along with which he also introjects the alpha function. As we have been seeing throughout the book, the development of this alpha function is associated with maternal reverie.

The tasks that the maternal reverie leaves unfinished fall upon the infant's rudimentary consciousness. Bion's illustration is interesting for this chapter, which deals with language: the infant evacuates into the breast his fear of dying through projective identification. The maternal reverie receives the primitive emotions and gives them a meaning: "if you have the fear of dying this means that you want to live". If reverie fails, the infant feels that the meaning and the source of meaning, the breast, have been destroyed, and what he receives back is a *nameless dread*.

The infant's personality, lodging undigested experiences and lacking adequate equipment, can evolve towards psychotic functioning, which Bion has described. What happens in autistic phenomena? In autism, we deal with human beings trapped in a world almost exclusively sensory–tactile.

Frances Tustin's investigations show that the autistic child has compensated for early psychological deficiencies by overvaluing tactile contacts and the sensations that they provoke. This "clinging to" tangible things leads to very serious disturbances in the mental processes that generate memories, images, fantasies, thoughts, and language, which are intangible. The mental functions needed for thinking and speaking, with their components of imagination and abstraction, are blocked. These children depend on contact with autistic objects of sensation and autistic figures, which are always present, for their feeling of existence and safety. This protects them from experiencing losses, but, at the same time, it prevents the development of those mental functions that depend on the possibility of conceiving presence and absence and of conceiving an object discontinuous in space and time. In a process of mental development, images, thoughts, ideas and language, the world of the intangible things occupies the place and the time where the object used to be and is not (Bion, 1965). The autistic object of sensation, always present, blocks the development of the capacity to play, "to dream" (Bion, 1962), and to speak. The catastrophic experience of experiencing separation as a hole in their own body, especially in their mouth, which prevents the process of mourning the loss of the "nipple–tongue" object that produces sensations, precludes the use of the mouth and the tongue to speak in a communicative way.

In this chapter, I attempt to show how these children use the emission of sounds as an inanimate object, which produces sensations. *The jargon is related to the production of sensations as an always-present object.* It is not a matter of bizarre objects, which, although they are an agglomerate, formed by projective identifications in inanimate objects, also have ego, superego, and mental functions traces, which maintain a certain vital spark.

The autistic objects of sensation belong to a devitalized world, immobilized and frozen. "The jargon" is not a true linguistic achievement and does not have possibilities of being transformed into communication. It is a kind of patchwork, in which pieces of isolated sounds appear, devoid of all meaning.

I want to mention now a contribution that seems interesting to me, because it shows the importance of the human relationship in the transformation of primitive emotions, in terms of mental development, including language.

The researchers of the evolution and development of language from the phylogenic and ontogenetic point of view, Greenspan and Shanker (2006), ask themselves how the first idea in the evolution of the human species and in the infant is born. Their amazing answer, which becomes obvious once one thinks about it, is that the first factor is the separation of perception from action.

A trout perceives a fly in the water, and immediately acts to catch what it perceives. An initial requirement, to be able to use the sensorial impressions of the perception as images for dream-thoughts, is to separate perception from action. These investigators have also studied the primary emotions and the role of the parental functions in transforming these emotions into emotional signs, which later on will also be able to be transformed into abilities to think and to communicate at a higher level of abstraction.

Their hypothesis is that our ability to form symbols, which allow us to represent the world and to think of it, has its origin in the transformation of our basic emotions into a series of more and more complex emotional signs, as mental development takes place. The ability to exchange emotional signs with other human beings (their care-givers) begins very early in infants, and a long period of exercitation of these exchanges leads to the development of symbols, language, abstract thought, and a variety of complex emotional and social abilities. A fundamental factor of this development is that meaningful emotional experiences must become associated with the formation of symbols.

Bion expresses this idea by saying that to have a notion of pain, one needs to have a registration in an ideogram, that is, for example, to have an image of a face in tears, the rubbing of an elbow, etc. To be able to use this ideogram for thinking, it must be contained and not evacuated by projective identification, which is equivalent to action. Images without emotion, without meaning, generate a memory without meaning, such as I could see in my little patient, Mary, who could mechanically recite numbers without understanding what it was all about. The need for association with emotional experiences for the development of thought is valid even for the most abstract notions, such as the understanding of numbers. First, it is necessary to go through the emotional experience of "much" or "little", related to partial or total object, as an emotional matrix for the acquisition of the notion of a mental number.

An autistic boy, when he had managed to make some emotional contact in analysis, was playing with a washtub and asked me to put water into it. I brought the washtub back half full. He then showed me a cup, which already was a gesture communication, but, instead of asking me to bring him more water, he said instead, "big water".

Bion says that the number is the name of a feeling. If this emotion can be detoxified (see Chapter Three), we can use numbers for thinking and to communicate. When the pain or the emotion is made bearable for the personality, it can then be assimilated and transformed in thoughts.

The authors mentioned earlier, Greenspan and Shanker (2006), stress the fundamental role that parental functions have in this development and how the emotional exchanges between care-givers and infants lead to this first step, the separation of perception from action, and, for the subsequent steps, the development of thinking and verbal communication.

I consider that the failures in the development of verbal language in autism have, as a central factor, difficulties in the primary link in the task of detoxifying the emotions, which are not being transformed into emotional signs of exchange. We often find in the life stories of autistic patients an infant with an extreme and premature sensitivity, which develops defences of isolation and disconnection as a way of dealing with the failures of maternal reverie associated with depressed mothers and absent fathers, which are another factor in hindering the transformation of emotions into signs of emotional communication in the relation-ship. These first failures in communication also block subsequent ones. The absence of the father as a buttress for the mother (Houzel, 2002) is another of the factors that needs to be considered.

Factors in the development of the thinking–speaking function

Three of Bion's contributions shed light on some aspects of the relationship between cognitive and emotional development, and between dream-thoughts and verbal communication. I have already described some in earlier chapters, especially in Chapter Eight, and I will repeat them again here to stress how their failures are factors in the development of verbal language.

1. *The alpha function* transforms sensory and emotional impressions into alpha elements. This alpha function makes possible the development of a conscious associated with an unconscious. Unlike a *rudimentary consciousness*, which perceives but does not understand, this is an *evolved consciousness*. *The conscious–unconscious binocular vision* offers the possibility of being aware of what is perceived in the world of common sense and also of psychic reality. The rudimentary consciousness perceives and acts through projective identification of what is perceived. If the transformational system of the maternal alpha function fails, or is lacking, this might produce a hypertrophy of the projective identification of the infant.

As we saw in Chapter Eight, in autistic children we meet with a stunted conscience, since they have blocked off contact with every human bond and replaced it with self-generated, spurious sensations and autistic objects and forms of sensation. This clinging to tangible things leads to serious disturbances of alpha function, which, through the alpha elements, provides the possibility of generating memories, images, phantasies, thoughts, and language, which are "no-things" and are intangible. The mental functions of thinking and speaking, with their components of imagination and abstraction, are blocked and mental growth is arrested.

These children use the production of sounds as an autistic object of sensation. The "jargon" *is related to the generation of sensations, as an always-present inanimate object.*

In these children, the catastrophic experience of separation blocks the mourning process. Frances Tustin helped us to understand that they live the loss of the object as a hole in their own body, because the "nipple–tongue" is a unity, and what is prioritized is its characteristic of giver of sensations and not the emotional experience. This prevents the use of the mouth and the tongue for speaking in a communicative form.

Camille, an autistic girl who began treatment when she was five years old, almost did not speak, and each time she had to face any evidence of separation between her and me, she put her thumb in her mouth, without sucking it. The sounds she produced sounded as if they were language, but they had no communicative function. It was as if she were wrapping herself up in sounds, with a function of isolation and disconnection.

2. *It is not enough to have thoughts; it is necessary to be able to use them for thinking.* Thoughts precede thinking and stimulate the development of an apparatus for thinking (Bion, 1962).

This *apparatus* is constituted by mental functions that are the different forms in which thoughts can be used. In *The Grid* (1977), Bion proposes two Cartesian axes, to classify any statement by the patient and by the analyst: the horizontal axis refers to the development of thoughts in increasing levels of complexity, which go from beta elements to the algebraic calculus. The vertical axis, the columns, represents the different uses by which a thought can be employed, whatever its level of complexity might be. Among the columns are memory, attention, inquiry, action, etc.

When we listen to a patient we need to observe not only the content of what he is saying, but also how he uses thoughts and language.

The clinical experience of listening to patients who use thoughts of a high level of complexity and abstraction in a mechanical way as devitalized intellectual schemes or voids, and of observing autistic children reduce to stereotyped rituals expressions that had a communicative level, inspired me with the idea of proposing to add an autistic use to the columns of The Grid: an autistic use of thoughts. If the use indicated in Column 6, use of the thoughts as action, is related to projective identification, sometimes as a communicative form and other times as an evacuative or manipulating form (which could be evidence of psychotic functioning, or one of lies), the autistic use of a thought implies its reduction to the equivalent of an autistic object of sensation with ritual characteristics or as a devitalized stereotype. Sor & Senet (1993) also proposed a fanatical use.

Echolalia illustrates the autistic use of language. Tustin (1981, p. 105) defined it as: ". . . a manipulation of words and sounds as if they were tangible physical objects, in order to make them into 'me' ". Thus, words can be sensation objects or Autistic Objects.

G, an adult patient with autistic nuclei, spoke without making any pauses, in a monotonous tone, which systematically made me sleepy. As a model, I would say that if, instead of speaking, he were writing, he would do it without ever raising the pen. As a ritual, each session began as a continuation of the previous one, as if the separation had not existed. Thus, a live communication, such as the exploration of a dream, was stereotyped until it lost all meaning.

3. *The matrix functions of thinking*. In my opinion, its disturbance affects verbal language, which is evidenced by the use of same in a non-communicative manner.

As was developed in Chapter Eight, Bion described two matrix functions of thinking: (a) the container–contained relationship, and (b) the oscillation PS⇔D between states of dispersion and integration. This function refers to the aptitude of the mind to open towards the "negative capability", which means to tolerate what is seen as dispersed, to tolerate indetermination, and the temporary lack of meaning; it also means to tolerate harmonization through the discovering of the selected fact that harmonizes, also temporarily, what was previously seen as dispersed. It is necessary to be able to develop tolerance to integration in transit, because every point of arrival reveals problems that were not seen before, which needs, in turn, to be able to tolerate the disarticulation of what was already articulated, so it can also be a point of departure for new developments.

The generation of an adequate container depends on detoxification of the emotions, because such a container is formed by connective tissue, made by threads, which are the emotions that are links receptive to the contents.

Words can function as containers of emotional experiences. If, between the verbal expression and the emotional experience, there is a symbiotic container–contained relationship, mutually beneficial, the nomination favours the detoxifying and transformation of the emotional experience at more mature levels, and this maturity in turn favours the development of achieved forms of expression. Bion says that the English language was never the same after Shakespeare; those of us whose native language is Spanish can think the same of Cervantes. The immaturity of forms of expression also leads to a vicious circle in relation to emotional maturity and *vice versa*.

I want to remind the reader again that the concept of the container–contained relationship is a transformation that Bion made of Klein's formulation of projective identification. He conceived this mechanism not only as an omnipotent phantasy, but also as a primitive means of communication. It is content in search of a container. If everything goes well, the reverie function, a factor of the mother's alpha function, will be the container that will house the content and give it a meaning. The content could be the "lallation" of the child: "da . . . da . . . da . . .", the container could be the name, when the mother says, "Yes, daddy", linking the name with the emotional experiences of the child with that man who is his father.

The two matrix functions of thinking, when they operate in a co-operative and complementary way, are the motor of the mental growth. The authentic factor of learning to speak is the discovery of the selected fact (SF), which harmonizes a conjunction of emotional experiences to which it gives a name: "daddy" is the name of a relationship, of a constant conjunction of emotional experiences. The container–contained relation tests the SF that was found through oscillation PS⇔D. The name "dad" includes a series of experiences, and, as is obvious, it excludes all those that are "not-dad". After a while, the child who related the name "daddy" with the emotional experiences, with a man, his dad, will have to open the constant conjunction when he hears some other child call another man "daddy".

If this modulation and transformation through maternal reverie do not take place, these tasks that imply contact with internal and external reality are imposed on the rudimentary consciousness of the infant, with different possibilities of damage in cognitive and emotional development.

Autistic infants have been described time and again as being of an extreme and premature sensitivity. As I have already said, too premature a contact stimulates anxieties, which are experienced as catastrophic and do not permit detoxification of the emotions so as to transform them into communicative signs. These children, who build their autistic barriers through isolation, disconnection, and the use of autistic objects and forms of sensation, lack the necessary nourishment for mental growth.

Klein said that a certain amount of anxiety is necessary, because it acts as a development motor. As opposed to psychotic functioning, where there is a parasitic container–contained relationship of mutual destruction and a hypertrophy of the apparatus for projective identification, autistic children, because of the arrest of projective identification as a primitive method of communication and the predominance of bi-dimensionality and adhesive identification, cannot conceive a container, which presupposes the notion of an interior, and a content, which implies capability for penetration. To illustrate this theme, I return to the autistic girl who tried time and again to put a bigger cube into a smaller one, without being able to realize that it was impossible.

Mimetic language

Mimetic language shows the failures of projective and introjective identification processes and the privileged use of adhesive identification. This type of identification not only occurs with the superficial aspects of the bi-dimensional object, without an interior, but, in autism, it is also a relationship at the sensory level with an inanimate object. An imitation of other people's voices takes place, one that has a mechanical intonation. This intonation is not to express an emotion, and seems to be related to the sensory qualities of the voices that autistic persons imitate and not with the emotional meaning of the words. They are not emotional experiences, nor do they express them. They are not the authentic voice of the child. They do not seem, either, to be voices and sounds in which there is a projective identification (which one hears as a caricature of the object), or an introjective, emphatic identification.

The arrest of the projective and introjective identifications obstructs the development of the symbiotic container–contained relationship. The devitalization of emotion and the substitution of living contacts with the mechanical relationship with inanimate objects, blocks the development of the other matrix function of thinking: the PS⟺D oscillation.

The bi-dimensionality of the object also implies failure in the constitution of the notion of an internal space, and this favours the failure of language development. The mouth cannot be transformed into a stage of vocal games and dramatizations. The processes of projective and introjective identification are arrested, as is, therefore, identification with talking objects.

In this paper I propose the conjecture that the imitation of voices acts as a second skin (Bick, 1968), which contributes to encapsulation and to mechanical functioning. There cannot be learning through emotional experience, since these experiences have been annulled by autistic defences. The learning is by copying and imitation of the objects' superficial aspects. This second skin works like a façade, behind which it seems that there is a void, but this second skin could have some type of support function, like a prosthesis. I formulated this conjecture after observing the incessant senseless movement and chat of these children and some adult patients. I asked myself time and again: why do they move, order the toys, and emit sounds? Is it that there might be something alive and vital that is trying to be maintained in such an inadequate way?

Camille, six years old, repeats things heard on television, and because of this she speaks the Spanish that is on television, a Spanish with a neutral accent and not as it is spoken in Argentina. Thus, she says "*cállate* (shut up)", "*aléjate* (go away)" with this neutral accent, or she repeats television jingles. She orders the little dolls in a circle, or she piles them up inside a truck, while she repeats in a mechanical voice, "Hello, boys . . . we're leaving, boys . . . let's go, boys . . ." Afterwards, the words are often transformed into unintelligible sounds. Also, at times, their verbalizations seem to constitute failed attempts to assimilate experiences via an extremely inadequate method. Thus, I sometimes see her knit her eyebrows, trying to imitate an expression of anger; I listen to her angry intonation, which is just an imitated intonation but without an authentic feeling of anger, in which she repeats bits of what seem to be fights between father and mother, or the mother angry with the children: "it is your fault", "you are punished", "penitence", etc. My experience is that unlike the "jargon", this mimetic modality has more possibilities of being transformed.

She uses "jargon" when she turns her back on me, and it is a part of her method of disconnection. The mimetic language, however, can at some moments acquire some meaning, as when I say to her, "You are telling me how mum and dad fight", or, "It seems that you are yelling like your mum when she is very angry." Sometimes, those interpretations are received with a look that sees and some communicative smile in which there is an expression of a contact and an understanding, as well as a feeling of being understood.

The Tarzan language

What I have called the Tarzan language appears when these children begin to tolerate contact with a living being, when they develop
curiosity and the need to communicate. Then we can observe
achievements in the configuration of the constant conjunction, but
it still lacks the narrative form. The use of nouns in a way that
makes sense and in communicative form is evidence that they have
the possibility of forming constant conjunctions, but they fail in the
narrative articulation. This failure is related to isolation, which does
not allow the development of verbal elements that articulate: they
lack the verbs, the conjunctions that act as bridges.

Mary, six years old, goes into the elevator, and says "I": she
wants to leave me outside; she makes a gesture as if to close the
door and says, looking at me, "stairs", leaving me to understand in
her "Tarzan" language that I should take the stairs. It seems to me
that it is the very significant beginning of discrimination and the
development of the notion of "I", a pronoun that until now she did
not use; at the same time she cannot say, "I will take the elevator,
you take the stairs". She registers the separation between session
and session. Each time I go downstairs and look for her, I see her at
the front door, behind the glass, speaking to me enthusiastically, as
if waiting for the encounter to tell me something.

The verbal, linguistic function is an articulator of time. A present
time, related to a past that is not there, and a future that is not there,
either. The problem of the constitution of the notion of time is associated with the verbal narrative, which is sequential and with the
verbs that mark time.

The construction of constant conjunctions depends on the
PS⇔D function: on the tolerance to the oscillation between dispersion and integration through the finding of the selected fact. The
nomination of the constant conjunctions implies naming the selected
fact.

The "Tarzan" language, unlike the "jargon" and the mimetic
language, is formed with alpha elements.

I shall now differentiate the processes through which one
arrives at an abstraction, which is what verbal language is, because
this differentiation implies that not everything that seems a thought
or a verbal language is such, at least to the aims of communication.
I differentiate, then, as follows.

1. The abstraction with potentiality to acquire meaning, which is originated in the complementary operation of the primary functions of thinking, where the emotional component has been detoxified. It is an abstraction that has been achieved with alpha elements, which assumes having achieved a differentiation between emotional experience and the images or signs that name it. It implies tolerance of uncertainty through patience (it includes the time factor) and tolerance of decision (it includes tolerance of choice and of a sense of infinite).

2. The abstraction that derives from a means of despoliation: when paranoid anxieties are so intense, abstraction is developed as an "escape" from these anxieties. The word is deprived of meaning, so that the word "table" only means table, in order to separate it from the emotional experience. And, if it only means "table", it lacks depth and has no meaning at all.

   Not being able to be used as a metaphor or analogy, it thus means nothing. Through a combination of a hypertrophied projective identification and an attack on linking, a deprivation of meaning takes place. This is expressed by Shakespeare in *Macbeth* as: "Life is a story told by a fool that means nothing."

3. The way autistic patients arrive at the use of jargon is produced through dismantling (Meltzer, 1975), which implies an isolation of sensations, not by attacks on linking. Mimetic language relates to adhesive identification and not to projective identification.

The technique of approaching these problems that I have been developing to achieve a meaningful emotional contact with these patients, to deal with their difficulties of verbal communication, implies, as I have discussed in previous chapters, a personification and dramatization of the emotions and the toys and, at the same time, naming them. This technical approach aims to help these patients develop a three-dimensional space, repairing the container–contained function. It is also proposed as a way of modulation of anxieties, transforming atavistic terrors into anxieties that are made tolerable for the personality.

A technical resource that I also use is the *interpretive action* of naming the emotional experience. In the clinical illustration that I present in what follows, one can observe how I use this technical resource.

The name that binds a constant conjunction of emotional experiences, linked also with the toys, the game, and with visual images, aims towards repairing curiosity as a mental function, what Bion nominated the K link. It is what Klein did with Dick when she inquired into what his interests were; she found out they were trains, and then she named them: "train mother", "train Dick". Mother is the name that binds a set of emotional experiences, and the "train mother" can personify those experiences. I also want to draw the reader's attention to the fact that Klein is the one that finds the SF* and names it.

In the clinical material that I am going to use to illustrate these ideas, I attempt to show how the use of nouns with meaning and in a communicative form is developed. I consider this naming as evidence that the patient has the possibility of forming constant conjunctions, which we see in the "Tarzan" language, although still the narrative articulation fails. Thus, the patient can name a horse but when she tries to tell me an episode she fails. The little girl of the clinical material still lacks the linguistic articulations and the conjunctions. This difficulty, in my opinion, is due to the obstacles in constructing the notion of time, which is related to the notion of a discontinuous and separated object, sometimes absent and at other times present, in contrast with the always-present autistic objects of sensation.

Clinical considerations

In what follows, I present a fragment of a session with a seven-year-old girl, Jane, who has been in treatment for two years. When she began, she practically did not speak in a communicative form; she almost always used what I called "jargon" and mimetic language. In this fragment, I attempt to illustrate the Tarzan language and the oscillation with the other forms in which isolation predominates. My conjecture is that the contact that implies the use of language in a communicative way stimulates depressive anxieties which are felt as intolerable at times, and also generates much frustration, since the continuous use of objects of autistic sensation and the language as an autistic object of sensation always present and available does not allow for excitation in the tolerance of frustration. In the session we can observe that the "Tarzanesque" reading of books and the game of "big–small" is followed by a retreat into the autistic world.

In the office, Jane sits on a chair and removes one of her sneakers, she frowns and looks at me as if she were defying me, and puts her thumb in her mouth.

A: It seems that you are angry; your mother told me that you didn't want to get out of the pool. Now, you look at me, you remove your sneaker, you are telling me that Jane doesn't do what Lía wants. But Lía isn't a thumb that does what Jane wants.

Jane shouts "shut up" and "stop it", goes to the cushions (which is one of her autistic corners in the consulting room), turns her back to me, looking at the wall, removes the other sneaker, and puts her thumb in the mouth.

A: "As Lía is not a thumb, Jane goes to the cushions, turns her back on me and with her thumb in her mouth, Lía is not there any more. Jane is at her house and in the pool."

Jane stands up, grasps the edge of the chest of drawers with both hands, and, with agility, sits on top, crossing her legs. I sit on a small chair in front of her; I look at her (she is looking at me).

A: "Now you're big and Lía is very small."

J (*shouts loud in playful tone*): "Lia!!!"

A (*dramatizing and personifying a very small girl*): "Oh I'm so scared! You're big, I am very small, and you are angry, angry!!"

Jane laughs and, looking at me, puts her hand on the phone that is on the chest of drawers, where she is seated). I say to her "no", we do not play with the phone. She accepts.

J (*again shouting and personifying an emotion of anger*): "Give me paper!" (*She looks at the place where the folder with sheets of paper is.*)

I give her some sheets, and, to my astonishment, she rolls them up, she hits with it, with the paper, on the edge of the chest of drawers and shouts loudly, looking at me and frowning.

J: "Lía, attention!" (She repeats this several times.)

A (*personifying a scared child*): "I am so scared! She shouts so loud! I am scared, she is angry."

She follows the game, shouting loudly and laughing. (It is the first shared game we have with an active participation of J, who also personifies a character who is an angry adult person, probably her mother.)

This game is the equivalent of sharing an experience as it happens in the moments when we are reading books together. Sharing an experience has a reparatory character in the relationship, and is an indicator of moments when she is getting out from the autistic world and from isolation.

Jane gives me orders, playing and pointing at the books that are on the smaller table: "Bring my library" (She says library instead of books: she has associated books with a visit she made with her kindergarten to a library, and, as often happens, she has difficulties naming things appropriately.)

A: "Do you want the books?" (I say the appropriate name.)

J: "Aha!" (It is an "aha" in a singing tone, as if she sang, as an exclamation. The beginning of the use of exclamation patterns is produced through the development of the function of attention in the relationship.)

A: "What books do you want?"

J (*with an imperative tone, but also with doubts*): "The jungle one, no, Pinocchio."

I think that, with my question, when I give her the option of choosing, I am opening a space for her for the development of the evolved consciousness capable of being aware of herself: *What does she want?* Also when giving her the option to choose I am stimulating the evolution of the container–contained function and the evolution of the PS⬄D function.

At the same time, I function as a part of her, container of this development, in which a certain awareness begins to take place, through the game of externalization related to a projective communicative identification, which has the possibility of evolving and be transformed in a dramatization. In the game, the necessary process of externalization of the emotions takes place. Through projective identification, with a touch of dramatization, I function as a part of her, and a transformation is taking place from an evacuative action (projective transformation) towards a personification, which is a transformation into dramatic action, and which has the connotation of representation and the creation of a representational space. Also, in the game, I function as an "other", as somebody else who asks what she wants, opening up a space for her ego.

I hand over the Pinocchio book that she had requested, she opens it and begins "to read" going through the pages:

J. "Here is Pinocchio, here is . . . what is it called? The fairy, here the friends. . . (she goes through the pages), and, "*colorín colorado*" (something like "Lo and behold!"), this story is finished." The intonation is similar to when I read to her, it is a soft, non-hyperkinetic tone, but she adds "*colorín colorado*", which I had never used with her. It does not sound mimetic.

I think there is the beginning of introjective identification of the alpha function because of the development and excitation of the function PS⟺D.

Jane finishes the book and again she points at the table.

J: "Give me."

A: "Which one do you want?"

The development of the ability to make choices increases tolerance of the pain of accepting the relationship between what is chosen and what is not chosen, that which is left out of the selection. It implies tolerance to the SF*, which is in turn associated with tolerance of the PS⟺D function.

J: "The jungle one."

I give it to her; she opens it and goes through the pages, looking slowly at the illustrations.

J: "Here sandwiches and Coca-Cola, here baby and nursing bottle, seals (she turns the page) here lion, angry." One can observe the development of the use of adjectives and the ability to name. She turns the page. "Here tiger, yellow, here black." She turns the page. "Here kangaroos." She stops at the illustration of the serpent, looks at me and says: "What is it?" I answer "serpent", she repeats the word with effort, trying to pronounce all the syllables. She does the same with the crocodile and the word crocodile. She turns the page.

J: "Here bears, they eat."

She turns the page, she points at the deer and asks me, "What is this?" I say "deer", and she repeats the word, also trying to pronounce the syllables.

She then turns the page and says, "A big monkey."

We are at a moment in the session in which there is an atmosphere of connection, tenderness, and sharing experiences. In that context Jane has a tolerance and a willingness to also tolerate the names of common sense of the conjunctions and pronunciation, as it should be, and not the arbitrary one, the way she does when she "speaks" in "jargon". It implies accepting living in a shared world. She throws away the book and asks for "the animal babies one". I give it to her and she looks at it.

J: "Here small dogs, here kittens, here little pigs, etc." She shows me the little pigs. She throws away the book and jumps down agilely towards the cushions. "Where paper?"

I give her the folder and she takes out some sheets. She opens the rucksack and gives me orders in "Tarzanesque" language to search for the "boys" and "girls" (the puppets) and she searches for the pencils. She distributes the sheets on the floor, puts a red pencil in the hand of each puppet and makes him draw. The emotional atmosphere has changed: she "makes" the "boys and the girls" draw, putting in their hands a pencil and repeating, "Very well, excellent" (in a voice that sounds like echolalia). She makes each one write letters or begins to speak in "jargon", which, as I described, are confused sounds, in which she makes noises, but does not say words. The letters that she does write, and the way she locates them on the page, are also chaotic.

She makes each puppet draw and afterwards she seats them neatly in a circle next to her. To each one she says, "Very well, excellent."

There is another emotional atmosphere here. The first one was of anger, shouts, and a shared experience of game, and afterwards, during the reading of the books, the atmosphere had a sharing nuance with tenderness. The emotional atmosphere that follows is the one of "schooling of children"; it is rigid, mechanical, but, at the same time, it gives the impression that she is trying "to digest" something that she does not understand and that is at the same time chaotic.

The contrast between the order in which she seats the little puppets and the mess that she is writing is remarkable. (See Figure 10.)

She treats the puppets as if they were an extension of herself, and it seems to me that, in this part of the session, the disturbance in the development of the alpha function can be observed. The reparation of the alpha function was shown in the session through her ability to plan a game with the puppets—that they are going to draw—and it also shows in her drawings. Later on, she starts with the mechanical "very well, excellent", said as if in the voice of a

Figure 10.   A patchwork mess of letters (perturbation in her capability for abstraction).

ventriloquist's puppet, and with attempts to write letters mechanically. The mechanical writing also goes with the naming of colours in a mechanical way, and the "jargon". It seems as if the mental organization she is achieving through the already introjected alpha function was disturbed when she was unable to tolerate the connection she made, and then she fell back in the mechanical repetition and the "jargon" that prevails over the "Tarzanesque" language and over the achieved attempts to pronounce words correctly. The evidence of the introjection of alpha function can be seen through her interest in the reading of books, through the way she could use my selected fact, in how the experience of the kindergarten's going to the library remained inside her, etc.

The calmer atmosphere at the book reading moment is transformed into a hyperkinetic activity, where the non-vital, autistic order prevails, and one can see it when she crosses out the drawing of the father elephant (blue and red—see the previously mentioned drawing of the "mess of letters"), and imposes over it a second autistic skin of a "mess of letters".

The Oedipal preconception and the function of the triangular relationship in the acquisition of verbal language

Bion described innate preconceptions, defining them as expectations capable of receiving a limited number of experiences. Thus, the infant has an innate expectation of the breast, a preconception of the breast, which, when matched with a positive "realization" of the breast, forms a conception. Bion also referred to the Oedipal preconception as a precursor, not in the sense of the early Oedipus of Klein, but as a part of the equipment of the ego's contact with reality. This preconception can be damaged.

In the case of autism, my conjecture is that there is a devitalization of the Oedipal preconception, associated with the situation of non-differentiation with the mother and the absence of the father with a function of discernment. My hypothesis is that this is also a factor of the disturbances in verbal language development.

Bion describes a situation in which the function of the mother is that of naming the selected fact that will allow the infant to correlate the lallation, da-da-da, with the emotional experiences in the relationship with the father. As I have said, when the baby says da-da-da, the mother gives it a name: yes, daddy. This name allows for binding a constant conjunction of emotional experiences with that man, who is associated with taking the child in his arms, taking him for a walk, with feelings of love and by whom he feels loved, etc. The function of the PS⇔D oscillation is to help to develop the next step in the process of abstraction: when the child hears someone else call another man "daddy"; the child must then open the constant conjunction already established, to be able to understand that "daddy" is the name of a relation.

Bion does not say too much about the Oedipal preconception. He says that it is part of the ego equipment for making contact with reality—external and internal—and it seems associated with the ability to create myths and dream thoughts. My hypothesis is that he refers to an ability to establish relations (that is, tolerate the relationship) or constant conjunctions through the PS⇔D function. In autistic functioning, as we have already described, this function is disturbed, because, at point D, the achieved conjunction becomes frozen, it loses vitality and is emptied of meaning (as we saw with Jane when she repeated "very well, excellent"), and at point PS there is no disarticulation, but a segmentation through isolation (as with the puppets sitting in their isolated order). The Oedipal preconception, in the sense of a non-saturated expectation, obviously loses vitality through stereotyping and ritualization. As I understand it, the Oedipal preconception allows the exploration of the relationship between parents and with between the child and the real parents, and when it freezes it becomes flat, bi-dimensional, losing all meaning and vitality. Jane, when she has to face her difficulties in speaking, made obvious when she tries to speak and it does not come out well, retreats into her autistic world, with the little puppets, where everything seems to be under her omnipotent control.

Tustin states that the constant use of autistic objects of sensation means that the autistic child has little possibility of learning to tolerate frustration. These children also have missed a stage of excitation that, in non-autistic children, takes place while the mother is absent. Many of them have missed the stage of lallation. They have missed early experiences of playing, in general, and especially playing with sounds. Children like this expect to do everything well on the first try, without any previous excitation. If they fail, they give up on the first try. This is what happens with Jane with her pronunciation defects, as well as when one does not understand what she says in her "Tarzanesque" language right away. If one asks her what she is saying, she answers "nothing". They have missed the opportunity of what Winnicott calls the transitional object or phenomenon. They therefore block the apprehension of a shared reality with another human being. Nothing can come in, and, even more importantly, nothing can come out. (A serious perturbation of the introjective and projective processes.)

If mother and child become autistic objects for one another, they live in a "cocoon" dominated by sensations in which each seems to adapt with the other in a predictable and perfect form.

In my experience, the father in the family has an important part to play supporting the "bonding couple" through the pains and tribulations aroused by the lack of perfect fit with each other and the realization that they cannot absolutely control each other. [Tustin, 1981, p. 107]

Clinical vignette

Jane is becoming able to name things and she is trying to tell me something. She names a horse Bobby, she tries to tell me her experience of riding a horse with her father, and when the narrative fails she shows me with gestures how Mary (her elder sister) rides a horse. Immediately, in a mechanical voice, she begins repeating "Raton Perez (Raton Perez, in English, Mouse Perez, is a tale for children: when they loose a tooth, he brings them money. It is also a film. He would be the equivalent of the Tooth Fairy of English-speaking countries.). I tell her that she wants to speak and tell me something, and, as it is difficult, she ends up repeating: "Raton Perez", etc., to avoid connecting with the difficulty of what she cannot say.

She begins to draw with a red pencil, and a part of the drawing gets a little "stained". She seems distressed, and stops using the red pencil. She continues with the blue one: to my astonishment, she draws, with a single line and a lot of skill, the figure of a shark; she says shark, draws the eye, and says eyes, underneath she sketches the nose, and says nose, later, she wants to draw the teeth, which she also names; they end up above and around the nose. I think that she is showing something of the traumatic situation with her teeth, her conflicts with aggressiveness and with teething, which has the meaning of weaning. (See Figure 11.) Then she draws the fin and tries to name it, finally, with my help, she finds the name. Jane takes

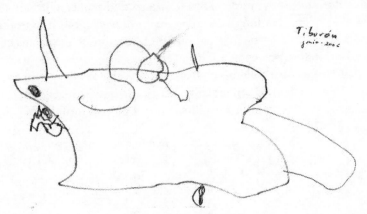

Figure 11. Jane's drawing of the shark, evidence of an amazing ability to draw images.

the red pencil again and sketches a kind of back tail. Then she leaves the drawing and begins to play with the horses: first she makes them caress each other, and then she makes them crash into each other in a way that seems a representation of a sexual relation.

A: "It seems as if you are telling me about daddy and mummy in bed."

Jane puts her hand inside the back part of her pants and says "piss".

I let her to go to the bathroom; she stays there a while, and I hear that she opens the tap; the door is half-open. I tell her that I am going to come in. I see her standing in front of the lavatory, with her pants down, but still without having urinated, rubbing and washing a red spot on her hand that she made with the red pencil when she was drawing. Jane seems distressed; she cannot wash off the spot. Later, she urinates and returns to the office. There she starts a usual stereotyped play with the taxi. When I tell her that we are going to finish the session and put the toys in the rucksack, she alternately puts her thumb in her mouth and on her genitalia. Again the separation seems to be experienced as a hole in her body, which she tries to fill with her fingers and through the privileged tactile sense.

Comments on the session

With the names and the attempt at narration, she is trying to produce articulated verbal language. At this point we can consider the problems of the formation of the constant conjunction through the PS⇔D function. The names, the nouns, are constant conjunctions, but what is lacking is the narrative articulation to relate these names.

She achieved the constant conjunction* that is bound together with the name, through the word "horse": it binds together an emotional experience in relation to the father.

The linguistic development is demanding a container. After a very simple interpretation, Jane again establishes a connection and makes a drawing that is the equivalent of a dream-thought. The Oedipal preconception is acquiring vitality and also emotions. Then anxiety emerges. The representation of the horses playing what seems a primal scene produces in her an intolerable state of excitation, with which she tries to deal through isolation and obsessive mechanisms: going to the bathroom, washing the red spot, urinating.

In the drawing, the choice of colours is probably influenced by the early oedipal configuration: blue might represent the mother, red the father. The mouth of the shark is very big: the conflict with the teething appears in the drawing of the teeth. She has a conflict with the red and with the stain. The red tail at the back, which has the form of what can be a penis, perhaps represents the beginning of a sexual differentiation.

Later on in her analysis, when Jane became much more connected, one of her attempts to make a differentiation was also through colours, such as the analyst's blue eyes and her brown eyes.

The father's function of making differentiations is shown in the following illustration: in an interview with her parents, I told them about the need to help Jane live in a shared world and with a certain notion of limits. These parents have tremendous rivalry between them that often shows in their relationship with Jane. In the interviews with them, I have tried to deal with this issue, which has become more mitigated, stressing the importance of the father's presence, so that they could understand that he should spend more time with Jane when he was not traveling. Thus, he began to take her horse-riding, with a double benefit for Jane, because, besides the meaning of sharing that activity with her father, there was also what is implied in the relation with a living being such as a horse. Jane also brought this to her session, as is seen in the horse material. The analyst's consulting room is, furthermore, also near a polo camp, so horses also began having a meaning in transference.

In an interview, the parents told me that Jane insists on sleeping in their bed, and that one day, she surprisingly approached her father and gave him a kiss on the mouth. After the interview, in which the parents were able to understand and elaborate on the importance of limits and differentiation, the father was able to tell Jane when she wants to kiss him, not to do so with a princess kiss: "You give me a dad kiss," showing his cheek, "and not a prince-and-princess kiss."

Tropisms

As I already stated in Chapter Four, in his posthumous book, *Cogitations*, Bion refers to tropisms, and he defines them as seekers of objects.

> Tropisms are the matrix from which all the mental life springs. For maturation to be possible they need to be won from the void and be communicated. Just as a breast, or its equivalent, is necessary for the infant life to be sustained, so it is necessary that a mental counterpart, the primitive breast, should exist, for the mental life to be sustained. The vehicle of communication—the infant's cry, tactile and visual senses—is engaged in order not only to communicate but also to control the tropism. If all goes well the communication, by projective identification, leads (as Melanie Klein has described) to the deposition in the breast of the tropisms that the infant can neither control, modify, nor develop, but which can be so controlled and modified after they have been modified by the object. [Bion, 1992, p. 34]

He says that if these tropisms do not find a suitable object, with which projective identification is possible, instead of being able to be transformed they remain retained within and disturb the communication channels.

I think that by characterizing them as tropisms, Bion on the one hand includes them in the characteristics of life: even parasites and predators are part of life or forms of life, and not of the inanimate world. This dominion of the animated world is different from the inanimate one, which can be observed as a reduction towards which tends psychotic functioning, and which can also be seen in the scientist who is trying to avoid the complexity of the scientific research of the animated being, research that becomes more complex now, when it has to deal with psychic reality. This reduction of the animated to the inanimate has been deeply investigated by Tustin for the understanding of autistic functioning. What happens with the tropisms in this functioning? The incorporation of a hostile primitive super-superego, an object hostile to projective identification, does not take place, nor is there a hypertrophy of projective identification as in the psychotic part of personality. What we observe is a non-relation through isolation and disconnection. Emotional links are annulled and replaced by self-generated sensations and autistic objects of sensations.

Bion draws attention to the fact that the lack of a primary object with which projective identification is possible has some sort of disastrous consequence in relation to the communication media: they seem to be engulfed or to engulf the tropisms. Instead of being vehicles for communication, they are taken over by tropisms.

This creates serious clinical problems, since we deal with patients whose communication with themselves and with others is seriously disturbed, as their communication media are receiving the weight of undigested and untransformed primitive tropisms that obstruct possibilities for communication.

In these cases, as analysts we have, in the first place, the task of generating a container that can transform the primitive contents, opening a field for the development of communicational means of expression of the emotions. The fact that such communication means are affected in this way is the reason why they cannot be used either for intrapsychic communication or for communication with the group. The tropisms are rejected by the object-breast as much as by one's own psyche.

This is an important element to take into account in treatments: how to undo this "vicious circle". One factor in the resolution of this problem is the analyst's tolerance of being an object with which projective identification is possible.

But what happens in the autistic functioning in which projective identifications are arrested? In psychotic functioning there is a level of psychic functioning, although a very disturbed one. Clinical experiences allowed me to observe that frequently, in patients with autistic functioning, when a traumatic situation occurs for which they do not have adequate equipment, what appears is a somatic answer. This made me remember Bion's hypothesis of *Experiences in Groups*, of a proto-mental apparatus, where the basic assumptions that are not active at a determined moment go.

I wish to propose the hypothesis that, in autistic functioning, tropisms lodge at proto-mental, neurophysiologic, hormonal, etc. levels, and are expressed as somatic symptoms.

Jane has to change school and go to one that has a first grade that is for children with cognitive difficulties. This fact makes the parents have to face, in a very traumatic way, the reality of Jane's problems, and they are overwhelmed with anxiety, which adds to the traumatic situation of the change of school for Jane. When Jane begins to attend school, a tremendous eczema appears over her whole body, which produces very impressive sores when she scratches. She shows me the eczema on the back of her legs and says "itches". We worked all the session and when it was ending, Jane said, in an expressive and distressed voice, "I want to get better." A few days later, the eczema disappeared, and she showed me at each of the following sessions that she no longer had it.

E, a thirty-five-year-old man, consults following his clinical doctor's suggestion because he had "explosions of adrenaline". In the course of his analysis, I became aware of strong autistic enclaves. He had made very important achievements in his business activities, which meant for him a certain professional prestige and becoming well known in his profession. This apparently had a somatic effect, which his doctor called "an adrenaline explosion" and a sexual dysfunction. His blood tests showed a testosterone level corresponding to that of a man of eighty years old.

Ideas in progress: openings?

The content of this chapter, as its title shows, is in a phase of exploration. I have proposed some hypotheses that aim to be, most of all, openings and an invitation to analyst colleagues that can follow this investigation, combining it with their own clinical experience. My future project is to explore how to further develop those technical instruments that help these patients leave behind their autistic world, one which condemns them to a life without the vital nutrients of contact with emotional experience.

It seems to me of vital importance to understand the emotional roots of autistic problems in relation to the development of verbal language. This is because what predominates today is approaching them either as problems that are resolved by means of genetics or confronting them as only cognitive problems, usually treated with mechanical methods, which strengthens the defenses of isolation, stereotypy and disconnection of the emotional experience.

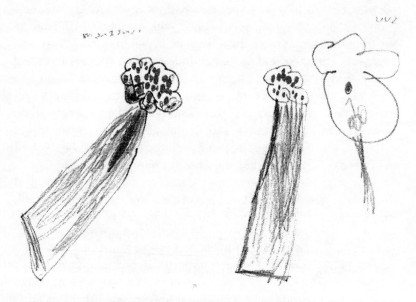

Figure 12. Apples. Demonstrates an increasing capability to draw representations where one could find meaning.

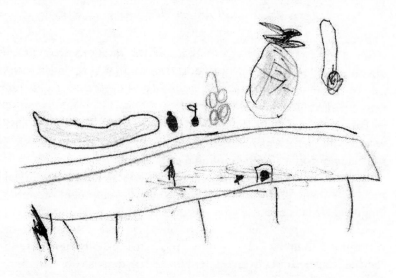

Figure 13. Fruits. Shows an increasing capability to draw representations where one could find meaning.

Figure 14. Oedipal preconception: triangle situation. Demonstrates capability in drawing representations where one could find meaning.

Figure 15. Evolution in the capacity of abstraction. There is a difference between her capability for representing images, which are not isolated, and the letters, each one isolated from the other.

THE GRID EXTENDED

	1 Definitory Hypotheses	2 ψ	3 Notation	4 Attention	5 Inquiry	6 Action	7 Fanatic use	8 Autistic use	...n
A β-elements	A1	A2				A6	A7	A8	...?
B α-elements	B1	B2	B3	B4	B5	B6	B7	B8	....Bn
C Dream Thoughts, Dreams, Myths	C1	C2	'C3	C4	C5	C6	C7	C8	....Cn
D Pre-conception	D1	D2	D3	D4	D5	D6	D7	D8	...Dn
E Conception	E1	E2	E3	E4	E5	E6	E7	E8	....En
F Concept	F1	F2	F3	F4	F5	F6	F7	F8	....Fn
G Scientific Deductive System		G2					G7	G8	...Gn
H Algebraic Calculus									

Figure 16. The extended grid.

Glossary of some Bionian terms

Alpha elements: Bion started using Greek letters and other abstract signs, with the model of algebra, as a means of avoiding the saturated meaning associated with psychoanalytical terms, which soon acquire a saturated meaning; the scientific use is soon lost because the words are the same as those derived from conversational language. Alpha element is the name of a hypothesis; it is not an empirical description. The theory of alpha function postulates a function that transforms sense impressions and emotional experiences of which one is aware into alpha elements. These, unlike the perceived sense impressions, can be used in a new process of transformation and can be stored and used for thinking. Alpha elements can be defined as the sense impressions of emotional experiences, which are transformed into visual, auditory, olfactory, etc. images. They function in helping to think in the field of investigation of what is unknown. These elements, which include, as I mentioned before, visual images, hearing and smell patterns, etc., and also emotional patterns, are the particles of thought, the "furniture of dreams", apt for being used in dream thoughts, in the mental state of being asleep, and in the unconscious thoughts of the mental state of being awake. These elements are produced when there is a differentiation between the sensuous impression as the recording of a concrete object, or of the emotional experience and the concrete object, as a thing-in-itself. As an example, we can take the baby that can differentiate the feelings of hunger as the need for a breast to feed it from the concrete experience of being breast-fed.

Alpha elements, produced by the operation of alpha function, can be articulated and disarticulated and form a reticule that constitutes the semi-permeable contact barrier. Alpha elements are the unavoidable precursors of memory, of unconscious thoughts when awake and of dream-thoughts. They are the elements with which models and dreams are formed.

Alpha function and dream-work-α: Function is a term used in mathematics to indicate the relationship or correspondence between two or more quantities. It also can be said that it fixes a relationship between two or more variables, or that it establishes a relationship between different parameters. A function has factors through which the function can be determined. A clinical observable is a function of factors that can be correlated. The value of a function will depend on the way in which the factors relate among themselves. Bion uses function and factor to define characteristics of the personality. He also uses function in a second sense, that of direction; used in this way one can say that it has an objective or a purpose. Walking has the function of moving from one place to another; a symptom, thus considered, "comes" from and "leads" to. Bion suggests that, when the function can be clarified in both senses in the psychoanalytical investigation, its unknown characteristic diminishes and it can now be taken as a factor.

The theory of functions and of "alpha function" is an instrument for observation in psychoanalytical practice that helps to work without prematurely proposing new theories. Alpha function is intentionally devoid of meaning, to provide psychoanalytic investigation with a counterpart to the mathematician's variable, an unknown that can be invested with a value when its use determines what that value is. It should not be prematurely used to convey meanings. Alpha function is an unknown whose value must be discovered through the psychoanalytic investigation.

Dream-work-alpha is an expression used in *Cogitations* (1992), Bion's posthumous book, published by Francesca Bion, which contains his unpublished thoughts. This expression appears transformed as alpha function in *Learning from Experience*. The investigation of alpha function deals with the development of thought, thinking, and of learning from emotional experience.

It is a function for digesting emotional experiences, which transforms the sensuous impressions of the external world's concrete objects and of those associated with emotional experiences into "dream-thoughts", which can then be stored as memory and used for thinking. Alpha function operates on sensuous impressions and emotions of which the patient is aware. If the operation is successful, alpha elements are produced which are suited to storage and the requirements of dream-thoughts. The evolved consciousness, capable of being aware, of perceiving and understanding what it perceives, depends on alpha function.

Bion extended the meaning of the word "dream" for understanding certain events in analysis of severely disturbed patients. Emotional experiences (either in the sleeping or waking state of mind) have to be "dreamt" so that they can be assimilated by the personality. All "dream-thoughts" arise from an "undigested fact". This function also operates the differentiation between conscious and unconscious by means of the creation of the contact barrier. "Dreaming" is part of the process of digesting truth. Bion here challenges Freud's view that a dream is a hallucinatory satisfaction of a repressed unconscious childhood's wish, since hallucination is aimed at unburdening the psyche of what it cannot tolerate, whereas dream-work-alpha operates in the opposite direction, towards containment and storage.

Alpha function can be reversed, and this entails the dispersion of the contact barrier. Alpha elements are then stripped of all that differentiates them from beta elements, and this produces objects which resemble bizarre objects with ego and super-ego traces which are added to beta elements.

Basic assumption (BA): This is a term that Bion uses in *Experiences in Groups* (1961) to describe a primitive functioning, and it qualifies the concept of *group mentality*. This concept refers to an emotional phenomenon that is always present in group functioning. Basic assumptions are shaped by basic, primitive emotions and are related to the fact that man is a "political animal", as Bion says, quoting Aristotle. This means that man's group functioning is related to the fact that he is as a herd animal, subject to the emotional turmoil of BA.

As we know from his descriptions in *Experiences in Groups* (1961), Bion had the opportunity to observe two modalities of group functioning: the BA group and the work group. The work group functioning implies organization and tolerance towards co-operation. The basic assumption group has an automatic functioning, it needs no organization or co-operation. The agreements in the BA group are based on a kind of automatic combination to which Bion, taking a chemical model, gives the name of *valency*. He uses this word "to indicate a readiness to combine on levels that can hardly be called mental at all but are characterized by behaviour in the human being that is more analogous to tropisms in plants . . ." (Bion, 1961, pp. 116–117). Valencies combine, and the outcome of such a combination is reflected in the unanimous collective omnipotent beliefs of the BA automatic organization. It has the characteristic of being anonymous and also unanimous.

Bion describes three BAs that always coexist, although, at different moments, one prevails. In each one, different collective beliefs and omnipotent expectations towards a leader predominate. The other two BA group functionings do not disappear; Bion conjectures that they remain at proto-mental levels.

1. The BA of *dependence*: the group has the conviction that it is meeting so that somebody on whom the group depends should satisfy all their needs and desire. The collective belief is that the *leader* (which is part of the BA group) should provide security for the group as an omnipotent deity.
2. The BA of *fight/flight*: the group's conviction is that there is an enemy who must be attacked or avoided.
3. The BA of *pairing*: in this kind of group functioning, the collective belief is that, independent of whatever the present needs and problems of the group are, something or somebody in the future, a still unborn genius, will solve it. It is a messianic hope, which has the condition that the Messiah will never be born, so that the omnipotent hopes can be maintained.

The three BAs are emotional states that tend to avoid the frustrations implied in learning from experience. They coexist always and alternate. In the same group, different BAs can prevail and also change, which prevails from moment to moment.

Bion introduced the idea of specialized work groups, as those who are in charge of dealing with emotions of the BA, trying to avoid a transformation into action.

If the work group is able to contain the BA-group functioning, the task can be carried out, although not without difficulties. Bion believed that specialized work groups, such as the church, the army, and the aristocracy, have as their function that of providing an outlet to the emotions of the BA without these being translated into action. Action inevitably means contact with reality, which in turn compels regard for truth and therefore imposes scientific method.

Beta elements: These elements are sense impressions and emotional experiences that are not differentiated from the "thing-in-itself". These elements cannot be used to form thoughts; they can only be evacuated. As an example, let us take the infant that does not differentiate between feelings of hunger from the "need for a breast", which is equated with a present bad breast.

These elements cannot be articulated; they can only agglomerate. However, if they are evacuated through realistic, communicative projective identification and find a transforming container, such as maternal reverie or the analyst's alpha function, they can be the origin of thinking. In *Cogitations* (1992) Bion ascribes them a communication function of the emotions within the group (Bion, 1992, p. 181).

At the beginning of the development of these ideas, Bion had not yet made these differentiations. It is only when he transformed the notion of projective identification, through the formulation of the container–contained relationship, in *Learning from Experience*, that the bizarre object and the beta element could be differentiated. The bizarre object, described in "Differentiation of the psychotic from the non psychotic personalities" (1957), can be visualized as a beta element with traces of ego and superego, which have been evacuated through a hypertrophied projective identification in inadequate and inanimate objects. We can give here Bion's example of a person who, through projective identification, projects his capacity to see in a gramophone, which is then felt by the patient as looking at him. An infant's beta elements at the beginning of life, when he lacks alpha function, are termed beta virginal elements by Meltzer, who, furthermore, proposes differentiating them from bizarre objects, for which he suggests the name *"betes"*. When *reverie function* between the mother and the infant fails, the emotional experiences cannot be metabolized, and remain as "things-in-themselves" or β elements, which only can be evacuated through projective identification. When the β elements are not evacuated, they accumulate and form what Bion calls the "beta screen".

Beta screen: This term is used introduced by Bion for those states of mind where there is no differentiation between conscious and unconscious, sleep and wakefulness. Beta elements do not have the capacity to relate to each other, the agglomerate. The beta screen is produced by the agglomeration of beta elements. Nevertheless, they are used for provoking or evoking emotional responses in the object, through massive projective identification, which can be clinically observed.

Caesura: This term appears in his paper "Caesura". Bion uses a quotation from Freud: "There is much more continuity between intra-uterine life and the earliest infancy then the impressive caesura of the act of birth allows us to believe" (Freud, 1926). Caesura stresses two aspects: separation (barrier, pause) and continuity. Emotional development takes place in layers, and between each layer there are caesuras. The mind establishes a number of gaps, splits, or caesuras, birth being only one of them. They are places of separation between different mental states: being awake or asleep, prenatal or postnatal, etc. With Freud, psychoanalysis discovered the caesura between unconscious and conscious.

Bion marks a caesura with the sign "/", in order to represent separation as well as a potential dynamic change that can be established between mental states separated by the line, without indicating the direction of the change. For mental growth and for psychoanalytic investigation, it is necessary to traverse caesuras, but also to be able to establish some, as, for example, between unconscious and conscious states of mind.

The capacity to establish adequate caesuras is a source of new developments and unexpected discoveries. Although establishing caesuras is necessary for development, if the gap becomes too impermeable, the personality becomes more and more split or dissociated, and wilts and deteriorates.

The technical approach in psychoanalysis that Bion suggests is to investigate the caesura: not the transference or the counter-transference, but, rather, the relation, what is "in between".

Catastrophic change: This term refers to a constant conjunction of facts that can be found in diverse areas: the mind, the group, the psychoanalytic session, and society. This particular type of configuration is inherent to different structures of psychic change and transformation.

It is unavoidably concomitant with mental growth, which is timeless and catastrophic. It implies traversing different situations of crisis.

The constant conjunction refers to facts that can be observed when a new idea appears in any of the mentioned areas. The new idea has a disruptive force that threatens with a more or less violent break of the previous structure and organization where it is expressed.

The idea of catastrophic change relates to the disarticulation of a constant conjunction of meanings that are in evolution. The change towards growth involves the transformation of a structure or part of it, which necessarily implies moments of disorganization, pain, and frustration. This change, felt as a threat, is the bearer of the idea or experience of imminent catastrophe, which does not necessarily imply the fact of a real catastrophe.

In *Attention and Interpretation*, Bion deals with the issue of catastrophic change from the point of view of the container–contained model.

This model can be used to study different vicissitudes: the new idea can be considered the contained, and the mind, the individual, the society, a container, or *vice versa*. The investigation of the relationship and the different kinds of interactions has a clinical importance. The development of the personality requires a symbiotic relationship (of mutual benefit) between container and contained.

In the analytic setting psychic change is catastrophic in several ways.

In a restricted sense of an event that causes a subversion of the previous order of things.

It is accompanied by feelings of disaster in the participants.

1. It is sudden and violent.

   Catastrophic change has the following characteristics: violence, subversion of the system and invariance. These elements are inherent in any situation of growth:

   (a) Invariance: elements of the previous structure can be recognized in the new one although not with a sense of permanence, but rather of transformation.

   (b) Subversion: an alteration of the previously existing system produces a rupture or disarticulation of an existing constant conjunction.

   (c) Violence: the sudden discovery of a fact that acquires and offers meaning is experienced with feelings of disaster.

Catastrophic should not be understood as implying a catastrophe, if it takes place in a direction in the sense of the transformation of something that evolves from O (the "formless and infinite void") towards K (the disposition to know). The concept of catastrophe should be understood here related with that of change, as a mutation, a phenomenon that marks a sudden leap, a discontinuity in evolution and mental growth. The "act of knowing" as a disposition, not as possession of knowledge, is in itself a catastrophic change. The act of learning from emotional experience involves successive catastrophic changes. Insight in the analytic process configures catastrophic change.

Mental growth is produced by the alternation between becoming oneself, which implies O → O transformations, and the disposition to knowing oneself, which supposes O → K transformations.

Catastrophic change implies becoming oneself; they are transformations into being, into existing, not into knowing about oneself.

Resistance in analysis to knowing oneself is due to the fear of becoming oneself. This fear, in turn, is associated with the inevitable feelings of loneliness and uncertainty, implied in this becoming in at-one-ment. The evolution towards becoming oneself means detachment from our groupishness, from the group mentality, from our primitive roots as political or group animals, and implies opening our mind to house the new idea, to house thoughts without a thinker.

When change occurs and it is contained by the analytic situation, it is a controlled catastrophic change. If the change occurs in a K transformational medium it is not a catastrophe but an evolutionary phenomenon towards mental growth. If it occurs in a −K medium, of active misunderstanding, it may very likely be a real catastrophe for the personality.

In *Transformations*, Bion distinguishes two stages in the catastrophic change: one pre- and one post-catastrophic. It may be compared to an explosion that transforms a pre-catastrophic moment into a post-catastrophic one associated with a transformation. It is not a disaster, but rather the point of departure of an evolution towards mental growth. Transformations towards O, through insight and being in at-one-ment with oneself, are experienced as a risk of catastrophic change.

Constant conjunction: This is a term that Bion borrowed from the philosopher David Hume, to which he gave a personal meaning, in the framework of his developments on the function of thinking. In this context, the term denotes a pattern that is the way in which the mind of each person assembles its emotional experiences; a way that is his own peculiar modality. Bion describes a series of characteristics of this modality of forming sets or conjunctions, associated with the function of thinking and the process of abstraction. Considering psychoanalysis as a science that investigates relationships and not related objects is also linked to investigation of the constant conjunction.

(a) For the constant conjunction to acquire certain durability it is necessary to bind it with a name that not necessarily has to be of the verbal kind. It can be bound by something pictorial, a gesture, etc.

(b) The formation of constant conjunctions is stimulated by anxieties that can be either paranoid or depressive. Naming the constant conjunction stops the dispersion of elements, with its primitive connotations of fragmentation and attenuates uncertainty and intolerance of frustration.

(c) The depressive anxieties linked to a loss or a separation also stimulate the formation of constant conjunctions, because, when faced with the pain of the loss, they are a means of retaining the experience.

(d) The denomination constant conjunction is related to the fact that it has a certain stability and perdurability. Notwithstanding, they are exposed to modification through catastrophic change. When these conjunctions are associated with growth processes, they can be considered as transitory or in transition. When they acquire a more fixed character, they are associated with symptoms, character traits, beliefs, and they function more as stereotypes that inhibit mental growth.

Contact barrier: Freud used this term to describe a neurophysiologic synapse. Bion borrowed it to name a structure that has both functions: of contact and of barrier. It is formed through articulation of alpha elements that in one moment cohere, and in another are disarticulated as they proliferate and form a reticule. It is in a continuous process of formation, and marks the point of contact and separation between conscious and unconscious elements, creating the distinction between them. The term emphasizes the establishment of contact between conscious and unconscious and the selective passage of elements from one to the other. Alpha elements form a semi-permeable barrier that allows, at the same time, exchange, so that emotional experiences can be "dreamed" and stored, but it impedes the intrusion of phantasies and emotions into the conscious, which might perturb an appropriate assessment of the facts of external reality; at the same time, it preserves dreams, the psychic reality, from being overwhelmed by a hyper-realistic vision.

The change of elements from conscious to unconscious and vice versa depends on the nature of the contact barrier. The nature in turn, will depend on the supply of alpha elements and of the kind of relationship these elements have with one another. They may cohere or agglomerate; be ordered sequentially as a narrative, as occurs in a dream; or be ordered logically or geometrically. Its function as a semi-permeable membrane allows for being awake or asleep, conscious or unconscious and to differentiate past from present and from future. It acts as a barrier that impedes the mutual invasion between "dreams" and realistic facts, acting also as an articulating caesura that makes thinking and communication possible.

Container–contained (δ $\female$): This term describes a relationship that has a model of a container with receptive qualities and a contained with a penetrating quality. In a significant manner, Bion uses for this model the masculine and feminine signs (δ $\female$), which have the characteristics of an abstraction, but also contain the common matrix of the emotional experience they emerge from. Both the container and the contained are models born of the emotional experience in relation to primary objects. Thus, the breast can be conceived as the container ($\female$) of the mouth (δ) or *vice versa*. This model also emerges as a way of conceptualizing the relation between the projective identification of the infant, a content (δ) with a capacity of penetration, and the receptive quality of the container ($\female$) the mother's reverie. This is also his model of the origin of thinking, as the realistic, communicative projective identification of the infant is received and transformed into alpha elements by maternal reverie. Bion does not conceive the isolated development of each of these terms, so that the object of study is the relationship they maintain amongst themselves.

According to the quality of the emotion that impregnates it, the container–contained relationship can favour development or not. If it is impregnated by envy, container and contained are stripped of their essential qualities, meaning, and vitality. This relationship is the antithesis of growth. Bion represents an emotion that denudes and a container–contained relationship, united by this parasitic emotional link, with the minus sign: $-\delta$ $\female$. This is in contrast with a relationship towards growth represented by: $\delta \cdot \female$, the point being the representation of an emotion, of a link of love (L), hate (H), and the disposition to know (K). The main difference between the two kinds of relationship is that the latter has the possibility of development, based on tolerance of doubt and a sense of infinite.

The $-\delta$ $\female$ relationship leads to deterioration.

Bion describes three basic types of relation:

1. Symbiotic: a container–contained relationship in which two get together to mutual advantage and/or for the benefit of a third

party. Projective identification, as the content, is used in a communicative way and is detoxified by the container and transformed into meaning, thus becoming a preconception open to new meanings. These characteristics of the relationship are factors for growth. The mother grows in her capacity to be a mother through the contact with her baby, and the baby in turn develops through the relation with his/her mother.

2. Commensal: a container–contained relationship in which both coexist side by side without making contact. The caesura is wide, thus no conflict ensues. We can think that the conflict has not yet arrived, because the conditions for the encounter of container and contained have not yet been given; as Bion illustrates with the heliocentric theory of Aristarchus of Samos, 500 BC, who went unrecognized in his time, since the geocentric theory predominated. This was, of course, until the evolution of culture and of instruments, when the telescope opened the way for a conflictive encounter (between science and religion); starting with Galileo, who, as we know, abjured his scientific discoveries but also said: "*eppur si muove*".

3. Parasitic: the relationship between container and contained is mutually destructive. Projective identification is explosive; it is destructive of the container. The container is also destructive for the contained. Container denudes contained of its qualities of penetration, and contained denudes container of its receptive quality. This parasitic relationship is of mutual denudement, not only of the already existing relationship, but also of its possibilities for future development. Container and contained are united by a malignant combination of envy and voracity. Bion named this type of link −K and considered that it was the matrix of the primitive super-superego, which usurps and/or assassinates the functions of the ego.

Emotional experience: This is a term that acquires growing importance in Bion's writings. Experience is in a sense related with "realization", but the latter of these terms is also associated with becoming aware of the experience. Experience denotes a broad spectrum within the order of human relations. It does not only have dramatic connotations: reading a book, recalling a memory, a conversation with a friend, having a child, breastfeeding an infant can also serve as examples of emotional experiences.

Enforced splitting: Bion described with this term a split between what is material and what is psychological–emotional. This mechanism arises as a kind of "solution" of a conflict between the infant's need to survive and the fear of violent and conflicting emotions stimulated by the contact with the nurturing breast-object.

A strong fear of emotions can inhibit the infant's impulse to obtain sustenance. If fear of death through starvation compels the baby to resume feeding, this is done, but at the price of developing an enforced splitting, which is characterized by relating itself to the material product, the milk, but not with the breast as an emotional link. This state originates in a need to be rid of the emotional complications of awareness of life and a relationship with living objects. Steps are taken to destroy or impede awareness of all emotions or feelings. Its object and effect is to enable the infant to obtain material comforts without acknowledging the existence of a live object on which these benefits depend. The need for love, understanding, and mental development is split off and transformed into the search for material comforts.

Language of achievement and negative capability: The last chapter of *Attention and Interpretation* begins with a quotation from Keats, by which Bion introduces the idea of negative capability as the quality of a person that is "capable of being in uncertainties, mysteries, doubts, without any irritable reaching after facts and reasons". This negative capability is akin to the discipline of eschewing memory, desire, and understanding, which analysts need for being in at-one-ment with themselves and with the O of the patient. This capability is linked to the concept of language of achievement. This language has an unsaturated quality that promotes transformations in evolution, towards the development of the expression of the emotional experience. It is the language of artistic or scientific creations, and has the capacity of traversing caesuras of time and space. Bion contrasts language of achievement with language of substitution, which is used as an action that is substitution of thought. It is not a prelude of thought, nor is it designed to express it. The latter arises from inhibition, due to a combination of envy and voracity towards growth-stimulating objects. The language of achievement is receptive, and transforms the stimulating objects towards growth. Analogy and symmetry are some of its main features.

Link: Bion maintained that psychoanalysis is a science of relationships, and that it is necessary to investigate the relationship between objects and not the objects in themselves, which are the anchors of the relationship.

Link is an emotion that relates container with contained. He described three links, which he named L (love), H (hate), and K (knowledge), as well as describing three stripping negative emotions, to which he added a minus sign: −L, −H, and −K. Meltzer describes them as anti-emotions, for which he gives hypocrisy and cynicism as examples.

Bion's developments are mostly dedicated to investigating the K link, as the disposition to know related to curiosity, and not as the possession of knowledge, and he also makes an important contribution to the understanding of the −K link as a link of active misunderstanding, characteristic of the psychotic part of the personality.

Model: Model making is part of the equipment available to the psychoanalyst. Its use is convenient for several reasons. It has the flexibility that you can change it at any time, in contrast with theories. *If the analyst can build appropriate models he will avoid the temptation to create* ad hoc *theories.* A model helps to find a correspondence between clinical problems and psychoanalytical theories. It can be easily discarded, because it does not have the status of theories; should it prove useful on different occasions, it could be eventually transformed into a theory.

The model is built with elements related with sense experiences and helps to bridge the gap between clinically observed facts and the psychoanalytic theories with the highest levels of abstraction.

When the analyst builds the model he must also be aware of the model used by the patient. The model is useful for restoring contact with the concrete experience of psychoanalytic investigation, when contact has been lost due to the use of abstractions far removed from experience and associated with the theoretical system.

Any experience can be used as a model for future experiences. This aspect of learning from experience is related to, and in a certain way is identical to, the function that Freud attributes to attention, a function which periodically goes out to seek "samples" in the outside world, so that its data might already be familiar in case an urgent need arises. Bion extends this notion to the psychic reality. The value of the model as a factor of the attention function for emotional experiences is that its familiar data are available for encounter with future emotional experiences. Before an emotional experience can be used as a model, its sensuous data need to have been transformed into alpha elements, in order to be able to be stored and be available for abstraction. If a model is needed for an emotional experience, those necessary elements can be taken from the storage of alpha elements which have (such as visual images) a reminiscence of the emotional experience in which the alpha element was formed.

Myth: The myth is a kind of thought that Bion classified in Row C of The Grid. He proposed using myths to form "a picture gallery" of verbal elements that can serve as models for different aspects related to emotional experiences that belong to the point of inter-section between clinical experience and psychoanalytic theory.

This implies using them as a preconception open to unknown facts, or to those facts that have not happened yet, and which the myth, acting as a receptive net, could help display and highlight. "The Oedipus myth may be regarded as an instrument that served Freud in his discovery of psychoanalysis and psychoanalysis as an instrument that enabled Feud to discover the Oedipus complex" (Bion, 1963, p. 92).

To the well known Oedipus myth, Bion added: the Garden of Eden, the Tower of Babel, the Death of Palinurus, and the burial at the cemetery pit in Ur. He suggested freeing myths from their narrative structure, which is only one form of relating the elements of a constant conjunction, and using each element in a form analo-gous to an algebraic unknown. He also proposed the myth as one of the dimensions of the psychoanalytical object, together with commonsense and passion. An interpretation has to take into account these three dimensions.

O: The letter O represents ultimate reality, absolute truth, or unknowable psychic reality, in the sense of Kant's *noumena*, which can only be known through its transformations in phenomena. Bion often quotes Milton, defining O as the *infinite and formless void*. He introduces this term in *Transformations*, which has, as subtitle,

"From learning to becoming". Transformations in O, from O to K, and from O to O, are complex concepts that describe the evolution of the personality towards becoming in at-one-ment, and the K link as disposition to know.

Prenatal states of mind: In *Caesura* (Bion, 1977), Bion asks if it is possible for psychoanalysts to think that there may still be, in the human being, vestiges which would suggest the survival in the mind of embryonic intra-uterine functioning. "Is there any part of the human mind which still betrays signs of an 'embryological' intuition either visual or auditory?" (Bion, 1977 [1989, p. 42]).

Bion takes up the hypothesis of a proto-mental system (Bion, 1961), where the physical and mental remain undifferentiated, expanding it with the conjecture of a mental/emotional functioning which is closer to neurophysiology than to psychology. He suggests that such primitive experiences as the ones of intra-uterine life can somehow find expression in the child or in the adult. Can we conjecture that, during intra-uterine life, the first stages of what after birth will be called fear, hate, etc., develop?

The usefulness of making conjectures as to the continuity between prenatal and postnatal PS⇔D functioning is that it allows widening the field of clinical observation and understanding of certain manifestations, seeing them as traces of the first stages of emotional development. Certain expressions on a bodily level, like an intense blush or an extreme pallor, for instance, might be understood as vestiges of intense thalamic or sub-thalamic fears of prenatal life. Thinking about the first stages of fear as thalamic fears might help to understand certain bodily manifestations, which we observe in today's child or adult patient, as vestiges of prenatal emotions in intra-uterine life.

PS⇔D oscillation: This is one of the two matrix functions for thinking that Bion has described. It refers to the oscillation between mental states of dispersion, the PS point (schizo–paranoid dispersion) and the integration or synthesis of the depressive position, the D point. Bion transformed Klein's positions into a mental function, the matrix of thought. It acquires relevance to the extent that, once primary emotions have been detoxified, this function allows tolerating the paranoid anxieties related with the experience of dispersion and depressive anxiety implicit in that the point of arrival is not definitive, but rather is, in turn, a point of departure.

This function allows tolerating that the facts to be understood be dispersed without knowing what they mean, until such time in which an understanding can be found through the discovery of the selected fact, which harmonizes them.

The D point is unstable, and in a new oscillation it will be transformed into a new PS, which will begin a new cycle. Once the PS⟺D oscillation makes possible the finding of a constant conjunction, the meaning can be investigated through the container–contained relationship. The PS⟺D function delineates observation of the total object; the exploration through the ♂♀ interaction permits finding a meaning. The PS⟺D function helps to tolerate the depressive anxieties derived from keeping different aspects of the same object in the D point. The experience of discovery and the finding of meaning also suppose tolerance of the pain of confronting conjectures, the pre-conceptions, with the observed facts.

Realization: Bion takes the word realization, which combines the materialization of the experience with becoming aware of it. Positive "realization" means that the infant's preconceptual expectations of the breast mate with the actual experience of the breast. By negative "realization", Bion means that the expectations mate with frustration. The tolerance of the emotional experience of the absence of the breast, meeting with a "no-breast", is the origin of the formation of thoughts. Positive realizations form conceptions, which, when there is another step towards abstraction, form concepts.

Reverie: Reverie can be defined as a detoxifying and digesting function that the mother performs for the infant through her alpha function. Bion used this term to designate the mother's capacity to receive the infant's projective identification of intolerable emotions and return them detoxified, that is, with the painful emotion made bearable, so that he can now introject them as part of his personality under a tolerable form. The infant, being in itself unable to make use of the sense data, for example, feelings of hunger, has to evacuate his emotions into the mother, relying on her to transform them into a form suitable for employment as alpha elements.

If the projection is not accepted, the infant feels that its feeling, for example, the fear of dying, is stripped of meaning; it returns to him as a nameless dread and therefore he does not reintroject an emotion made tolerable, which he can assimilate. Bion also defines reverie as the "psychological source of supply of the infant's needs for love and understanding". "If the feeding mother cannot allow reverie or if reverie is allowed but is not associated with love for the child or its father this fact will be communicated to the infant even though incomprehensible to the infant" (Bion, 1962, p. 36).

The tasks that the breakdown in the mother's reverie leave unfinished are imposed on the rudimentary consciousness of the infant. This can lead to the establishment of an internal object, hostile to projective identification, which means that, instead of an understanding object, the infant has a wilfully misunderstanding object, with which he is identified.

Selected fact: This term was used by the mathematician Poincaré, who thought that the facts science selects as valuable are those that harmonize and give coherence to known facts that were previously scattered and seemingly foreign to each other. Bion thinks this formulation closely resembles Klein's description of schizo-paranoid and depressive positions. He uses this term to describe the "fact" the psychoanalyst must experience in the process of synthesis. A selected fact is an emotion or an idea that gives coherence to what is dispersed and introduces order into disorder. The selected fact is the name of an emotional experience, the emotional experience of a sense of discovery, of coherence. The name of the element that appears to link together elements not hitherto seen to have a connection is used to particularize the selected fact.

The Grid: Bion was concerned with achieving instruments that would make possible the recording of the emotional experience of the sessions, which otherwise is ineffable. Among its objectives, as well, was managing to work in psychoanalytic inquiry, in the absence of the object and thus outside the emotional turbulence of the session. He also aspired that the instrument could help the communication between psychoanalysts, with a system of analogous notation, as musical notation is for musicians. This kind of notation would help to avoid sterile polemics. The Grid is an instrument designed by Bion to record and classify statements, expressed by the analyst and by the patient in the analytic session. It is not an instrument like the microscope or the telescope, which are extensions of the senses; it is designed to record transformations. It records linguistic formulations and the emotional experience that occur in the session. It is a tool that helps the psychoanalyst to think post-session about problems that arise in daily clinical practice and elaborate on different observations made during the session. It is not to be used during the session, but, rather, in the way that a musician practices, before and after a concert.

The Grid is constructed on the basis of theories, but it is not a theory in itself. It belongs to the field of clinical observation.

The formulations categorize progress from apparently simple elements, like a gesture, an exclamation, to complex formulations, like dream-thoughts, concepts, the scientific deductive system, etc. It may also be used to classify thoughts and interpretations of the analyst. It applies to everything that is part of the communication between analyst and analysand.

In its formal aspects, it consists of co-ordinates with two axes: the vertical, which marks the development of thoughts in growing degrees of abstraction, and the horizontal, which defines the use of the thoughts. According to Bion's innovative epistemological posture, thoughts are prior to thinking, and stimulate the development of an apparatus for thinking. This apparatus is equivalent to the functions that are categorized in the columns of uses.

1. Vertical (is the genetic axis): the *rows* categorize thoughts and statements based on growing degrees of abstraction. They are given letters, from A to H, and Bion leaves the open the possibility of adding more. This progression nominates formulations, which are categorized in accordance with their state of development in degrees of abstraction or complexity.

    Row A: Beta elements: Simple statements of an evacuative character. They have all the characteristics of beta elements.

    Row B: Alpha Elements

    Row C: Dreams, dream-thoughts, myths.

    Row D: Pre-conceptions: formulations that have a non-saturated component that can go from innate expectations to any complex formulation that has a non-saturated element.

Row E: Conceptions: Formulations that originate in the mating of a pre-conception with a positive realization.

Row F: Concepts: Abstract formulations that have the possibility of articulating on the basis of logical considerations in a scientific deductive system.

Row G: Scientific Deductive Systems: A combination of hypotheses logically related to each other.

Row H: Algebraic Calculus: A row empty for the time being, since it has no realization in psychoanalytic practice. Nonetheless, Bion left open the possibility of using Row C elements as algebraic unknowns.

2. Horizontal (columns, classify uses)

The *columns* categorize uses of the statements. The columns have numbers from 1 to 6, and Bion leaves one column marked as "n", to indicate the possibility of future expansions of The Grid when clinical requirements demand them. The same statement can be classified in any of its uses without varying its formulation. In this regard, in Chapter 9 I included a column for autistic use.

Column 1: Definitory Hypothesis: a use to join a constant conjunction.

Column 2: Resistance: sometimes carries the Greek letter ψ, and marks a resistential use.

Column 3: Notation: marks a recording use.

Column 4: Attention: a use to draw attention. Bion attributes to it a pre-conceptual use of non-saturation.

Column 5: Inquiry: the attention directed to inquiry of a specific point of the psychoanalytic material.

Column 6: Action

Transformations: "Transformations" refers to a theory developed by Bion to facilitate the observation of clinical facts; it is not a new psychoanalytical theory, it is an observational theory, which belongs to the theory of technique. All types of communication, both from the patient and from the analyst, can be investigated using this concept. Bion's Kantian epistemological position leads him to postulate an unknowable ultimate reality, which he terms O, an unknown and unknowable point of origin, from which something evolves in different transformational forms in each session. Bion differentiates three types of transformations: (1) transformations in rigid movement, which we can also call transformation in thinking, (2) projective transformations, and (3) the transformations in hallucinosis. To these groups of transformations he adds: transformations towards O (→O) and transformations from O → K.

The model of the projective identifications finds its inspiration in projective geometry, whose invariants are more difficult to find, as in the apparently incoherent speech of a psychotic patient, which is different from the narrating of a dream by a neurotic patient. The transformation in hallucinosis is characterized by always being carried out in a medium of rivalry: in analysis, the patient feels that the psychoanalytic method is in rivalry with his hallucinotic method, which he considers superior.

Bion also refers to transformations of O towards O (→O), which are related to at-one-ment; which is not a knowing about something, it is becoming, becoming one with oneself. The transformations from O towards K are formulations of what has already been won from "the formless and infinite void". This phrase is a quotation from Milton used by Bion as a model for O. They imply circularity. The qualities of these transformations towards K depend on the diameter of the circle: if it is only a point, the field for inquiring the meaning is too small, if it is a line, the field too big. Transformations towards K need the toleration of the restriction implied in thought and in the definitory hypothesis.

Vertex: Investigating the problem of development and the use of abstractions in psychotic patients, or in patients whose psychotic part of the personality prevails, Bion began proposing mathematical terms, used as models or analogues. Vertex, which is one of these terms, defines the point of view or perspective from which an investigation is carried out, and it also denotes an opinion. Bion says that one cannot say "from the point of view of smell" to a patient with thought disturbances, since he could answer "My nose can't see".

For a discussion to be able to be carried out at scientific levels, it is necessary to state the vertex from which one is speaking. Correlations can then be carried out between vertices, and disagreements between different points of view can be specified. One can speak from a vertex that is financial, aesthetic, religious, psychoanalytic, etc. If the vertices are specified, and there is respect for each angle, understanding differences is made easier and sterile controversies are avoided.

Vogue: Bion uses this term in *Cogitations* (Bion, 1992, p. 374). This expression does not mean fashion, but something invariant of the mind and of the human being's primitive groupishness, which takes on different forms in different cultures. These differences in the ways of expressing the invariant primitive emotional experiences, show that there is a difference in the forms, related with their affinity to different historical moments and cultures, which create forms in which these invariants are expressed. The transformations in music or in language show this "vogue", which might not be understood or even sound agreeable from one generation to the other.

REFERENCES

Bateson, G. (1972). *Steps to an Ecology of Mind.* New York: Chandler.

Becket, S. (1952). *En attendant Godot.* Paris: Les editions de Minuit [English edition, *Waiting for Godot*, 1954].

Bick, E. (1968). The experience of the skin in early objects relations. *International Journal of Psychoanalysis, 49:*484–486.

Bion, W. R. (1950). The imaginary twin. In: *Second Thoughts.* London: Heinemann, 1967.

Bion, W. R. (1957). Differentiation of the psychotic from the non psychotic personalities. In: *Second Thoughts.* London: Heinemann, 1967.

Bion, W. R. (1958). On hallucination. In: *Second Thoughts.* London: Heinemann, 1967.

Bion, W. R. (1961). *Experiences in Groups.* London: Tavistock.

Bion, W. R. (1962). *Learning From Experience.* London: Heinemann.

Bion, W. R. (1963). *Elements of Psycho-analysis.* London: Heinemann.

Bion, W. R. (1965). *Transformations.* London: Heinemann.

Bion, W. R. (1967). *Second Thoughts.* London: Heinemann.

Bion, W. R. (1970). *Attention and Interpretation.* London: Tavistock.

Bion, W. R. (1977). *Two Papers: The Grid and Caesura.* Brazil, Rio de Janeiro: Imago [reprinted London: Karnac, 1989].

Bion, W. R. (1979). Making the best of a bad job. In: *Clinical Seminars and Four Papers*. Oxford: Fleetwood Press, 1987.

Bion, W. R. (1980). *Bion in New York and Sao Paulo*. Perthshire: Clunie Press.

Bion, W. R. (1987). *Clinical Seminars and Four Papers*. Oxford: Fleetwood Press.

Bion, W. R. (1991). *A Memoir of the Future* (Book 1: *The Dream*, first published Brazil, Imago, 1975; Book 2: *The Past Presented*, first published Brazil, Imago, 1977; Book 3: *The Dawn of Oblivion*, first published Strath Tay, Perthshire, Clunie Press, 1979; Book 4: *A Key*, first published Strath Tay, Perthshire, Clunie Press, 1981). London: Karnac.

Bion, W. R. (1992). *Cogitations*. London: Karnac.

Bion, W. R. (1997). *Taming Wild Thoughts*. F. Bion (Ed.). London: Karnac.

Borges, J. (1944). Funes el memorios (Artificios). In: *Obras Completas*, Volume 1. Buenos Aires: Emecé, 1974.

Borges, J. (1980). *Siete noches* (Seven nights). México: Fondo de Cultura económica.

Brecht, B. (1943). *Leben Des Galilei*, first performed in Zurich. [*The life of Galileo* (English), 1947].

Carroll, L. (1982). *Alice in Wonderland, Alice Through the Looking Glass*. Crown.

Cortázar, J. (1996). *Imagen de John Keats*. Buenos Aires: Alfaguara.

Eco, U. (1994). *Six Walk in the Fictional Woods*. Cambridge, MA: Harvard University Press.

Freud, S. (1892–1899). Unpublished drafts, *S.E.*, 1. London: Hogarth.

Freud, S. (1895). A project for a scientific psychology. *S.E.*, *1*: 283–397. London: Hogarth.

Freud, S. (1900a). *The Interpretation of Dreams*. *S.E.*, *4–5*. London: Hogarth.

Freud, S. (1911b). Formulation of the two principles of mental functioning. *S.E.*, *12*: 213–226. London: Hogarth.

Freud, S. (1911–1915). Papers on technique. *S.E.*, *12*: 89–156. London: Hogarth.

Freud, S. (1920a). The psychogenesis of a case of homosexuality in a woman. *S.E.*, *18*: 145–172. London: Hogarth.

Freud, S. (1920g). *Beyond the Pleasure Principle*. *S.E.*, *18*: 7–64. London: Hogarth.

Freud, S. (1925h). Negation. *S.E.*, *19*: 235–239. London: Hogarth.

Freud, S. (1926d). *Inhibitions, Symptoms and Anxiety*. *S.E.*, 20: 87–178. London: Hogarth.

Freud, S. (1927c). *The Future of an Illusion. S.E.*, 21: 3–56. London: Hogarth.

Freud, S. (1927e). Fetishism. *S.E.*, 21: 152–158. London: Hogarth.

Freud, S. (1930a). *Civilization and Its Discontents. S.E.*, 21: 59–145. London: Hogarth.

Greenspan, S. & Shanker, S. (2006). *The First Idea*. Cambridge: Da Capo Press.

Houzel, D. (2002). *L'aube de la vie psychique*. France: ESF.

Kaufman, G. (2001). *La Fábrica Audiovisual*. Buenos Aires: Facultad de Arquitectura, Diseño y Urbanismo, UBA.

Kandinsky, V. (1926). *Punkt und Linie zu Fläche* (Point and line in front of the plane). Munchen: Albert Langen.

Kant, I. (1781). *Critique of Pure Reason*. Max Muller edition. London: Macmillan.

Keller, H. (1954). *The Story of My Life*. New York: Modern Library.

Keats, J. (1819). *Ode on a Grecian Urn*. London: Annals of the Fine Arts.

Klein, M. (1926). *The Psychological Principles of Early Analysis* [reprinted in *The Writings of M. Klein*. London: Karnac, 1995].

Klein, M. (1929). *Personification in The Play of Children* [reprinted in *The Writings of M. Klein*. London: Karnac, 1995].

Klein, M. (1930). The importance of symbol formation in the development of the ego. *International Journal of Psycho-Analysis*, 11: 24–39 [reprinted in *The Writings of M. Klein*. London: Karnac, 1995].

Klein, M. (1933). The early development of conscience in the child. In: *Contributions to Psycho-Analysis, 1921–1945* (pp. 267–277). London: Hogarth Press, 1950 [reprinted in *The Writings of M. Klein*. London: Karnac, 1995].

Klein, M. (1940). Mourning and its relation to manic-depressive states. In: *Contributions to Psycho-Analysis, 1921–1945* (pp. 311–338). London: Hogarth Press, 1950 [reprinted in *The Writings of M. Klein*. London: Karnac, 1995].

Klein, M. (1946). Notes on some schizoid mechanisms. *International Journal of Psycho - Analysis*, 27: 99–110 [also in: *Developments of Psycho-Analysis*. London: Hogarth Press. Reprinted in *The Writings of M. Klein*. London: Karnac, 1995].

Klein, M., Heimann, P., Isaacs, S., & Riviere, J. (1952). *Developments of Psycho-Analysis* (pp. 292–320). London: Hogarth Press [reprinted in *The Writings of M. Klein*. London: Karnac, 1995].

Langer, S. (1954). *Philosophy in a New Key*. New York: Harper.

Levy Montalcini, R. (1988). *Elogio dell'imperfezione*. Milan: Garzanti.

Liberman, D. & Pistiner de Cortiñas, L., et al. (1982). *Del cuerpo al simbolo*. Buenos Aires, Kargieman.

Mankiewicz, R. (2000). *The Story of Mathematics*. London: Cassell/Orion.

Meltzer, D. (1962). *The Psychoanalytical Process*. London: Heinemann.

Meltzer, D. (1967). *The Psychoanalytic Process*. Perthshire: Clunie Press.

Meltzer, D. (1973). *Sexual States of Mind*. Strath Tay, Perthshire: Clunie Press.

Meltzer, D. (1975). *Explorations in Autism*. Strath Tay, Perthshire: Clunie Press.

Meltzer, D. (1983). *Dream Life*. Strath Tay, Perthshire: Clunie Press.

Meltzer, D. (1986). *Studies in Extended Metapsychology*. Strath Tay, Perthshire: Clunie Press.

Meltzer, D. (1990). *The Apprehension of Beauty*. Strath Tay, Perthshire: Clunie Press.

Meltzer, D. (1996). *On Sincerity*. London: Karnac.

Money-Kyrle, R. (1961). *Man's Picture of the World*. London: Duckworth.

Money-Kyrle, R. (1968). Cognitive development. In: *The Collected Papers of Roger Money-Kyrle*. Strath Tay, Perthshire: Clunie Press, 1978.

Money-Kyrle, R. (1971). *The Aim of Psycho-analysis*. In: *The Collected Papers of Roger Money-Kyrle*. Strath Tay, Perthshire: Clunie Press, 1978.

O'Shaughnessy, E. (1990). Can a liar be psychoanalyzed? *International Journal of Psychoanalysis*, 71: 187–195.

Pirandello, L. (1921). *Sei Personaggi in cerca d'autore*. First performed in Rome: Teatro Valle (5 October 1921).

Pistiner de Cortiñas, L., & Bianchedi, E. (1988). Theory of anxiety in Freud and Melanie Klein. *International Journal of Psycho-Analysis*, 69: 359–368.

Pistiner de Cortiñas, L., & Bianchedi, E. (1999). *Bion Conocido/Desconocido*. Buenos Aires: Lugar.

Pistiner de Cortiñas, L., & Liberman, D. (1982). *Del Cuerpo Al Símbolo*, Buenos Aires: Kargieman.

Proust, M. (1913). *À la Recherche du Temps Perdu: Du Côté de chez Swann*. Paris: Grasset.

Rhode, M. (1999). Echo or answer? The move towards ordinary speech in three children with autistic spectrum disorder. In: *Autism and Personality*. London: Routledge.

Segal, H. (1957). Notes on symbol formation. *International Journal of Psychoanalysis*, 38: 391–397.

Segal, H. (1981). Phantasy and other psychic processes. In: *The work of Hanna Segal. A Kleinian Approach to Clinical Practice*. London: Free Association.

Semprún, J. (1994). *L'écriture ou la vie*. Paris: Gallimard.

Sor, D., & Senet, M. R. (1988). *Cambio catastrófico*. Buenos Aires: Kargieman.

Sor, D., & Senet, M. R. (1993). *Fanatismo*. Santiago: Ananké.

Spitz, R. (1958). *La Première Année de la Vie de L'Enfant: Genèse des Premières Relations Objectales*. Paris: Presses Universitaires de France.

Steiner, J. (1993). *Psychic Retreats*. London: Routledge.

Tustin, F. (1981). *Autistic States in Children*. London: Routledge & Kegan Paul.

Tustin, F. (1986). *Autistic Barriers in Neurotic Patients*. London: Karnac.

Tustin, F. (1990). *The Protective Shell in Children and Adults*. London: Karnac.

Van Buren, J. (1989). *The Modernist Madonna*. London: Karnac.

Van Buren, J. (1992). *Saint Anne and Two Others: The Discovery and Signification of Maternal Reverie*. California Psychoanalytic Center.

Winnicott, D. (1972). *Playing and Reality*. London: Tavistock.

Wittgenstein, L. (1945). *Philosophical Investigations*. Oxford: Blackwell.

BIBLIOGRAPHY

Bion, W.R. (1950). The Imaginary Twin, in *Second Thoughts*, London: Heinemann, 1967.

Bion, W.R. (1980). *Bion in New York and Sao Paulo*, Perthshire, Clunie Press.

Eco, U. (1994). *Six walks in the fictional woods*. Harvard University Press.

Kaufman, G. (2001). *La Fábrica Audiovisual* Buenos Aires, Edit. Facultad de Arquitectura, Diseño y Urbanismo, UBA.

Klein, M. (1933). The early development of conscience in the child. In *Contributions to Psycho-Analysis, 1921–1945*. London: Hogarth Press, 1950, pp. 267–277. (Reprinted in The Writings of M. Klein, London, Karnac, 1995).

Klein, M. (1940). Mourning and its relation to manic-depressive states. In *Contributions to Psycho-Analysis, 1921–1945*. London: Hogarth Press, 1950, pp. 311–338. (Reprinted in The Writings of M. Klein, London, Karnac, 1995).

Klein, M., Heimann, P., Isaacs, S. & Riviere, J. (1952). *Developments of Psycho-Analysis*, pp. 292–320. London: Hogarth Press, (Reprinted in The Writings of M. Klein, London, Karnac, 1995).

Mankiewicz, R. (2000). The Story of Mathematics, London: Cassell & Co./Orion P. Group.

Meltzer, D. (1996). *On Sincerity*, London: Karnac.

Money-Kyrle (1961). *Man's Picture of the World*, London: Duckworth.

O'Shaughnessy, E. *Can a liar be analyzed?* International Journal of Psycho-Analysis, 71: 187–195.

Pirandello, L. (1921). *Sei Personaggi in cerca d'autore*, First performing in Rome: Teatro Valle. (5/10/21).

Pistiner de Cortiñas, L. & Bianchedi, E. (1988). *Theory of anxiety in Freud and Melanie Klein*. International Journal of Psycho-Analysis, 69: 359–368.

Pistiner de Cortiñas, L, & Bianchedi, E. (1999). *Bion Conocido/Desconocido*, Buenos Aires: Ed. Lugar.

Rhode, Maria (1999). Echo or answer? The move towards ordinary speech in three children with autistic spectrum disorder. (in *Autism and Personality*); London, Routledge.

Semprún, J. (1995). *L'écriture ou la vie*. Paris: Gallimard, Version in spanish of the author, *La Escritura o la Vida*, Buenos Aires: Tusquets, 1995.

Van Buren, J. (1992). *Saint Anne and two others: The discovery and signification of Maternal Reverie*, California Psychoanalytic Center.

Winnicott, D. (1971). *Playing and Reality*. London, Tavistock.

Wittgenstein, L. (1945). *Philosophical Investigations*, Oxford, Blackwell.

INDEX